THE BOOK OF MORMON MADE HARDER

The Book of Mormon Made Harder

Scripture Study Questions

James E. Faulconer

NEAL A. MAXWELL
INSTITUTE *for*
RELIGIOUS SCHOLARSHIP

Brigham Young University
Provo, Utah

THE BOOK OF MORMON MADE HARDER
Scripture Study Questions

Cover and book design: Jenny Webb

Cover image: Samuel Cheney, courtesy of MorgueFile

The paper used in this publication meets the minimum requirements of the American National Standard for Information Sciences—Permanence of Paper for Printed Library Materials. ANSI Z39.48-1984.

ISBN 978-0-8425-2862-7

Printed in the United States of America

maxwellinstitute.byu.edu

Contents

Wherever you look about you, in literature and life, you see the celebrated names and figures, the precious and much heralded men who are coming into prominence and are much talked about, the many benefactors of the age who know how to benefit mankind by making life easier and easier, some by railways, others by omnibuses and steamboats, others by the telegraph, others by easily apprehended compendiums and short recitals of everything worth knowing, and finally the true benefactors of the age who make spiritual existence in virtue of thought easier and easier. . . . You must do something, but inasmuch as with your limited capacities it will be impossible to make anything easier than it has become, you must, with the same humanitarian enthusiasm as the others, undertake to make something harder.

JOHANNES CLIMACUS
Concluding Unscientific Postscript

Introduction

FOR SOME OF US, scripture study is difficult because the scriptures, particularly the Book of Mormon, are too easy. I sometimes hear people say things like "I've read it several times. I know what it says, so I don't get anything new out of it." This is a book that I hope will help remedy that problem. Perhaps it will also help those who are only beginning to take scripture study seriously to keep their scripture study fresh and educating.

To those ends, this is a book of questions. Just questions, no answers, though occasionally I will throw in some answer-like material to help make the question easier to understand. It is a book of questions because in my experience—in both personal scripture study and in teaching Sunday School and other lessons—questions are of more help for reflective, deep study. We learn new things when we respond to new questions, and the person who says, "I no longer get anything out of the Book of Mormon" has stopped running up against questions to think about as he or she reads. This book is intended to make reading harder—and therefore fresher—by giving such readers questions for study.

Sometimes when we study we may ask questions to which we can give answers based on some type of research. Often, however, we learn the most when our questions are of a different sort, ones that don't require specific answers as much as they require application. They cause us to reflect on our lives and our associations with others. They make us consider whether or not we are continuing to live the covenants we have made. They help us ask once again what repentance means in *our* particular lives, what it requires us to do as individuals or as a people. You'll find here questions of all kinds (though none, I think, that require research), but I have hoped to focus mostly on questions to which you can return more than once, questions that will help you, as I believe they have helped me, "liken all scriptures unto us" (1 Nephi 19:23).

I understand Nephi's phrase to mean that I will find that the scriptures call me to faith in Jesus Christ and to repentance. In Alma's words, they call me to receive Christ's image in my countenance (Alma 5:14) and to continue "to sing the song of redeeming love" (Alma 5:26). As I study the scriptures prayerfully and thoughtfully, they call me in the same way that they called those who first heard their sermons, stories, songs, and poems.

So perhaps the most important reason for focusing on questions when we study, either privately or preparing for a lesson, is that questions about scripture help us think and ponder. They give us material to consider and ideas to contemplate. Questions help us to existentially hear again the divine call to come to Jesus Christ.

In contrast, when we focus on answers rather than questions, we tend to see scripture study as something that we can finish and check off rather than as an ongoing process. Thinking that I know the answer tends to make me feel there is nothing left to do. But focusing on questions helps me come back to passages fresh, ready to learn new things as I read rather than returning to them with an implicit attitude of "I already know what this is about."

A good example may be Doctrine and Covenants 121:43. This and the previous verses tell us that we can use priesthood power only through persuasion and love, "reproving betimes with sharpness, when moved upon by the Holy Ghost." Many in the LDS Church have read verse 43 to mean that *sometimes* we should reprove with sharpness, assuming that they know the meaning of the word *betimes*. Had they approached reading this verse with questions, they might have asked themselves, "Do I know what that word means?" and then checked a dictionary, where they would have discovered that it means "early." Using that newly understood meaning, such a reader might well go back to Doctrine and Covenants 121:41–43 and rethink his or her understanding of those verses—as well his or her relations to others.

I hope that those who use this book will find that they have questions of their own to add to mine. Obviously there is no exhaustive list of all the possible questions about the Book of Mormon. I have written down the questions that have come to me as I read the Book of Mormon. As a result, for some chapters and verses I have detailed questions. For others, I have only a question or two.

That doesn't mean that the chapters or verses for which I have more questions are more important than those for which I have fewer. Were I to write this book again, I would revise the questions I have already asked and add new ones. I would almost certainly focus on different chapters, and I would surely expand or contract some of my previous questions. My questions change each time I go through the scriptures anew.

So as you read the Book of Mormon, think of this book as a starter for study. Keep a notebook of your own questions and the reflections and ideas that my questions and yours inspire, and return to your notebook the next time you study the same passage, adding new questions and new insights. I believe that as you do, you will find your appreciation and love for the scriptures growing. I also believe that there is no better method for learning what the scriptures have to teach us. They do not say the same thing to every person every time or even to the same person every time.

Most who study the scriptures have had the experience of reading a familiar passage as if for the first time, seeing something in it that they had never seen before. Such experiences are almost always enlightening. Sometimes they are deeply moving spiritually. They are the reward of scripture study, the way in which the scriptures come to bear on our lives. They give us insights into ourselves and our relations to others. They remind us of our duties. They help us understand and appreciate the Atonement. They carry us to a remembrance of the blessings we have received and, so, to humility and gratitude. I believe that using questions to help us think about the scriptures fosters these kinds of experiences, so I offer these questions to other students of scripture as "seed money" that I hope will increase the value of their scripture study as they add their own questions and reflections to this seed.

Naturally, there are many more questions that can be asked about any part of the Book of Mormon; I have asked only a few of those possible. As I said, were I to write this book a second time, I would doubtless create a very different set of questions than these. Nevertheless, I hope my questions will help someone studying for a Sunday School or other lesson from the Book of Mormon. I also hope they will help those who are preparing to teach those lessons. Given those hopes, these sets of questions correspond to the material suggested in the *Class Member Study Guide* for Sunday School lessons. Because those lessons sometimes cover a lot of material, not every set of study questions in this book covers all of the chapters designated in the study guide.

If you don't have questions of your own around which you can organize your lesson, perhaps mine will help you. If you are preparing a lesson, perhaps you will find a question or two among mine that you can use as foci for your lesson. Perhaps reading my questions will help you think of your own questions. In either case, the purpose of this book will have been fulfilled.

In my experience, one or two good questions in the hands of a prepared teacher are sufficient for an excellent lesson. Of course, that presumes that the teacher has learned to control the discussion in a class so that it does not get away from the scriptures into personal flights of fancy or onto the gospel hobby horses we sometimes take such pleasure in riding. Leading good discussions takes practice, enough practice to give you confidence.

But there is a variety of methods that can help. Here is one that I have used and can recommend: Class begins with a brief review of the lesson from the week before (perhaps about five minutes), followed by an overview of the reading for the current week (another five or ten minutes). Then the class spends most of the time discussing one or two salient questions that are specifically about the scriptures assigned for the week.

The class discussion will not cover everything in the assigned material or in the lesson manual. There is always more in the material suggested for any lesson than can be covered in one lesson. But approaching the lesson in that way will cover something sufficiently well to help class members appreciate the reading and be prepared to do more individual study. When it goes well, as it usually does in the hands of a teacher who has prepared effectively through study and also the prayer of faith (see D&C 88:118 and 109:7, 14), a lesson of this sort not only is a good experience in itself; it also encourages those in the class to learn from the scriptures after the class is over.

A good question or two about a passage of scripture can also be the basis for an excellent talk for sacrament meeting: If the passage on which you are focusing is sufficiently brief, read it at the beginning of the talk, restating the parts most important to your talk in your own words. Make a point of raising your question in the context of the scriptures that brought it to your attention. Then discuss your thinking about the question. Explain the ideas that came to you in thinking about it. Talk about the implications of what you have learned. Show how what you have learned is relevant to your life and to the lives of those to whom you are speaking. To conclude, summarize what you have said, if your talk has been long enough to need a summary, and bear your testimony.

Over the years, many colleagues, friends, fellow members of the LDS Church, and university students have helped me think about the scriptures. Nate Noorlander has been invaluable in helping put these into publishable form, not only with formatting but also with questions about my questions and suggestions for improvement. Pat and Larry Wimmer and Art and Janet Bassett, who were willing to talk with me for hours about the Sunday School lessons, were especially helpful. I owe all of them thanks.

As always, I owe more than thanks to my wife and children, who have borne with my idiosyncrasies for many years. Finally, I am grateful to my grandchildren—and to the rest of my posterity—simply for being. I hope this work will help them have and increase their testimonies of Jesus.

Overview

Joseph Smith said that the Book of Mormon is the most correct book and the keystone of our religion. This chapter looks at what it means to say that it is the most correct book by comparing the Old Testament, the New Testament, and the Book of Mormon.

The Old Testament

Compiled largely by scribes after the Babylonian exile period

Parts may have been heavily edited after the Babylonian exile (Ezra); Deuteronomy may have been inserted

Missing books are mentioned (see "Lost Books," LDS Bible Dictionary [BD], 725–26)

Apocryphal writings (see D&C 91)

Pseudepigrapha (e.g., the Book of Enoch, various apocalypses) are not included

The Dead Sea Scrolls, discovered in Qumran in 1947/48 (BD, 654–55), verify some of the manuscripts on which we base our Bible and show us other books we didn't know about

Other missing books were revealed to the Prophet Joseph Smith:

- Book of Abraham, including the record of Enoch
- Book of Moses
- Quotations from the plates of brass (see below)

The New Testament

Gospels, Epistles, and revelation of Jesus Christ gathered by various branches of the church and individuals around the second century AD

Missing writings (BD, 725–26)

More pseudepigrapha (e.g., the *Gospel of Thomas* and *Gospel of Peter*) are not included

John's writings revealed to the Prophet Joseph Smith (D&C 7; 77; 93:1–6)

The Bible as a whole

Final form not decided until the mid-fourth century

Old Testament: The Law and the Prophets were canonized early; the Writings were perhaps not stable until about the time of Christ. Nevertheless, even during the first century, there was no Jewish notion of a closed canon

New Testament: Not fixed until the fourth or fifth centuries

- Paul's letters seem to have existed as a collection by the early second century, though they were not widely known among Christians

• The Gospels began to be collected at about the same time, and began to be treated as scripture as a group rather than individually

• No collection of non-Pauline epistles until the third century, and 1 Peter and 1 John were not included in any early collection

• Acts became part of collections in the second century; sometimes it was collected with the Gospels, sometimes with the non-Pauline epistles

• The book of Revelation was accepted in the second century, rejected in the third, and reaccepted in the fourth

• Some early canon lists: Muratorian canon (ca. AD 350) Eusebius's (ca. AD 325)

• First list to name the twenty-seven books we currently accept: Athanasius's (AD 327)

Transmission: prophets to various editors and compilers over a long period of time to us

The Book of Mormon

Written by commandment of God from the beginning, with portions (the gold plates) delivered by Moroni, the last custodian of the records, to Joseph Smith, who translated them under the guidance of God from the original "reformed Egyptian" text. The descriptions below are of the records referred to by

Book of Mormon writers, not all of which are themselves included in the Book of Mormon.

Plates of Ether

Jaredite history, begun at the Tower of Babel and continued to the end of their society

From twenty-four gold plates discovered by people
of Limhi (Mosiah 21:25–27) and translated by King
Mosiah

Abridged by Mormon and translated by Joseph Smith
as the book of Ether

Plates of brass *(1 Nephi 5:10–14; Alma 37:3–4)*

Acquired from Laban by Lehi's family when they left
Jerusalem

Is this a Jewish record? An Israelite record? A Josephite
record?

Genealogy of Joseph's posterity from the beginning

Five books of Moses *(perhaps differing from our own)*

Record of Jews from the beginning to the reign of
King Zedekiah

Prophecies of some of the holy prophets of same period to the time of Jeremiah (e.g., Zenos and Zenoch,
not known in the Old Testament record). The bulk of
their writing centers in incidents from the life of the
patriarch Joseph, who was sold into Egypt

Small plates of Nephi *(included in their original form in the gold plates)*

Firsthand narrative account of Nephi and Jacob, primarily from the time of leaving Jerusalem until the time of King Benjamin

Primarily a sacred record (1 Nephi 19:3, 5–6)

Contained in current Book of Mormon as 1 Nephi through Words of Mormon

Differs from rest of the Book of Mormon in that it is also a firsthand narrative

Large plates of Nephi

Primarily narrative records of Nephite history (begun with emphasis on secular aspects, pre–King Benjamin) from the first Nephi to end of the Nephite civilization (1 Nephi 19:1–2, 4)

Translation of a portion (from Nephi to Benjamin) was contained in 116 pages of manuscript lost by Martin Harris

An abridgment of the rest is currently in the Book of Mormon: Mosiah through Moroni, excluding Ether

Sealed portion of the gold plates

Transmission: prophets to editors to prophet to us

Questions

How are these books of scripture the same? How are they different? For example, what difference does the mode of transmission make to each book?

Grant Hardy has written an important piece on how the Book of Mormon is different: "How the Book of Mormon Is Not Like the Bible (and Why We Should Celebrate That!)" http://www.ldsmag.com/component/zine/article/5866?ac=1.

Lesson 1

Book of Mormon title page

Most scripture divides the world into "Israel" and "Gentile" or "Jew" and "Gentile," but the title page of the Book of Mormon does not. For what two groups was the Book of Mormon written? What is the significance of that division?

What is the point of saying that the Book of Mormon was "written by way of commandment"? Why not just say "by commandment"?

The second paragraph of the title page gives the purposes of the Book of Mormon. What are they?

Who is "the remnant of the House of Israel"? Why is it important to show them "what great things the Lord hath done for their fathers"? (Compare 1 Nephi 1:20.)

How does the Book of Mormon convince people that Jesus is the Christ? (Compare Mormon 5:14–15.)

Why does the title page end with a warning? What is the significance of that warning? (See 1 Nephi 19:6.)

Doctrine and Covenants 84

Verses 54–57: In what ways might the early latter-day church have treated the Book of Mormon lightly? Why might its people have done so? Have we continued to treat it lightly? (See President Ezra Taft Benson's talk "The Book of Mormon—Keystone of Our Religion," *Ensign*, November 1986, 4–7.)

What is the condemnation of which verses 56–57 speak?

How is the Book of Mormon a covenant? A *new* covenant?

Doctrine and Covenants 20

Verses 8–10: What does it mean to say that the Book of Mormon contains "the fulness of the gospel" (verse 9)?

Verse 10 begins "Which was given by inspiration . . ." Is it referring to the Book of Mormon or to the power to translate it?

Verse 10 also speaks of the witnesses to the Book of Mormon. Why are they important? (See Ether 5:2–4.) How do the two testimonies of witnesses (that of eight witnesses and that of three) differ? Why was it important to have two sets of witnesses? Why is it significant that Oliver Cowdery, Martin Harris, Hiram Page, and all of the Whitmers but Christian were for a significant part of their lives disaffected from the Church but did not deny the testimonies they signed for the Book of Mormon? What other witnesses of the Book of Mormon are there?

Verse 11: What proves that the Book of Mormon is true? The witnesses? The book itself? Something else?

Verses 14–15: What does it mean to receive the Book of Mormon "in faith"?

We often speak of being righteous, but verse 14 speaks of working righteousness. Do those phrases mean different things? Does the second have a different connotation than the first?

What does it mean to receive a crown of salvation? How can the Book of Mormon be so directly connected to receiving one?

What does it mean to *turn* to one's own condemnation (verse 15)?

How does one harden one's heart in unbelief in response to the Book of Mormon?

"Keystone of our religion"

President Benson said that there are three reasons that we should study the Book of Mormon: (1) it is the keystone of our religion, (2) it was written for our day, and (3) it helps us draw nearer to God than any other book. How are these reasons related to the purposes of the Book of Mormon given on its title page?

What does it mean to say that the Book of Mormon was written for our day? How is it relevant to us today in a way that it might not have been relevant for those before the Restoration? (See 2 Nephi 25:21–22; 27:22; Moroni 1:4; and especially Mormon 8:26–41.)

Referring to Joseph Smith's statement (*History of the Church*, 4:461), President Benson gave three ways in which the Book of Mormon is the keystone of our religion: "It is the keystone in our witness of Christ. It is the keystone of our doctrine. It is the keystone of testimony."

How are these three related to the purposes given on the title page?

A keystone holds an arch together, distributing the weight that bears down evenly to the two sides of the arch and preventing the two sides from toppling under the sideways pressure. How is the Book of Mormon the keystone of our witness of Christ? Of our doctrine? Of testimony? How are "our witness of Christ" and "testimony" different?

Lesson 2

1 Nephi 1–7

Historical background for Lehi's flight from Jerusalem (all years are BC)

837 Syria takes the border cities of Israel captive.

c. 795 Israel defeats Judah in battle and plunders the temple.

792–697 Isaiah prophesies in Judah.

732 Assyria defeats Syria.

730–722 Assyria conquers Israel; the end of the northern kingdom.

708 Judah rebels against Assyria's domination, making an alliance with Egypt—against Isaiah's advice.

670 Assyria defeats Egypt.

605 Nebuchadnezzar's armies defeat Egypt, making Babylon the dominant power of the region. Babylon's armies attack Jerusalem as an Egyptian ally and take thousands captive, including Daniel.

598 Concerned about rebellion, Nebuchadnezzar again sends his armies and confederate armies from Edom, Ammon, and Moab against Jerusalem. King Jehoiakim dies, and his eight-year-old son, Jehoiachin,

is placed on the throne. Jehoiachin reigns for three months, giving Nebuchadnezzar all of the temple treasures as tribute. Nebuchadnezzar takes thousands more into captivity, including Ezekiel and especially those from leading families, the artisans, and the government officials. Nebuchadnezzar appoints another son of Josiah, Mattaniah, as king, changing his name to Zedekiah. Lehi is called as a prophet and leaves Jerusalem with his family.

c. 590 In spite of his promise of loyalty to Nebuchadnezzar, Zedekiah forms an alliance with Edom, Ammon, Moab, Phoenicia, and Egypt, and they rebel against Babylon. Jeremiah prophesies that the rebellion will be unsuccessful and Babylon will continue to dominate Judah.

587 Under the personal leadership of Nebuchadnezzar, the Babylonian army lays siege to and conquers Jerusalem. Zedekiah flees and is captured at Jericho. One month after the fall of Jerusalem, Nebuchadnezzar's army burns the city, destroying the temple and the palaces and tearing down the city walls. The ark of the covenant disappears. Much of the remaining population is taken into captivity; many flee to Egypt. But a significant portion also remain behind.

1 Nephi 1

Verses 6–15: Lehi has two visions, and the second begins with him seeing "God sitting upon his throne, surrounded with numberless concourses of angels in the attitude of singing and praising their God" (verse 8). Why is *that* the way he sees the celestial kingdom, as a place of praise rather than a place of celestial work?

In verses 9–11, Christ appears to Lehi and gives him a book to read. Is it significant that this revelation occurs by means of a revealed book rather than by Christ speaking to Lehi or in some other way? (Compare Ezekiel 2:9; Revelation 5:1–5; 10:2, 8–10.)

Verse 13 tells of the woes that are to come to Jerusalem, and verse 14 follows immediately with Lehi's praise of God. Then verse 15 tells us that Lehi's heart was filled with joy because of the things he had seen. Since the only thing we are told about what he has seen is that Jerusalem will be destroyed, how do you explain his joy?

Verse 20: In the last sentence of this verse, Nephi stops to talk about why he is writing: to "show . . . that the tender mercies of the Lord are over all those whom he hath chosen, because of their faith, to make them mighty even unto the power of deliverance." The phrase "tender mercies" is from the Psalms. In them the phrase is almost always used to refer to salvation from sin. (See, for example, Psalm 51:1.) Is Nephi using the phrase differently here?

What does it mean to be chosen? Compare D&C 95:5–6; 105:35–36; 121:34–36; Matthew 20:16; 22:14; John 15:16; and Revelation 17:14. If we read the verb phrase, omitting the insertion, Nephi says "chosen . . . to make them mighty even unto the power of deliverance." How would you paraphrase that in contemporary English? What does it mean to be chosen to be made mighty?

Who has the power of deliverance, those chosen or God? Presumably the answer is the latter, but if so, what does it mean to be chosen to be mighty "even unto the power of deliverance"? Is Nephi thinking about being chosen in the same way that the other scriptures I've referred to are?

What does it mean to say that people are chosen "because of their faith"? (Compare 1 Nephi 2:19.)

Ending as it does with the total destruction of the Nephites, how does the Book of Mormon show us that the tender mercies of the Lord are over all those chosen because of their faith "to make them mighty even unto the power of deliverance"?

1 Nephi 2

Verses 16–17: Did Nephi initially believe his father's visions? If so, then what does it mean that his heart was softened, and why was he "crying unto the Lord"?

What is Nephi's explanation for why he didn't rebel against his father as his older brothers had done?

What is the difference between Nephi's belief and Sam's? Compare D&C 46:14. Does that difference necessarily say anything about the faith of either of them?

1 Nephi 3

Verses 7–8: Compare verse 7 to D&C 124:49. How do you explain the difference between the teachings of these verses?

Verse 8 tells us that Lehi knew that Nephi had been blessed. The suggestion is that he knew because of what Nephi said in verse 7. How is Nephi's statement in verse 7 evidence of having been blessed?

How is what we see in these verses connected to 1 Nephi 2:16?

Verse 16: What does it mean to be "faithful in keeping the commandments of the Lord"? What does the word *faithful* or *faithfully* add that is important? Why not just say "keeping the commandments"?

How is keeping the commandments faithfully connected to being chosen for deliverance because of faith (1 Nephi 1:20)?

1 Nephi 4

Verses 1–2: In verse 1, Nephi again exhorts his brothers to be faithful in keeping the commandments of the Lord. Then, in verse 2, he appeals to the experience of Moses, asking them to remember what the Lord did for Israel at the Red Sea. Book of Mormon sermons often begin in this way, by calling on the listeners to remember something from scriptural history or their own history and then basing their preaching of the gospel on that remembrance. Nephi is using a version of that pattern here. Why is remembering the Lord's deeds in the past so important to keeping the commandments faithfully? How does the Book of Mormon call us to remember? What does it call us to remember?

1 Nephi 5

Verses 20–21: Lehi and Nephi have been faithful in keeping the commandments, and that has enabled them to obtain the brass plates. How is that an example of what Nephi said he would show, namely, "that the tender mercies of the Lord are over all those whom he hath chosen, because of their faith, to make them mighty even unto the power of deliverance" (1 Nephi 1:20)?

They have found that the plates are "desirable; yea, even of great worth" because they will allow the people to "preserve the commandments of the Lord unto [their] children" (verse 21). If we were to change *unto* to *for,* would that change the meaning of that statement? In other words, is *unto* just an archaic usage, or does it mean something other than what we might expect?

The plates contain the five books of Moses, a chronicle of the history of Judah, and a collection of prophecies, including those of Jeremiah. How will those preserve the commandments for Lehi's descendants?

1 Nephi 6

Nephi says that he intends to write "the things of God" (verse 3). In verse 4 he expands on that, saying that he intends to persuade people to come to the God of the patriarchs and be saved. Compare this description of his intent with what we saw earlier in 1 Nephi 1:20.

1 Nephi 7

Verses 11–12: Nephi again appeals to Laban's and Lemuel's memories to try to help them repent. One of those memories (verse 11) is quite specific, but the other is much more general: "the Lord is able to do all things according to his

THE BOOK OF MORMON MADE HARDER: SCRIPTURE STUDY QUESTIONS

16

will" (verse 12). What would make it possible for them to remember the second of these?

In both of these verses, Nephi asks how Laman and Lemuel could have forgotten. Does 1 Nephi 2:16 suggest an answer?

At the end of verse 12, Nephi uses "exercise faith in him" and "be faithful to him" to mean the same thing. How does the second of these help us understand better what it means to have faith? What does it mean to be faithful to someone? The scriptures often use the metaphor of betrothal or marriage to describe the relation of the faithful to Christ. Does that help us understand what it means to have faith in him? My wife and I are faithful to each other, but it seems odd to think of either of us as obedient to the other.

How is obedience related to faithfulness? Does this way of thinking suggest a different way of thinking about obedience?

Lesson 3
1 Nephi 8–11; 12:16–18; 15

To keep the study materials for this lesson within a usable limit, I have focused on chapter 11, referring to other chapters in the context of that one.

1 Nephi 11

Verse 1: Compare the personage who responds to Nephi's desire with the one who responded to Lehi (1 Nephi 1:5–6). Are they the same being?

How does Nephi's desire to know what his father had seen (see 1 Nephi 10:17), presumably a desire expressed in prayer, differ from his prayer in 1 Nephi 2:16?

Three things seem to precipitate Nephi's vision: he wants to know what his father has seen, he believes that God can reveal that to him, and he is pondering in his heart. The word *ponder* originally meant "to weigh," and based on that meaning it came to mean "to weigh something mentally." What meanings does the word *heart* have in the scriptures? What does it mean to weigh something in your heart? What might Nephi have been weighing in his heart?

Why does this vision occur on a high mountain? How is Nephi's experience like that of others? Is there any significance to that parallel?

Verses 2–7: The Spirit already knows the answers to the questions that he asks Nephi in verses 2–4, so why does he ask?

Having asked Nephi what he wants and what he believes, the Spirit then praises God before proceeding with the revelation (verse 6). Why?

The word *hosanna* means "save, please" or "save now." Why does the Spirit's address to Nephi, a praise of God, begin with *hosanna*? Does the fact that the second clause begins with *for,* meaning "because," help us understand the cry of hosanna?

According to the Spirit, what will explain why Nephi will see the vision he wants to see?

Verse 7: The Spirit tells Nephi that he will see the tree that his father saw. Then he will see and bear record of the Son of God descending from heaven. And he begins the verse by telling Nephi that this combination of things will be a sign. A sign of what?

The Spirit uses the word *witness* to mean "see" in this verse rather than to mean "testify" or "bear record." Why does he use the word *witness* rather than the word *see*?

Verses 8–10: Before Lehi saw the tree, he went through a dark and dreary space and a large and spacious field (1 Nephi 8:7–9). Why do you think those things are omitted from Nephi's experience?

Is it significant that Nephi says the tree he saw was *like* the tree his father saw (verse 8)? What tree does Nephi see? What justifies your answer?

Why is beauty a representation of good and godliness? Is there a connection between truth, goodness, and beauty?

How does Nephi know that the tree is precious (verse 9)?

Verse 10: Here the Spirit asks the same question that he asked in verse 2. Why? Is there some sense in which this is the beginning of a second vision? If so, can you explain the connection of the two visions?

Verse 11: What has Nephi seen so far? When he asks for "the interpretation thereof," what does he want to have explained for him? As you read the interpretation, compare it to what Lehi says about the tree (1 Nephi 8:11–12).

Nephi identifies the Spirit as the Spirit of the Lord. Does that phrase refer to the Holy Ghost or to the Son?

Why does Nephi tell us that he spoke with the Spirit as one person speaks with another? How is that relevant to this particular story?

How does the vision that follows correlate with Lehi's vision, and if what follows is an interpretation of the beautiful tree, what does that tell us about Lehi's vision?

Verses 12–15: Do you see any significance in the repetition of *look* in verses 8 and 12?

As you read these verses and those that follow, keep in mind that they are the answer to the question "What does the tree mean?" Ask yourself how this vision answers that question. How does this interpretation fit into Lehi's vision? Why doesn't Lehi's vision include this interpretation?

What do you make of the fact that verses 13 and 15 describe the virgin in the same language used in verses 8–9 to describe the tree?

In the Old Testament, the prophets frequently have to deal with people who worship the goddess Asherah, whose symbol is a pole or tree. In Canaanite religion, Asherah was the queen of heaven, the consort of El, and the mother of the gods. Does Nephi's vision help us understand better why the Israelites might have found Canaanite religion so easy to adopt? One LDS author has argued that the asherah was legitimately part of preexilic Hebrew worship and that Nephi's vision reflects that fact: Daniel C. Peterson, "Nephi and His Asherah," http://maxwellinstitute.byu.edu/publications/jbms/?vol=9&num=2&id=223.

An angel appears before Nephi (verse 14) and continues the pattern of asking Nephi questions about his beliefs and, now, what he has seen. What is the point of that pattern?

Verses 16–18: As used here, the word *condescension* means "a voluntary stoop or descent from one's rightful position." Why does the angel ask Nephi about the condescension of God rather than about something else? It is relatively easy to see what condescension has to do with the part of the vision that is about to come, but does it have anything to do with what Nephi has already seen?

How is Nephi's answer, "I know that he loveth his children," an answer to the angel's question (verse 17)?

Why does Nephi add, "I do not know the meaning of all things"? Since no human being does, that is a strange thing to say.

How is verse 18 related to the question of verse 16?

Verses 19–24: There is a kind of empty spot in the vision here: the virgin is carried away and then, after a while, reappears, and as far as we know Nephi sees nothing in the interim (verse 19). Why do you think the vision might have been given in that way? Why not proceed directly to the part of the vision that we see in verse 20?

Having shown Nephi the birth of Jesus, the angel asks (verse 21) whether Nephi now understands the meaning of the tree. How is the birth of Christ the interpretation of or explanation of the tree?

Having seen the birth, Nephi says that the tree is the love of God (verse 22). How does he get that from what he has seen? What does it mean that the love of God "sheddeth itself abroad in the hearts of the children of men"? (Compare Romans 5:5.)

In verse 8 Nephi saw that the tree was the most beautiful thing and the most white, in other words, the brightest thing. In verse 9 he saw that it was most precious. Now Nephi sees that it is most desirable (verse 22), and the angel says that it is the most joyous thing to the soul (verse 23). How are these things connected to each other? What does "joyous to the soul" mean? Does it mean the same as "joyous *for* the soul"?

How is verse 24 related to the verses that precede it? For example, does it explain what the angel says in verse 23?

Verse 25: How do the fountain of living waters and the tree of life both symbolize the love of God?

Why do you think that Nephi doesn't mention the contrasting river of filthy water in this part of his account, though he seems to have seen it? (Compare 1 Nephi 8:13; 15:26–29.)

Do you think that Nephi saw, as Lehi did, his family in his vision? (Compare 1 Nephi 8:14–18.) If so, why doesn't he mention them? If not, why not?

Verse 26: Why are the vision of Christ's birth (verses 17–23) and the vision of his life (verses 27–34) both preceded by the angel describing them to Nephi as "the condescension of God"? In other words, why does verse 26 repeat verse 16?

Verse 27: Is there any particular reason that the name "Lamb of God" is used in this context?

Verses 28–29: Notice that the chronological order of the elements of the vision doesn't correspond to the historical order. What does that tell us about visions? About historical order?

Why might there be a break in the vision at this point, with a kind of end to the vision, followed by a new beginning in verse 30?

Verse 30: When did the event of this verse occur?

Verse 31: Why does the vision include this relatively lengthy description of the physical and psychological healings that Jesus did? How were they important to his mission of salvation?

Verses 32–33: Why does Nephi see a vision of the crucifixion of Jesus, but not of his resurrection?

Verses 34–36: Verse 35 tells us that the building is the wisdom of the world. If we compare that to 1 Nephi 8:26–27, we see that the world with its wisdom engages in derision of those who are outside. What does that mean? 1 Nephi 12:18 says that the building is human vain imaginations and pride. How do those three versions of the building fit with one another?

How do we participate in the "wisdom" of the world?

Why does the angel describe the occupants of the building as the house of Israel (verse 35)? Don't the events to which this corresponds occur after the loss of the ten tribes?

What does "pride of the world" mean here (verse 36)?

All three of these verses speak of those who fight against the apostles. What fight are they speaking of? Why is it a fight against the apostles rather than against God?

Lesson 4
1 Nephi 12–14

Why would the vision recounted in these chapters have
been important to Nephi? What difference to him would
this information about the future have made? What difference might having a record of this vision have made to
Mormon? How is this vision, a vision of mostly past events,
important to us?

1 Nephi 12

Verse 9: Why would the descendants of Lehi have a different
set of twelve judges than the descendants of Israel since, after
all, the descendants of Lehi are also descendants of Israel?

Verse 10: How do we understand the doctrine taught in
these verses: the twelve judges from among the Nephites
"are righteous forever"? Why? Because their faith has
made their garments white through the atonement? Why
doesn't the angel say anything about keeping the commandments?

Verse 18: The manuscript of the Book of Mormon says
"even the *sword* of the justice of God" rather than "even the
word of the justice of God," as we now have it. How would
that change the meaning of this verse, if it does?

Verse 22: We find here the phrase "dwindle in unbelief"
for the first time, though it occurs often in the rest of

the Book of Mormon. It is a distinctly Book of Mormon phrase; it doesn't occur in other scripture, ancient or modern. To dwindle is to shrink in size. What does it mean to dwindle in unbelief? Does it mean to decrease in number? What evidence from the Book of Mormon might there be for that interpretation? Or is *dwindle* being used metaphorically? If so, can you explain the metaphor? In what sense does someone who doesn't believe, or particularly someone who no longer believes, shrink or get smaller?

1 Nephi 13

Verse 3: To what is the angel referring when he points to "the nations and kingdoms of the Gentiles"?

Verses 5–9: The angel points out three things that this abominable church does:

> Verse 5: It slays, tortures, binds down, and yokes the Saints of God.
>
> Verses 7–8: It desires gold, silver, silks, scarlets, fine-twined linens, and harlots.
>
> Verse 9: It destroys the Saints "for the praise of the world."

How are these three related to each other? Is the third same as the first? Whether it is or not, what's the connection between the ideas of these three points?

Verses 10ff.: In context it is fairly clear that the Gentiles in these verses are the western Europeans. Why is it important that those people be identified as Gentiles? How does that fit into Nephi's understanding of the world? How is it important to our understanding of the world?

Verse 23: The Bible was written by many different people, some prophets, some not. Unlike the Book of Mormon, there is no single voice, such as that of Mormon, that gives it unity. What does it mean, then, to say that the book came "out of the mouth of a Jew"?

This verse appears to refer to the Bible as a whole, both the Old Testament and the New. What does its insistence that the Bible is one book and a Jewish book suggest about seeing a sharp dichotomy between the teachings of those two testaments?

Why does the angel focus so much on the covenants of the Bible?

Verse 26: "Parts which are plain and most precious" and "many covenants of the Lord" appear to be parallel. If so, then in scripture it wouldn't be unusual for them to mean the same thing. How might a covenant be plain and precious? What covenants have been taken away from the Bible?

How do you suppose the abominable church has taken away the plain and precious things and the covenants? Does the angel's earlier description of the church give any clues?

Verse 29: How does the absence of the plain and precious things from the Bible cause people to stumble if those things are texts that used to be in the Bible? How does it do

29

so if those things are doctrines or beliefs? How does it do so if those things are covenants?

Verse 33: The angel puts two things in parallel here: being merciful to the Gentiles and exercising great judgment on the remnant of Israel. (The parallel is conceptual, however, rather than grammatical.) How is exercising great judgment on Israel an act of mercy to the Gentiles?

Verse 34: What does it mean to say that the gospel is plain? Does the word mean "simple" or "unadorned"? Does it mean "clear and obvious"?

Verse 37: In the name of the Lord the angel says, "Blessed are they who shall seek to bring forth my Zion at that day." Why does the Lord speak of *bringing forth* Zion rather than establishing it or creating it? What does the metaphor of bringing forth suggest?

Verse 39: To what does "other books" refer? To Restoration scripture?

Verse 40: This verse tells us that the Book of Mormon restores the plain and precious things that have been lost from the Bible. That suggests that those things are not, mostly, lost texts since the biblical texts that are repeated in the Book of Mormon are, for the most part, like the biblical texts as we now have them. So what is it that the Book of Mormon restores that was lost from the Bible?

1 Nephi 14

Verses 1–2: These verses are one long sentence. Here is a paraphrase and outline of them:

If the Gentiles will *(a)* listen to the Lamb of God

> when he shows himself to them in word, power, and deed, removing what has previously kept them from believing—
>
> and *(b)* not harden their hearts against the Lamb of God,

then they will *(1)* be numbered among the descendants of Nephi's father;

> they will be numbered among the house of Israel;
>
> and *(2)* always be a blessed people on the promised land;
>
> they will not be made captives again;
>
> and the house of Israel will not be confounded any more.

In short, the first two verses say that if the Gentiles will listen to Christ and not harden their hearts, then they will be counted as Israelites and receive the blessings of Israel.

When does the Savior show himself to the Gentiles "in word, and also in power, in very deed"? There seem to be two possible interpretations of verse 2: (1) the Gentiles will be numbered among Lehi's (Nephi's father's) seed; (2) the father the angel is referring to is Jacob (Israel). Which do you think makes the most sense and why?

Verse 3: This is another long sentence. It tells of how the pit that Satan dug will be filled, no longer being a place to capture humankind. How does the last part of the verse, "not the destruction of the soul, save it be the casting of it into that hell which hath no end," relate to the rest of the verse grammatically? Whose destruction is it denying?

Verse 7: What is the marvelous work to which the angel refers here? Is it the Restoration? The Second Coming? Something else? Does it have a definite reference, or is it a scripture that can have more than one meaning?

Depending on your answer to that question, you will understand differently what it means that this will be "a work which shall be everlasting." In any case, however, *everlasting* describes either the convincing of the Gentiles or their being delivered over to the hardness of their hearts. What would an eternal convincing be? What would it mean to be delivered over to the hardness of one's heart eternally?

In the last half of this verse, "the deliverance of them to the hardness of their hearts and the blindness of their minds," "being brought down into captivity," and "[being brought] into destruction, both temporally and spiritually" seem to be ways of saying the same thing. How is hardness of heart the same as being destroyed? How is it the same as being made captive? What is "the captivity of the devil"?

Verse 8: To what does "the covenants of the Father unto the house of Israel" refer? Why does the angel ask Nephi whether he remembers those covenants before he shows Nephi a vision of the two churches?

Verse 10: If there are only two churches, that of the Lamb of God and that of the devil, to what do those two phrases refer? Though some have assumed that the church of the devil refers to the Catholic church, most use this verse to argue against that assumption. What does their argument look like?

Verses 11–12: What is the world like for those who are members of the church of the Lamb of God?

Verse 13: What is the promise to them?

Verses 15–16: How does this passage explain the wars of the time period that Nephi sees in vision?

Verse 17: Does this verse explain the angel's question in verse 8? If so, how so?

Verses 18–28: Why was it important for Nephi to have the same vision as John? Why is it important for us to know that he did?

Verse 23: We know what it means for something someone writes to be true, but what does it mean for it to be "just and true"? Is "just and true" a case of using two words to mean the same thing (such as "without form and void" in Genesis 1:2 and Moses 2:2; compare Abraham 4:2)?

Verse 26: What does this verse promise?

Lesson 5
1 Nephi 16–22

As usual, I've not written questions on every chapter or for every verse in the chapters I've covered in this lesson.

1 Nephi 16

Verses 1–2: Nephi's brothers tell him that the things he has said are too hard to bear (verse 1). What have they heard that has caused that response?

In verse 2, Nephi explains why they find the truth to be hard. Which meaning of *hard* is relevant, "difficult to understand" or "difficult to bear"?

What does the fact that the wicked are cut to their center by the truth tell us about wickedness and truth?

Verses 9–10: Why does the Lord wait until only the night before to tell Lehi when they will leave (verse 9)?

Why does he deliver the Liahona in such an unusual way (verse 10)?

Verse 11: Why might Laman and Lemuel not complain at this departure, especially given its suddenness? What could anyone with the party have assumed from the fact that they were taking "seed of every kind" with them?

Verses 14–18: Verses 14 and 15 tell us that there was more than one bow among them. Why, then, when Nephi broke his bow the result was that they had no food (verse 18)? (See also verse 21—why does Nephi wait to answer that question for us?)

Verse 15 says they had been killing animals with their slings; how does the breaking of Nephi's bow change that?

Verse 20: Laman, Lemuel, and the sons of Ishmael didn't murmur when they departed quickly (verses 10–11), but they do murmur now. What does that difference tell us? What does Lehi's murmuring suggest?

Verse 23: Why does Nephi make only one arrow? Why didn't anyone else in the group think to make a new bow and arrow?

For what kinds of reasons might Nephi have asked his father where he should go to hunt?

Verse 28: It is relatively simple to see the Liahona as a metaphor for other things in our spiritual lives that "work according to the faith and diligence and heed which we . . . give unto them." What are some of those things? Why are our spiritual lives like that?

Verse 29: Nephi himself draws a lesson from the Liahona: "by small means the Lord can bring about great things." Why might the Lord choose to work by small means? What are some of the small means in your own life that have brought about great ends?

Verses 34–37: Notice the strangeness of these events: Ishmael dies and his daughters mourn exceedingly (verse 34). Presumably that includes Nephi's wife. In response, the husband of one of those wives, Laman, urges the husband of another, Lemuel, that they should kill Lehi, their own father. What motivates Laman's plan?

Do you think that when Nephi tells us that the daughters mourned exceedingly he means that they mourned excessively? What might excessive rather than "normal" mourning be? Are there any indicators in these verses that they mourned excessively?

Verses 37–38: Of what do Laman and Lemuel accuse Nephi? What evidence do they have for their accusation?

1 Nephi 17

Verses 2 and 20–21: Compare and contrast these two perspectives on the same event, asking yourself which things each includes that are the same and which things are different and what those similarities and differences suggest.

Verses 7–10: In chapter 16, Nephi fashioned a bow and asked his father where he should go to hunt. Here, in 17:9, he asks the Lord where he should go to find materials for the boat he is to build. Is that parallel instructive? What does this show us about Nephi? Does it suggest something for us?

Verse 14: What does the Lord mean when he says, "*After* ye have arrived in the promised land, ye shall know that I, the Lord, am God"? Doesn't Nephi already know that?

Verse 15: Nephi begins this verse with "Wherefore . . ." In other words, what follows is a consequence of what preceded: Because the Lord promised that after arriving in the promised land Nephi would know that the Lord is

God, that the Lord delivered them, and that he brought them out of Jerusalem, Nephi strove to keep the commandments. How does that promise motivate Nephi's striving for obedience?

Verses 22–23: In verse 22, Nephi's brothers say that they know that the people of Jerusalem were righteous because they kept the law of Moses. Were they wrong about that, or is their standard of righteousness the problem?

In verse 23, Nephi responds to their complaints by asking them to remember the Lord's dealing with Moses and Israel. (Remembrance is, I believe, one of the major themes of the Book of Mormon.) How will that remembrance answer their complaints?

Verse 31: What does this verse mean by "there was not any thing done save it were by his word"? What things is Nephi talking about—what the children of Israel did or what happened to them? What does "by his word" mean in this context?

Verse 35: What does it mean to esteem—to value—all flesh as one but to favor the righteous? How do esteem and favor differ?

Verse 40: How does Nephi explain Israel's salvation? Is it because Israel was worthy of salvation?

What does it mean to say that the Lord remembers his covenants? What does Nephi's teaching in this verse suggest about us today? About our children?

Verse 45: What does it mean to be "slow to remember the Lord"? Explain why that metaphor is appropriate.

1 Nephi 19

Verse 6: Nephi tells us that he has written only sacred things on the plates. How can that be? How can the material of 16:11–13, where we learn that they took seeds with them and that they went south-southeast and called one of their stopping points "Shazer," be sacred? What makes a narrative sacred?

Verse 7: At the end of the verse, Nephi says that some people set the Lord "at naught, and hearken not to the voice of his counsels." Is he using parallelism to explain what he means by "setting the Lord at naught"?

Why do the scriptures so often use verbs of hearing, such as *hearken*, to talk about obedience?

Verse 15: Here Nephi uses a different metaphor: turning away from God. How is this metaphor related to that of verse 7? Could we paraphrase this verse to say, "When Israel remembers its covenant with the Lord, then he will remember his covenant with them"? If so, of what covenant is Nephi speaking?

How does Israel remember its covenant? How does the Lord remember his?

Verse 18: Compare this verse to 1 Nephi 1:20 and 6:4. Nephi describes his purposes in writing in three different ways. How are those ways related to each other?

Verse 24: Nephi introduces his readings from Isaiah by telling them to hear those words and to "liken them" to themselves. Given what Nephi has just been talking about, how are Isaiah's writings relevant to Nephi's people? How are the particular chapters that Nephi chooses relevant?

1 Nephi 20

Verses 3–4: Do these verses help us understand why Nephi is reading from Isaiah?

Verse 9: When the Lord says "for my name's sake I will defer mine anger," what is he saying?

What does he mean by "my name" in this verse? Is it parallel to "my praise"? If so, what is the point here, and how are we to understand that point? Does verse 11 answer those questions?

Verse 10: In verse 4, the Lord described Israel as obstinate. Here he says they have been refined and were chosen in affliction. How do those go together?

Verse 11: The Lord says he will save Israel for his own sake. Does this mean he won't be doing it for Israel's sake? Does this contradict Moses 1:39?

1 Nephi 21

Verse 1: How does this verse explain the scattering of Israel, including the scattering of Lehi's family? Who were the pastors—shepherds—of the Israelites? (Compare Ezekiel 34:1–10.)

Verse 3: How is the Lord glorified in Israel? Does this help us understand better what Isaiah said in 1 Nephi 20:9?

Verse 14: What is promised here? How does this compare to what Nephi said in 1 Nephi 19:15?

Verses 22–23: What is promised here? To whom?

What is the role of the Gentiles?

How does this promise compare to the prophecy in the last part of chapter 13?

Are there other parallels between Nephi's vision and these parts of Isaiah's writings?

What does the word *wait* mean in "they shall not be ashamed that wait for me"? Does it mean "to await," "to be quiet" (as in Psalm 62:1), "to serve," or something else?

1 Nephi 22

Verses 1–3: In verse 1, the brothers ask Nephi whether what he has read has spiritual meaning rather than temporal meaning. He responds to their question in verse 2, but verse 2 isn't an answer to their question. Why not? He answers the question in verse 3, but why does he interject the material of verse 2 before he does?

Why is it important for Lehi's people to know that Jerusalem is shortly to fall?

Verses 10–11: In the scriptures, what does it mean for a man to make his arm bare, that is, to reveal his arm? How does restoring his covenants make his arm bare?

Verse 23: What definition of the devil's kingdom does Nephi give here? How is it relevant to the vision he had of the abominable church?

Verse 26: What will bind Satan, or prevent him from working, during the millennium? Does that suggest anything about our own relation to him? Is James 1:13–15 relevant?

Lesson 6
2 Nephi 1–2

If you know me or a little about me, such as that I'm a philosophy professor, you won't be surprised to learn that I'm going to focus on chapter 2. I recognize that is a problem. Chapter 2 is full of such interesting material that chapter 1 gets overlooked, and there are also interesting things to think about there, such as the implications of the fact that the land to which Lehi was led is covenanted to "all those who should be led out of countries by the hand of the Lord." In spite of that, I'm going to focus on parts of chapter 2.

2 Nephi 2

Verse 1: Why might Lehi have given his firstborn son in the wilderness the name Jacob? Is there any reason that his wilderness experience might make him particularly attached to that patriarch? Or does Jacob's name have more to do with something else?

Verse 2: What does it mean to have afflictions *consecrated* for one's good? To think about that, we probably have to think about what the word *consecrate* means. In Webster's 1828 dictionary (a dictionary that reflects American usage of Joseph Smith's time), the first definition is the one that comes from the Latin root of the word: "to make or declare something sacred." If we take that meaning, what does it mean for affliction to be made sacred? How does that occur?

Verse 3: Jacob is blessed that he will be safe and that he will spend his days in the service of God. How often do we think of our service as a blessing? We speak of our service in terms of our callings—which makes a lot of sense—but do we sometimes think of it as a duty rather than a blessing? What is the difference, and what difference does that make?

Notice that Lehi says, "I know that thou art redeemed, because of the righteousness of thy Redeemer." We sometimes speak as if our obedience brings our redemption. In the New Testament, Paul warns against thinking in those terms. But Paul's doctrine isn't only New Testament doctrine. Here we see Lehi attributing redemption to Christ rather than to us. (Joseph Smith said, "That man was not able himself to erect a system, or plan with power sufficient to free him from a destruction which awaited him is evident from the fact that God . . . prepared a sacrifice in the gift of His own Son who should be sent in due time, to prepare a way, or open a door through which man might enter into the Lord's presence, whence he had been cast out for disobedience" [*Teachings of the Prophet Joseph Smith,* comp. Joseph Fielding Smith (Salt Lake City: Deseret Book, 1976), 58]). How do we square what Lehi says here with our usual understanding?

What does it mean to say that the righteousness of the Redeemer redeems us rather than he himself does? What does it mean to say to Jacob, still a young man, that he *is* redeemed rather than that he will be?

Verse 4: The ideas in this verse move from "you have seen Christ in his glory" to "your experience is the same as that of those who will know him when he comes to earth" to "the Spirit is the same at every time" to "the way for salvation has been prepared from the beginning and salvation is free." It is not difficult to see the connection of the first three ideas, but how is the fourth idea connected to the three that precede it?

Why is it important to know that the way is prepared "from the fall"?

What does Lehi mean when he says "salvation is free"? How does that fit with what he says in verse 3?

Verse 5: What does Lehi mean when he says that men are instructed sufficiently to know good from evil? Where and when do we receive that instruction? When is the law given to us? Is it given to everyone? If so, what does Lehi mean by *law* here?

What does it mean to be justified? What does justification have to do with justice? Is it relevant that both words have the same root?

Lehi says we are cut off from that which is good by the law—both by the temporal and by the spiritual law. What does it mean to be cut off from the Father by the temporal law? By the spiritual law?

What is Lehi referring to when he says "that which is good"? If he means "the presence of the Father," why does he not state it that way?

Verse 6: This verse begins with "Wherefore . . ." meaning "because." Redemption comes through the Messiah *because* the law cuts us off. What does that teach? And it comes to us through him *because* he is full of grace and truth. Presumably the contrast is between Christ and us: as fallen beings, we are not full of grace or truth, but he is. What is grace? What is truth? What does it mean to say that Christ is full of them? What does it mean to say that we are not?

Verse 7: What are the ends of the law? *Ends* usually means "purposes." Does it mean that here? What does "to answer the ends of the law" mean?

Why does Lehi tell us that we must have a broken heart and a contrite spirit to partake in Christ's redemption? Why doesn't he mention obedience or ordinances if they are necessary?

Verse 8: Jacob is in the wilderness of a new land and presumably has little chance to tell very many others this gospel. So why does Lehi tell Jacob that it is important to make these things known to everyone?

Why does Lehi connect resurrection to redemption?

What does the phrase "merits, and mercy, and grace" mean? Should we understand each of those three terms separately, or should we understand the phrase as a unit?

To think about what is being said here, ask yourself what it means to rely only on the merit of the Messiah. Then ask yourself what it means to rely only on his mercy, and then only on his grace.

Verse 9: Why is the Savior said to be the firstfruits? Notice that in the Old Testament, the word is mostly used to describe the first grain or other produce to ripen. How is that description appropriate? Is it related to his title of Firstborn?

What meaning does the phrase "unto God" add to "first-fruits"? Lehi tells us that Christ is the firstfruits *inasmuch as,* or because, he intercedes. How does his intercession make him the firstfruits?

Verse 10: Notice that this verse speaks of the law as something that the Father has given. What does that mean?

Sometimes Latter-day Saints speak of the law as something to which even the Father is subservient. Is that compatible with what Lehi says? (Those wishing to pursue the theology here—rather than the scriptural teachings—may wish to read Brigham Young's response to Orson Pratt's teaching of related doctrine in James R. Clark, ed., *Messages of the First Presidency of the Church of Jesus Christ of Latter-day Saints, 1833–1964* [Salt Lake City: Bookcraft, 1965], 2:233–40, 214–23.)

According to this verse, what are the ends of the law?

Verse 11: In the ancient Mediterranean Basin and Near East, many religions understood the world as a continuum: ultimately there is no difference between the lowest insect and the highest god; there is a unity of all-in-all, a state that could be described as "compound in one." Some religions today hold similar beliefs. Perhaps Lehi has such religions in mind here. If so, why would he think it important to teach Jacob that they are false?

If there must be opposition in all things for there to be good, why are those who oppose God's law punished?

What does *opposition* mean, "contrariety" or "difference"? My dictionary says that in the nineteenth century one of the meanings of *opposition* was "contrast." Could that be

47

the meaning here? Does that change our understanding of the verse?

Does it follow from what Lehi says here that there must be evil acts?

Verse 12: Why would the world have been created for nothing, without purpose, if there were no opposition? Why would that "destroy the wisdom of God and his eternal purposes, and also the power, and the mercy, and the justice of God"?

What is God's wisdom? His purpose? His power, mercy, and justice? Does Lehi mean this phrase to be understood as one thing, or does he mean us to understand each thing separately?

What does *destroy* mean in this case?

The phrase "no purpose in the end of its creation" is odd since *purpose* and *end* seem to mean the same thing in this case. What do you make of that odd phrasing?

Verse 13: Look at each step in the chain of this argument. Can you explain why each step is true? For example, why is it that if there is no righteousness, then there is no happiness?

To what does "these things" refer in the phrase "if these things are not there is no God"—to righteousness, happiness, punishment, and misery, or only to the last two?

Variations of the phrase "to act and not to be acted upon" occur in several places in Lehi's address (verses 14 and 26). If we are affected by something, we are acted upon, so if we have bodies or emotions, we are acted upon. Since Lehi doesn't deny that we have bodies or emotions, he must mean something different. What does "acted upon" mean to him? What things act? What things are acted upon?

Verse 14: The first part of the verse answers the string of if-then statements in 13: Verse 13 says "if this, then not that," and so on. Verse 14 says "but that is true." It follows that the first *this* in verse 13 isn't true.

Verses 15–25: Why is the story of Adam and Eve in the Garden such an important scriptural story, so important that it is repeated for us more often than any other if we attend the temple regularly? If we think in types and shadows, how does their story give us a type for understanding our own lives?

Verse 17: Why does Lehi add "according to the things which I have read"? Does this perhaps suggest that he wasn't familiar with the story of Adam and Eve until he read the brass plates?

What did the devil seek that was "evil before God"? Are there times when we seek something similar? How?

Verse 18: Why is the devil called "the father of all lies"? Why use the metaphor of fatherhood? What is the devil's lie? (Compare what he tells Adam and Eve with Genesis 3:22 and Moses 4:28.)

Verse 21: What does it mean that all are lost because of Adam and Eve's transgression? How does that square with the second article of faith?

Verse 23: This verse connects having children directly to the necessity of opposition, with being able to have joy and being able to sin. Can you say explicitly what that connection

49

is? Why is it that if Adam and Eve could not have had children they could not have known what joy was (because they wouldn't know misery) and they couldn't have done any good (because they wouldn't know sin)?

Verse 24: Does verse 14 shed any light on what this verse means by "knoweth all *things*" (italics added)? Does verse 18 shed any light on what it means to say that God *knows* all things?

Verse 25: Isn't there a sense in which this is a restatement of verse 23? If so, each might help us understand the other. Does this verse tell us what Adam intended to do in falling or what the Lord intended him to do?

Is the word *Adam* being used here of only Father Adam, or is it being used as it is used in Genesis 1:27, "God created man [*adam*] in his own image, . . . male and female created he them"?

Verse 26: Why does Lehi use the present tense here: "They *are* redeemed from the fall" (italics added)?

How does redemption make us free? Lehi seems to equate three things: being free, knowing good and evil, and acting for oneself rather than being acted upon. How are those the same? What understanding of free agency does Lehi seem to have here?

Verse 27: In this verse Lehi returns to a theme he took up in verses 6–10: the Messiah. Why was the interlude in verses 11–26 necessary?

What does it mean to be free "according to the flesh"? Is that different from being free to act rather than to be acted upon?

Lehi says that "all things are given them which are expedient unto man." Then he says that we can choose life through Christ or death through the devil. Is that the choice to which "all things . . . which are expedient" refers? What does this verse tell us about moral agency?

Why is the devil miserable? Does the answer to that say anything about verse 25?

Verse 28: When Lehi began, he was speaking to Jacob. Now he is speaking to all of his sons (compare verse 30). How would you explain that?

Earlier Lehi referred to Christ as the Redeemer. Now he refers to him as the Mediator (here and in verse 27). Why?

Are "hearken unto his great commandments" and "be faithful unto his words" parallel? Does the word *hearken* suggest anything that *obey* might not?

Verse 29: Verse 28 spoke of choosing "eternal life, according to the will of his Holy Spirit." Here in verse 29 Lehi speaks of choosing "eternal death, according to the will of the flesh." How would you explain what those two "according to" phrases mean?

Lehi says that the will of the flesh has evil in it. What is that will? (Compare Mosiah 3:16, 19.) How does the will of the flesh give the devil power to take us captive?

Verse 30: Lehi says he has "chosen the good part, according to the words of the prophet." What does he mean by saying that he has chosen the good part? What does "according to the words of the prophet" add to what he says? Is he referring to a specific prophecy or to something else?

Lesson 7
2 Nephi 3–5

2 Nephi 3

Verses 1–25: Notice the use of types and shadows: Lehi blesses his son Joseph by telling him of Joseph of old, who prophesied of Moses and the latter-day Joseph. Presumably this blessing to Joseph was more than just information and gave him something he could use in his own life. In addition, it compares Moses and Joseph Smith in a way that helps us understand each of them better. There is a general concept or form of things, a type, to which each conform as an instance or shadow, a copy in history. For what types do we see shadows in today's world? Is this use of types and shadows the way that we are to apply the scriptures to ourselves?

Verse 5: To what degree has this prophecy been fulfilled? If you think it is still being fulfilled, what would it take for it to be completed?

Verses 7–8: Who are these verses about? What does it mean to say "he shall do none other work, save the work which I shall command him"?

Verse 12: Lehi says that the writings of Judah and those of his descendants "shall grow together." What does that metaphor mean? What does it tell us about the relation of the Bible and the Book of Mormon?

Verse 15: How is the Prophet Joseph like Joseph of Egypt? How did the ancient Joseph bring the Lord's people salvation, and how is that like what the modern Joseph did?

Verse 16: What is "the promise of Moses"?

Verse 17: How were the ancient Joseph and Moses the same? What is the significance of a rod? What rod did Joseph Smith have?

Verse 18: How many spokesmen did Joseph Smith have? How does the fact that he had more than one cohere with this verse? What does this tell us about prophecy?

Verse 23: What does it mean to say that Lehi's son Joseph is blessed because of the covenant? How is he blessed? Why is it an important blessing to know that your descendants many generations hence will not be destroyed?

Verse 24: To whom is this verse referring?

2 Nephi 4

Verses 5–6: If Lehi is speaking to his sons and his daughters (verse 5; see also verse 3), on whom does he say the curse will be placed (verse 6)?

What do you make of Lehi's explanation of his children's rebellion? What do you make of the self-sacrifice implicit in Lehi's promise?

Verses 15–35: Is this a reasonable outline of these verses?

> 15–16: Nephi's thesis: he delights in the things of the Lord
>
> 17–19a: Nevertheless, sorrow and woe
>
> 19b: Nevertheless, trust
>
> 20–25: Why he trusts
>
> 26–29: The response to sorrow and woe
>
> 30: The praise of God
>
> 31–33: A prayer for deliverance
>
> 34: A promise to trust God
>
> 35: A testimony of God's faithfulness

If so, explain the movement from one section to another. How do these verses cohere as a unit?

Verses 15–16: What makes Nephi begin to think about the scriptures? What has just happened that motivates verse 15? What are "the things of the Lord" (verse 16)? Surely a good part of what Nephi means has already been mentioned in verse 15, namely, the scriptures. But what else might he have in mind?

Verse 17–18: Why does Nephi, of all people, grieve about his iniquities? What is the connection between seeing the goodness of the Lord and grieving about one's iniquities? What does Nephi's grief teach us? What iniquities might Nephi have had? Given the context, what sins might he have found particularly tempting? Do verses 13 and 27–29 suggest an answer to this question?

Verse 19: Here we see Nephi turn from grief in the beginning of the verse to hope in the end. What does the change we see happening in this verse tell us about our own sorrows? Is sorrow or guilt bad?

What is the difference between Nephi's sorrow and harmful sorrow? Compare 2 Corinthians 7:10. What is the sorrow to death? When do we find ourselves in the kind of sorrow Nephi is experiencing? If someone is experiencing the sorrow to death rather than the sorrow to life, how can that change?

Verses 20–25: What things is Nephi grateful for? Can you draw specific parallels to the things we should be thankful for? Are these some of the "things of the Lord" mentioned in verse 16?

How does memory serve Nephi in this verse? How ought it to serve us?

Verses 26–30: What is Nephi's answer to the troubles he has—to his weakness in the face of temptation, for example?

Why is *enemy* singular in verse 27 and plural in verse 29?

When did Nephi's soul "droop in sin"? What was that sin?

Verses 31–35: Why does this psalm of Nephi end in a prayer? In our more ordinary terms, what are the things Nephi prays for?

Verse 32: Since obedience seems to be what I do rather than what the Lord does for me, what does it mean to pray to be obedient?

Verse 33: What does it mean to be encircled in the robes of the Lord's righteousness? (Compare Isaiah 61:10 and

Baruch 5:2. Baruch is in the Apocrypha.) What surrounded Nephi in verse 18?

Verse 34: Is there a significant difference between faith in God and trust in God? What does it mean to trust in the arm of flesh? When might we find ourselves doing that?

Verse 35: Compare this verse to James 1:5. What might Joseph Smith have thought as he translated this verse?

2 Nephi 5

Verses 1–7: Contrast verse 1 with 2 Nephi 4:27–29. Following the pattern of Moses and Israel that Nephi has referred to on several occasions, Nephi leaves Laman and Lemuel, taking his family and those who would follow him into the wilderness. The Doctrine and Covenants uses related imagery when it commands us to leave Babylon (See, for example, D&C 133:5, 7, 14). What kinds of meanings can this type have for us today? How can we leave "Babylon" and go into the wilderness? Where is the wilderness today?

Verse 19: When Nephi says he became his people's ruler and teacher, is he using these two words to say the same thing (as Genesis 1:1 does when it says that the world was "without form and void" in the beginning), or is he saying he was two things, a ruler and a teacher? If we think of "ruler" and "teacher" as two ways of saying the same thing, what might that tell us about being a ruler? A father or mother? Does it say anything about contemporary politics? If we think of "ruler" and "teacher" as different things here, what does that tell us about Nephi's relation to his people?

Verses 20–25: What is the curse that came upon those who followed Laman and Lemuel? Was it the darkened color of their skin or something else? If it was the darkness of their skin, how does that explain their idleness and mischief? If it was something else, what was it?

Verse 27: Nephi says that he and his people "lived after the manner of happiness." What does that phrase say that the phrase "we lived happily" doesn't say? What is "the manner [or 'way'] of happiness"?

Lesson 8
2 Nephi 6–10

This chapter is *much* longer than previous ones. It isn't that there is so much more material, but that I decided this time to cover the whole assignment rather than only part of it. We often stop reading the Book of Mormon when we get to Isaiah, and I want to see how Isaiah's teachings are connected to the events of the Book of Mormon as well as its teachings.

Consider the context in which Jacob's sermon occurs. The people to whom he is speaking left Jerusalem to wander in the wilderness, cross the ocean, and end up in a new land. Now they have just left those who came with them and, as it were, gone into the wilderness again. Why does Jacob think he needs to warn them at this particular time?

2 Nephi 6

Verse 2: What is the difference between being ordained and being consecrated? (Or is there a difference?)

Why does Jacob remind them that he was consecrated by Nephi when he tells them of his priesthood calling?

Was Nephi their king or not? Second Nephi 5:18 says that Nephi didn't want to be their king but indicates that he might have been anyway—though verse 19 suggests that he was something other than a king. If Nephi wasn't their king, why does Jacob speak of Nephi in this way?

How could the Nephites depend on one person, Nephi, for safety? What does it mean to say that he was their protector?

Verses 4–5: Jacob says he is going to read them the words of Isaiah, for they are meant for the house of Israel. What are the different senses of the phrase "house of Israel"? In what ways do they apply to each of the meanings of the phrase? In what ways might these words apply to us? In what ways do they apply to a narrower sense of "the house of Israel"?

Jacob tells us (verse 4) that he will read from Isaiah because Nephi asked him to. Why do you think Nephi picked these sections of Isaiah?

Verses 6–7: Jacob begins quoting Isaiah at Isaiah 49:22. The theme of Isaiah 49 is the redemption of Israel from captivity, and we understand the chapters from which Jacob reads (Isaiah 49–52) to be prophecies of the Messiah. Why does Jacob begin where he does rather than earlier?

When the Lord says he will lift up his hand to the Gentiles (verse 6), what does he mean? What do you think is the significance of lifting up the hand?

What does "set up my standard" mean? As it is used here, a standard is a flag. Of what might it be a symbol here? What does the Lord mean when he says he will set up his standard to the people?

What service is it that the Gentiles will perform for Israel (verse 7)? What is the Lord promising the house of Israel?

Verses 8–18: Compare what is in these verses to verses 6–7. Those verses say that the Lord will lift up his hand to the Gentiles and will set up a standard to them. They also say that the Gentiles will serve the house of Israel and will bow down to them in subservience, and they say that Israel will know that he is the Lord and won't be ashamed of him. These verses say that Israel has been scattered but will be gathered and scattered again when Christ is killed, and that Israel will be persecuted but allowed to continue until it comes to know Christ, when it will be restored to its inheritance. These verses also say that the Gentiles who believe will be blessed. The passage also tells of the Second Coming. How do these verses explain verses 6–7?

Verses 16–18: Jacob resumes his quoting of Isaiah again, taking up where he left off. (See Isaiah 49:24ff.) Notice that Jacob shifts back into quoting Isaiah without saying anything about the fact that he is doing so. Why not? Does that tell us anything about the office of a prophet?

The usual answer to the question of verse 16 would be no, but in reference to the children of God, as verse 17 shows, the answer is yes. What is the point of verses 16–17?

What might the image of feeding on one's own flesh mean (verse 18)? It has an obvious literal meaning, but is there any other meaning as well?

2 Nephi 7

Verse 1: The Lord addresses Israel as if it were a child: Have I cast you off, or divorced your mother, or sold you? Fathers in dire circumstances have sometimes had to sell their children to satisfy their creditors (see 2 Kings 4:1 and Nehemiah 5:5), but the Lord has no such creditors. Though Israel has been separated from the Father, the separation isn't permanent. It is a consequence of their unrighteousness.

Verse 2: To whom is the Lord speaking in this verse and the next?

To what time is the Lord referring when he says, "When I came, there was no man"?

Who was absent? Who didn't hear him?

After the Lord speaks to them of his power to redeem and deliver, what might Israel think of when he mentions his power to dry up the sea?

Verses 4–9: There are two interpretations of these verses. According to one, the Lord is speaking; according to the other, Isaiah is speaking. What do we learn from each interpretation?

Verses 10–11: These two verses compare those who trust God (verse 10) and those who do not (verse 11). What does it mean to say that those who trust in God walk in darkness? What does it mean that those who will have sorrow surround themselves with sparks and walk in the light? Usually the righteous are portrayed as walking in light and the unrighteous are portrayed as walking in darkness. Why is that imagery reversed here? What is the origin of the light in verse 11?

2 Nephi 8

Verses 1–25: How would this speech, a speech of consolation to Israel, be an appropriate thing for Jacob to repeat to the Nephites at the time of Nephi? Later? To us?

Verse 1: What does it mean that the righteous should look to the pit (or quarry) from which they were cut?

Verses 2–3: Does this passage explain the pit and the hole of verse 1? How?

How would one "look unto Abraham . . . and unto Sarah"? What is the Lord commanding here?

Isaiah mentions that Abraham was called "alone"—in other words, when he was the only one in Israel—and that he was blessed. Presumably the blessing referred to is that of numerous posterity. How is it relevant that he was alone?

In verse 3 the comparison is to verse 2: just as Abraham and Sarah were blessed when she was barren and supposedly beyond hope, so will Israel be blessed and made fruitful. Why the reference to Eden? What does it mean that the new Eden will be filled with gladness, thanksgiving, and song? What is the comparison?

Verses 4–6: These verses may help us understand 7:10–11 better: The Lord will give light to the earth by giving divine guidance, instruction, and salvation rather than what is offered by the world. How do we distinguish between the two sources of light?

Verse 7: In Isaiah the word *law* could also be translated "instruction." Presumably the same is true of whatever

Nephite word Jacob used in quoting Isaiah. What does that say about the law?

What does it teach? What does it mean to say that the righteous have the law/instruction written in their hearts?

Why do those who are righteous need not fear the reproach of others?

Verse 9–11: Who is calling out "Awake!" (verse 9)? Who is being addressed? Do verses 10–11 explain the references in verse 9?

Notice how scripture refers to the type of Israel—leaving Egypt, entering into the promised land. How is that type relevant to Lehi's family? How might Jacob and Nephi have understood these verses to apply to them? To the Nephites in particular? To us?

Verses 12–16: If verses 9–11 are Israel's prayer for deliverance, these verses are the answer to the prayer. How are that prayer and this answer relevant to the Nephites? To us?

The word translated "comfort" in Isaiah (verse 12) originally meant "strengthen" as well as "soothe." Does that change your understanding of the verse?

Why is it important in this context to remind Israel that the Lord is the Creator (verse 13)? Verse 13 describes the man at the end of verse 12 "who shall die" and "who shall be made like unto grass."

What is the contrast between the pit mentioned in verse 14 and that of verse 1?

In verse 15 we see that the Lord has power over all nature. How does this compare to the power feared by those who have forgotten him?

In whose mouth have the words of verse 16 been put? Israel's? Isaiah's? What does it mean to be covered in the shadow of God's hand?

Verses 17–25: These verses describe the end of Israel's captivity and their reentry into the promised land. What historical event or events might this describe? The original return from Babylon? The gathering at the Second Coming? The entry of the latter-day church into the Salt Lake Valley? Some incident in Nephite history?

In verse 17, what does the cup of the Lord's fury or anger stand for?

What does it mean to say that Israel has no sons to guide her (verse 18)? Notice that in verse 19 the only two sons remaining are desolation and destruction. What does that mean?

In verse 20, the "head" of the streets means the street corners.

Does *rebuke* help us understand the meaning of *fury* in the previous clause?

In verses 21–23 we see that the oppressors will become the oppressed. Who are the oppressors? Who will oppress them? How?

If those the Lord is addressing are drunk with something other than wine (verse 21), what is it? (See verse 22 for some hints.)

Notice that the first part of verse 24 is a repetition of the first part of verse 9. Who was speaking in verse 9? Who is speaking in verse 24? The prophet? The Lord? Israel?

Who are the uncircumcised and unclean?

In verse 25, what dust is Israel to shake off of itself? Does referring back to verse 23 give you any ideas? What would shaking the dust off be a symbol of? Does this reference help us understand references such as D&C 24:15; 60:15; and 75:20 (as well as Matthew 10:14; Mark 6:11; Luke 9:5; Acts 13:51)?

Has Jacob used the chapters from Isaiah the way we might expect him to use them? We take them to be prophecies of Christ's coming. How does he use them?

2 Nephi 9

Jacob gives us chapter 9 as a commentary on Isaiah 49:22–50:11. But 2 Nephi 9 is a chapter on the Atonement. How is this discussion of the Atonement a commentary on that part of Isaiah?

Verses 1–3: Why has Jacob read this passage from Isaiah to the Nephites? How will it help them to know that Israel will be restored in the last days? How could they apply this passage to themselves? How can we apply it to ourselves?

Verse 4ff.: How is a discussion of the Atonement an explanation of the passage from Isaiah? How are the two related? How does the prophecy of Isaiah typify the Atonement? (Such things as bondage and redemption from bondage occur in both discussions. Thinking about how those are alike can help us understand the Atonement better, and thinking about the Atonement can help us understand Isaiah better.)

Verses 8–9: What would happen to us if there were no resurrection? Since there is a resurrection, what do we learn from verse 9? Does that teach us anything about the traditional Christian understanding of hell, where those not saved are punished by being eternally in the presence of Satan?

Verse 9: What are "secret combinations"? Webster's 1828 dictionary says that a combination is an intimate union of several persons that has the purpose of bringing something about together. The *Oxford English Dictionary* says that when the word has that meaning, it is usually used in a pejorative way. Does secrecy make a combination bad? If so, why? If not, why is it the modifier used here? How are secret combinations antithetical to the gospel? (2 Nephi 26:22–28 discusses this.)

What kinds of things might count as secret combinations today—beyond the things that we sometimes hear mentioned in very conservative political discussions? Given the definition I cited, can we be part of a secret combination without knowing that we are? How do we avoid such combinations? How did the Book of Mormon people avoid them, when they did?

Verse 10: When Jacob mentions "death and hell," he seems to mean two things. This doesn't seem to me to be a repetition for emphasis. What does he mean by *death*? What does he mean by *hell*? What does he mean by "death of the body"? By "death of the spirit"? How are these pairs of terms related to each other?

Verse 13: What is the paradise Jacob is talking about? What do we usually call it?

Verse 14: What kind of symbolism do you see in the contrast between guilt, uncleanness, and nakedness on the one hand and enjoyment and the clothing of purity and the robe of righteousness on the other hand?

Does reference back to 2 Nephi 4:33 add any meaning to this verse?

Why does Jacob identify himself with the wicked at the beginning of the verse ("we shall have a perfect knowledge of our guilt")?

Verse 18: What are the crosses of the world? Who are those who have endured those crosses? Does this verse and those that follow have any connection to the passage from Isaiah that Jacob read?

Why is the cross an important symbol in the Book of Mormon?

Verses 21–22: Does this prophecy help us understand better the promises made to Israel by Isaiah?

What does *hearken* mean? How do we hearken to the voice of the Lord? Is it possible to have faith but not to hearken or to hearken but not to have faith?

Verse 24: What reason does this verse give for the damnation of those who refuse to repent? Why is that the appropriate explanation for this discussion? In fact, what are we to make of an explanation like that?

Verses 25–26: We sometimes speak as if the Atonement is required because there is a law that God must obey. Does Jacob speak that way? What does he say? Who has given the law? Whose justice is it that must be satisfied?

Verses 28–33: What part of Isaiah's prophecy do these verses refer to and amplify?

Verses 28–29: What kind of "wisdom" does Jacob warn against? What makes that supposed wisdom foolishness?

Verse 30: What does it mean to be "rich as to the things of the world"? Why does Jacob warn the rich? Does he warn all of those who are rich or only some? How much does one have to have to be described that way? Does this verse give us any understanding of such scriptures as Matthew 19:21–26 and Mark 10:21–27?

Together, verses 29–30 seem to connect learning with riches. Why might they do so? What is the connection? Given the small population to whom Jacob is speaking, all of them family, who could be either wise or rich?

Verses 34–37: Does Jacob's warning turn to a different kind of sin here? If so, what is the difference? What is the similarity of the sins of these verses to those of verses 28–33?

Verse 37: In what sense is this verse the culmination of the list that began in verse 28?

Verse 38: What does it mean to die in one's sins? How do we avoid that?

Verse 39: Compare this verse to Romans 8:6 and 1 Corinthians 2:11–16. What does it mean to be "carnally-minded"? To be "spiritually-minded"?

Verse 40: When Jacob asks us to remember the greatness of the Holy One of Israel, what kinds of things does he want us to remember? What kinds of things show that greatness did he mention in the quotation from Isaiah? What other things has he mentioned?

Verses 41–43: As you read through these verses, focus on the various types or symbols Jacob uses. What do they show us? How do they connect his prophecy to other prophecies, specifically to what he has quoted from Isaiah?

Notice that Jacob once again connects learning and wealth in verse 42, as he did in verses 29–30.

Verse 44: Might Jacob's shaking of his garment have anything to do with 2 Nephi 8:23, 25 and 9:14?

Verse 45: Notice how the command to shake off our chains resonates with the previous verse (and its reference to other verses) to tie these things together.

Verses 47–48: What does Jacob imply about our feeling that we mustn't ever say harsh things to one another? Under what circumstances would such harshness be permitted? How do we avoid using verses like this as an excuse for unnecessary and unkind harshness?

Verse 50: Jacob quotes Isaiah again (Isaiah 55:1–2). Isaiah's words seem never to be far from his thoughts as he delivers his sermon. Why might that be? The connection between the two seems to demand that we think about the relation of what he says to what Isaiah says if we are to understand fully Jacob's message.

What is the point of this verse? How does it relate to such things as Paul's letter to the Romans where he teaches that salvation comes by grace?

Verse 51: How does verse 50 help explain this verse? What is of value? What is free? What is of no worth?

Verse 52: What is the relation of this verse to the two that immediately precede it?

Verse 53: In what sense is this a repetition of everything that has been said in the last several chapters?

Does thinking in terms of types and shadows throw any light on this verse?

Is Jacob drawing a parallel between covenants and condescensions? If so, what does that parallel teach us?

2 Nephi 10

Verse 2: What does Jacob mean when he says the promises that have been made are promises according to the flesh?

Verse 3ff.: The word *Christ* is a title, not a name. Why does Jacob speak of it as a name? Why does Jacob repeat once again the prophecy of Christ's coming and death? Why does he feel the need to tell the Nephites of this over and over when they aren't going to have part in it? Is there anything here that they can apply to themselves? How?

Verses 20–23: Does this answer the previous question? How? Why would knowing that our knowledge is from

71

God mean that we ought not to hang down our heads? (Compare this to 2 Nephi 4:26ff.)

In verse 20, does Jacob assume that he is on an island?

Why does Jacob connect his teaching to what his father taught (compare verse 23 with 2:27–29)?

Verse 24: What does Jacob mean when he says that it is only in and through the grace of God that we are saved *after* we are reconciled? How have we seen that explained in the previous chapters?

Lesson 9
2 Nephi 11–25

Here is an outline of 1 and 2 Nephi that might help your study of these chapters:

* 1 Nephi 1–18: Creation of Lehites

** 1 Nephi 19–2 Nephi 5: Fall of Lehites

** 2 Nephi 6–30: Undoing of the fall of Lehites (i.e., Atonement)

* Jacob's words (2 Nephi 6–11) [2 Nephi 7–8 quotes Isaiah 50–51]

** Isaiah's words (2 Nephi 12–24) [a quotation of Isaiah 2–14]

* Oracle against Judah (2 Nephi 12–14; Isaiah 2–4)

** Oracle against Israel (2 Nephi 15; Isaiah 5)

*** Isaiah's call to prophesy (2 Nephi 16; Isaiah 6)

** Oracle against Assyria, Israel's destroyer (2 Nephi 17–18; Isaiah 7–12)

* Oracle against Babylon, Judah's destroyer (2 Nephi 23–24; Isaiah 13–14)

* Nephi's words (2 Nephi 25–30) [note: 2 Nephi 27 is a commentary on Isaiah 29]

* 2 Nephi 31–33: New creation of Lehites (restoration, beyond the veil)

2 Nephi 11

Verses 2–3: Nephi tells us he has two reasons for delighting in the words of Isaiah and writing them down: he can liken them to his people, and Isaiah, like Nephi and Jacob, is a witness of Christ, so the three stand together as witnesses of him. What reasons might there be for the words of Isaiah to be given to us? For other reasons, see 1 Nephi 19:23; 2 Nephi 11:2–6, 8; 2 Nephi 25:3.

Verse 4: What does it mean for something to typify another thing? Nephi says that everything typifies Christ. What does that mean? How, for example, does the natural world typify him? How do we go about seeing everything else as typifying Christ?

Verse 5: What covenants is Nephi referring to? The Abrahamic covenant? Covenants with the children of Israel? Covenants with Lehi?

Verses 6–7: Why would there be no God if there were no Christ? If, as Joseph Smith taught, we are coeternal with God, why does our existence depend on the creation?

Verse 8: Why would Nephi want his people to rejoice for all men? Why does he want them to see how these things can be likened not only to the Nephites but to all men? What might such rejoicing and concern indicate? (Compare Enos's experience in Enos 1:9. What brought about Enos's concern?)

2 Nephi 12

This begins Nephi's long quotation from Isaiah, extending from here to the end of chapter 24. As he recorded his brother's sermon, which included chapters from Isaiah that Nephi asked Jacob to read aloud, Nephi seems to have been inspired to record more of the words of Isaiah. Since these chapters were on the brass plates and the brass plates were available to the Nephites, why did Nephi copy them onto his own plates? There are only slight variations between these chapters as they are recorded here and as we have them in the King James Version of the Bible, so why do you suppose they were recorded for us in the Book of Mormon as well as the Bible? When you find Isaiah's writings difficult, remember that the Nephites too found Isaiah difficult to understand. This was because Nephi didn't teach them how to understand the prophesying of the Jews since he was worried that they might pick up some of the Jews' ways of sinning in the process (2 Nephi 25:1–3). Despite the difficulty of reading Isaiah if we do not understand well how the Hebrews prophesied, we can learn a great deal by reading slowly and trying to connect each verse to the preceding and following verses as well as by paying close attention to the symbols Isaiah uses. If we want to understand how Nephi and Jacob understood Isaiah, we must do three things: First, we need to see how what we read typifies Christ and how God and Christ have revealed themselves in history. Second, we need to understand how Isaiah's prophecies are about covenants. (See 2 Nephi 9:1.) Finally, we need to pay attention to how Nephi and Jacob interpreted Isaiah in *their* context.

The study questions for Isaiah 2–6 (*The Old Testament Made Harder*, lesson 36) may be helpful for these chapters.

Rather than try to cover all of these chapters, I will focus on only parts of two, chapters 19 and 25— that is, one chapter from Isaiah and another chapter in which Nephi talks about studying Isaiah.

2 Nephi 19

Verse 2: Why does the prophet use the past-tense verb form *have seen* to describe something in the future?

One way to understand this light literally is as the light from the destruction by fire of the Assyrians. On the other hand, the symbolism of light is fairly obvious. What might the relation be between the literal and the symbolic meanings?

Verse 4: In "thou hast broken the yoke of his burden," to whom does *his* refer? ("Yoke of his burden" and "staff of his shoulder" may mean the same thing.) It is relatively easy to think of literal meanings for this verse, but what might be some spiritual readings? From what spiritual burden and spiritual oppressor will Israel be saved? What would that have meant to those who heard Isaiah prophesy? To the Nephites? To us?

Verse 6: This is one of the most famous verses in Isaiah (and perhaps one of the most famous verses in scripture, thanks to Handel). As a result, we may be overconfident that we understand fully what it means. Consider a couple of questions: The verse begins with *for*, or *because*, so it must explain something that came in the verses before. What does it explain?

Why does Isaiah focus on Christ as a child?

What does it mean to say that the government will be on the shoulders of the Christ child? What is the alternative? In other words, what would it mean for the government *not* to be on his shoulders?

Do the names used here have particular significance? (Why, for example, speak of Christ as a child, as the verse does in the beginning, and then use the title of "Father"?)

Verse 7: What is an increase of government?

After the phrase "peace there is no end," it is difficult to understand this verse. Looking at a more modern translation of Isaiah 9:7 may help you make sense of it. Here, for example, is the verse according to the New American Standard Bible:

> *There will be no end to the increase of His government or of peace,*
>
> *On the throne of David and over his kingdom,*
>
> *To establish it and to uphold it with justice and righteousness*
>
> *From then on and forevermore.*
>
> *The zeal of the Lord of hosts will accomplish this.*

What is coming on David's throne and kingdom? How will that order his kingdom? (Some translators use *establish* instead of *order*—and *uphold* instead of *establish*.)

How will this coming thing establish (or uphold) David's throne with judgment and justice?

The sentence "The zeal of the Lord of Hosts will perform this" is ambiguous. It could refer to either the zeal for the Lord or the Lord's zeal for his people. What understandings are created by each of these possibilities? Does one seem more likely, or are they both useful?

Verses 8–21: Notice that there are three balanced sections within these verses, each ending in the phrase "For all this his anger is not turned away, but his hand is stretched out still." (The sections are verses 8–12, 9–17, and 18–21.) Does the repeated ending tell us something about how we are to understand the sections it ends?

These verses are some of the most poetic in scripture; they clearly show Isaiah's artistic ability. Why does Isaiah write so poetically? Why not present the material in a more straightforward way? Is Isaiah's use of poetic language essential to his message, or is it just his idiosyncrasy?

2 Nephi 25

Verses 1–3: Because he knows they will not understand, not having been taught to understand this kind of prophecy, Nephi appends his quotation with an explanation.

Verse 3: What does Nephi think is the point of these chapters from Isaiah? Does that differ from our usual way of understanding these chapters? If so, how?

Verse 4: To whom are the prophecies of Isaiah plain? What does that say about the Nephites? What does it say about us?

What would it take to have the spirit of prophecy? Is that limited to particular persons or callings, or is it a gift anyone may have?

Verse 5: In verse 4, Nephi said his soul delights in plainness. Here he says his soul delights in Isaiah. Does that mean that Isaiah is plain? (He does say, after all, that the Jews understood Isaiah.)

What would it mean to be "taught after the manner of the things of the Jews"? Has Nephi been so taught? Jacob? Nephi's people?

Verse 7: What does Nephi mean when he speaks of "my plainness"? His plainness compared to what? How does he describe his plainness, and why is that description important?

Verse 8: What reason does Nephi give for the writings of Isaiah being of value in the last days? Why does Nephi address particularly those who don't value Isaiah's work?

What does he mean when he says he will confine his words to his own people?

Verses 9–19: Nephi gives an overview of the scattering, gathering, rescattering, and regathering of Israel, including an account of Christ's first coming. Is this intended as only a restatement of what he has quoted in Isaiah? If so, why did he quote so many chapters from Isaiah? Or is it something like an outline or interpretive key to the book, something given to help us understand Isaiah better but not to take its place? If that, can you think of specific things you wouldn't have understood without Nephi's overview?

Verse 20: How does the reference to the miracle of the bronze serpents on Moses's staff serve as a testimony that what Nephi has said is true?

Verse 23: What are the two purposes for Nephi's writing?

How does the Book of Mormon persuade us to believe in Christ? How does it persuade us to be reconciled to God? What does it mean to be saved by grace? (Compare 2 Nephi 31:19; Mosiah 2:21; and Luke 17:7–10.)

Why does Nephi's point about being saved by grace follow his statement of his purposes for writing? Why make that point here?

Verse 25: What does it mean that the law of Moses is dead to them? What does it mean that they keep the law though the law is dead to them? Is he teaching the same thing that Paul teaches in various places, such as Romans 3:20–24 (footnote b)?

What does it mean to be alive in Christ?

What does it mean to say that they do what they do "because of the commandment," especially if the law is dead to them?

Verse 27: Why do their children have to know the deadness of the law in order to have life in Christ? Why must they look forward to that life? It makes sense to say that they must look forward to the coming of Christ, but why do they have to look forward to life in him?

What does Nephi mean when he says that after Christ fulfills the law they will not need to harden their hearts against him? Does that mean they harden their hearts because of the law? If so, how so? If not, why not?

Verses 28–29: In the middle of verse 28, Nephi says that "the right way is to believe in Christ and deny him not." At the beginning of verse 29, he says the same thing. Why is that repetition necessary?

Verse 29: What does it mean to bow down to Christ? How do we do that in our lives now? What does worship mean here? What does it mean to be "cast out"?

Verse 30: What might this verse say about our own "law"?

Lesson 10
2 Nephi 26–30

These questions will concentrate on 2 Nephi 26:20–31; 27:24–30; and 28:11–15, 19–24.

2 Nephi 26

Verse 20: To whom does "the Gentiles" refer? Why must we understand that to understand the import of these verses?

What image does the phrase "lifted up in the pride of their eyes" convey? How is that appropriate to the meaning conveyed?

What is their stumbling block?

Though in the nineteenth century the word *church* meant pretty much what it means today, according to the *Oxford English Dictionary* (a historical dictionary) it seems originally to have meant "that which has to do with a lord." So we can understand a church to be more than a religious institution; in principle, any organization that has a lord can be called a church. What is a lord? How does it differ from a boss? From a parent? Perhaps the broader meaning of the word *church* can help us understand the many churches that have been built up as a description of our culture as a whole rather than as a description of only its religious life.

Note the comparison created by the use of "put down" and "preach up." What does that say about the people being described? Specifically, how does one preach his own wisdom and learning? How does doing so allow one to "get gain and grind upon the face of the poor"?

What does "grind upon the face of the poor" mean? (This is Nephi's variation of a phrase from Isaiah. See Isaiah 3:15 and 2 Nephi 13:15.) How and when do we do that?

Verse 21: Can you give examples of how churches create envyings and malice and strife? Does envy, malice, or strife ever find a place in our congregations? How?

Verse 22: What is a secret combination? (See 2 Nephi 9:9 and the corresponding study questions.) What is the point of the *flaxen* cord? What does the fact that it is flaxen—made of flax (linen) or looking like flax—indicate?

Verses 23–25: Notice that the point of verse 22 seems not to have been so much an explanation of how Satan works as it is a comparison to the Lord, so we will understand how the Lord *doesn't* work.

Verse 23 is a hinge that swings us from the description of how Satan works to a description of how the Lord works.

In verse 25, what contrast does Nephi make between the Lord and Satan?

In verse 25 we see Nephi use a phrase from Isaiah: "buy milk and honey without money and without price." What is the significance of milk and honey? What is the significance of buying it "without price"?

In what sense is the gospel a free gift? Why might Nephi have been reminded of Isaiah's phrase in this context? How is the theme of these verses related to the last part of verse 20?

Verses 26–28: What is the point of these verses? Why are they formulated as rhetorical questions? Why are the messages of these verses important to us?

Verse 29: Why is this called *priest*craft? Is it something found primarily among priests? How do we go about setting ourselves up for a light to the world? Compare this to 3 Nephi 12:16. What's the difference? What does it mean to seek the welfare of Zion?

Verse 30: Instead of priestcraft, the Lord has commanded people to have charity. Why is charity the antidote (or is it the response?) to priestcraft?

Why is it that without charity we are nothing? What is the difference between this nothing and the nothing that Benjamin says we must recognize ourselves to be if we are to receive salvation (Mosiah 4:11)?

Verse 31: Is *perish* used here in the same sense it is used at the end of verse 30? If so, we are commanded not to allow the laborer in Zion to labor for money. It isn't just that he shouldn't *do* it, but that we are told that if we have charity we won't *allow* it. What is a laborer in Zion? (Am I not laboring in Zion when I take up my occupation?) What would it mean for such a person to labor for money? How would we prevent that for ourselves? Can we prevent it or help prevent it for others?

2 Nephi 27

Verses 24–25: The Savior quoted a version of verse 25 to Joseph Smith (Joseph Smith—History 1:19). How did it apply to the people among whom Joseph found himself? In what sense might it apply to us today?

What is fear toward the Lord? (Notice that 2 Nephi 27:34 suggests that *sanctify* and *fear* may have similar meanings.) What are the precepts of men? What would it mean to have our fear of the Lord taught by the precepts of men?

Verses 26–27: Whom is the Lord warning in these verses? Of what is he warning them? How would we "seek deep to hide [our] counsel [i.e., deliberations] from the Lord"? Why might a person think that his or her acts are hidden? What does it mean to compare a person's worldview to potter's clay? How does Nephi explain the fact that the Lord knows all our works?

Verses 28–30: Nephi quotes from Isaiah again (Isaiah 29:17ff.). Isaiah gives a list of miracles: Lebanon (in those days a forest) will become a fruitful field and the fruitful field will become a forest, the deaf will hear the words of the book and the blind will see, and the meek (the gentle, i.e., those without worldly power) will increase. What is the point of this list of miracles? There are obvious literal fulfillments of these, but beyond that what do they say to us?

Isaiah and, therefore, Nephi mention the poor over and over again, and they regard the deliverance of the poor as tantamount to the Second Coming. Why do Isaiah and Nephi take such a keen interest in the poor, and in what sense do the poor have a special relation to the Lord? What does this say to us?

2 Nephi 28

Verse 11: Who has gone out of the way and become corrupted? Once again Nephi seems to be quoting scripture. This is a variation on or another translation of the beginning of Psalms 14:3 and 53:3. (See also Romans 3:12.) Does looking at those psalms help us understand the point Nephi is making?

Verse 12: Why is pride mentioned twice in this verse? You may have heard of chiasmus, a rhetorical form of inverted parallelism found in scripture and other writings. This verse is in another, similar rhetorical form: inclusion. An inclusion is like a sandwich, with two pieces of bread and a filling in between. Inclusion creates a set of parentheses around something to help us understand that thing. Here the "bread" is the mention of pride; the "filling" is what comes between: false teachers, false doctrine, corrupt and lifted-up churches. What is the relation between the "bread" of this inclusion" and its "filling"?

What is doctrine? A look at a fairly comprehensive dictionary (perhaps the *Oxford English Dictionary*) or at the 1828 edition of *Webster's* can give you good ideas as to what this word might mean. Also use a concordance to look at some of the ways the word gets used in the scriptures, and ask yourself how those uses differ from what you thought the word means.

Verse 13: How do fine sanctuaries rob the poor? Is this something we must be cognizant of?

How does fine clothing rob the poor? Our society puts a great emphasis on fashion. Might we sometimes be guilty of robbing the poor with our fine clothing? How? What is the alternative?

Who are the meek and the poor in heart? How are they persecuted? Are there ways in which we persecute the meek and poor in heart? Can you give specific examples of how?

Verse 14: Only a few haven't gone astray. To whom does *they* refer in the phrase "nevertheless, they are led, that in many instances they do err"? To those with stiff necks and high heads, or to the few who are humble followers of Christ? Does the word *nevertheless* help us answer that question by pointing to one of these groups more than the other?

Verse 15: What is the connection between pride, preaching false doctrine, committing whoredoms, and perverting the way of the Lord? In what ways are these kinds of acts related? Is "pervert[ing] the right way of the Lord" one of a list of four things, or is it the general description of the three things that come before it?

As we read verses 19–24, it is often tempting to see someone else as the person described, often someone outside the Church, but if someone inside, then someone with whom we disagree. However, the scriptures are most useful to us when we apply them to ourselves, so our questions should be about us: how do *I* anger at that which is good, become lulled into carnal security, or accept flattery and deny the existence of hell?

Verses 19–20: When will the kingdom of the devil shake? Will it shake with its power or be shaken by something external to it? Who is in the kingdom of the devil? (Review 1 Nephi 14:10 in context.)

Why do we sometimes anger at that which is good? How do we justify such anger to ourselves and others?

Verse 21: In what ways might we be pacified in Zion?

Can you explain what it means to say that the devil cheats the souls of those who are pacified? How does he do that? Of what does he cheat them?

Verse 22: Can believing Latter-day Saints be duped in the manner described in this verse? How?

Verse 24: What does it mean to be at ease in Zion? Isn't Zion a place of rest (ease) and security? Is the ease this verse warns against a cessation of labor or the ease of conscience?

Lesson 11

2 Nephi 31–33

2 Nephi 31

Verse 2: What does the word *doctrine* mean?

Why is what Nephi and Jacob have written sufficient? Sufficient for what?

The phrase "the doctrine of Christ" can be understood to mean "the doctrine that comes from Christ" or "the doctrine about Christ." Which meaning do you think Nephi intends?

Verses 2–3: Nephi uses variations of the word *plain* three times, twice in the second half of verse 2 and once in the beginning of verse 3. Why does he delight in plainness? Does what he has said about the manner of prophesying of the Jews help us understand that? (See 2 Nephi 25:2–8.)

A common meaning of *plain* is "unornamented." However, Webster's 1828 dictionary also gives "honesty" as one of its meanings. Is that meaning part of what Nephi intends with the word? If you say yes, what makes you think so?

When Nephi says he delights in plainness, "for after this manner doth the Lord God work," what is he telling us?

Given the highly figured language in works such as Isaiah and Jeremiah, and the importance of types in the Old

Testament as well as the Book of Mormon, how can Nephi say that the Lord works plainly?

Verse 5: What does "to fulfil all righteousness" mean? To think about that, begin by asking what the word *righteousness* means? After you feel that you have a satisfactory definition, ask yourself why Nephi uses the qualifier *all* and what it means to fulfill righteousness.

We usually say that baptism is for the remission of sin. Though that is true, apparently it isn't the only reason for baptism, for if it were, Christ wouldn't need to be baptized. What other purpose or purposes might baptism also serve?

Verses 6–8: Nephi's rhetorical question in verse 6 suggests that these verses tell us what it means to fulfill all righteousness. How do they do so? Does this have something to do with other reasons for baptism besides the remission of sin?

Verse 8 begins with "Wherefore . . .": because the events of verse 7 happened, the event of verse 8 happened. What does this teach us? Does it say anything about the gift of the Holy Ghost?

Verse 9: Nephi gives another reason for Jesus's baptism. What is it? Why is that an important lesson for us? How is it related to the teaching of verses 7–8?

Verses 10–12: These verses begin and end with admonitions to follow Christ. What do they teach in between, and what has that to do with following Christ?

Compare what Nephi teaches here with 3 Nephi 18:24. How are these two teachings related?

Usually when someone tells us to keep the command-ments, that person mentions the law of chastity, the Word of Wisdom, tithing, or things like them. Here, Nephi men-tions only repentance and baptism. Why does he focus on those particular commandments?

Verse 13: Does Nephi give a list here (follow with full pur-pose of heart, acting no hypocrisy, acting no deception be-fore God, having real intent, repenting of sin, witnessing that you are willing to take the name of Christ, and so on)? Or is he naming one thing (following with full purpose of heart) and then explaining what that means in the list that follows?

How is this teaching related to that of Moroni 7:6–11?

What does it mean to speak with the tongue of angels? Is it significant that *tongue* is singular rather than plural, though *angels* is plural? What is the connection between having the Holy Ghost and speaking with the tongue of angels?

Why is the Holy Ghost necessary if we wish to shout praises to the Holy One of Israel? To whom does "the Holy One of Israel" refer? What is the significance of that name?

Verse 14: How does one deny Christ?

Verses 15–18: How do these verses define enduring to the end? What circumstances might have been the catalyst for Nephi's emphasis on being baptized because Christ was?

Verses 19–20: What does "relying wholly upon the merits of him who is mighty to save" mean? (Compare Moroni 6:4.) What would it mean not to rely wholly on his merits? On what other merits might we rely?

Does the first part of verse 20 tell us that if we are to rely wholly on the merits of the Savior, then we must press forward in perfect hope and love? What does it mean to have perfect hope? Perfect love?

Consider the context; then ask yourself what "feasting upon the word of Christ" means in that context.

To what does "the word" refer here? That phrase is used in verses 19 and 20. Does one use help us understand the other? Is there a referent for the phrase in some of the earlier verses of the chapter?

Verse 21: Why does Nephi say this doctrine is "the only and true doctrine"? What do the words *only* and *true* each mean that helps us understand his point when they are put together?

2 Nephi 32

Verses 1–3: Notice the strangeness of these verses: Speaking to his extended family, Nephi notes that they may wonder what they should do after they have entered in by the way. Then he answers by reminding them that after they receive the Holy Ghost, they can speak with the tongue of angels. How does that answer the question of what one does after entering the way? What does verse 3 teach us about what it means to speak with the tongue of angels? What does it mean to speak the words of Christ? Nephi tells them that if they have the Holy Ghost they will speak with the tongue of angels. Then he tells them that angels speak the words of Christ by the Holy Ghost. And he concludes by saying that the words of Christ will tell them everything they should do. Given that series, are they to speak the words of Christ or hear them? Is it significant that in 2 Nephi 31:20 Nephi told us to feast on the word (singular) of Christ but now he says we should feast on the words (plural)?

Verse 4: To what does "these words" refer?

Verse 6: To what does "this is the doctrine of Christ" refer? Does it refer to what Nephi teaches in verse 6?

Verse 7: Is Nephi speaking of his own people here or of his family, including the group with Laman and Lemuel, or of humanity in general?

If knowledge is given in plainness, what need is there to search it?

Verses 8–9: About what are Nephi's listeners pondering? Why do you think they might be doing so?

What kinds of things do we "perform to the Lord"? What is the significance of using *to* rather than *for*?

What does it mean for a person to have a certain performance consecrated to him or her? What would it mean for that not to be the case?

2 Nephi 33

Verse 2: Is Nephi describing his own people here or warning them of what might happen to them by telling them what has happened to many people?

Verse 4: What might Nephi mean when he says that he has written these words in weakness? Notice that doing good and believing in Christ are parallel in this verse. The scriptures very often use parallel phrases or ideas to mean the same thing. Is that the case here?

Verse 6: What does it mean to glory in Jesus? Do we glory in Jesus? How?

Verse 8: Why does Nephi add the note about Jews at the end of this verse? How is his own background relevant to understanding this note?

Verse 9: Why does he add what he says about the Gentiles in this verse when there is nothing comparable in what he says about his people and the Jews?

Verse 10: Nephi says that "if ye shall believe in Christ ye will believe in these words." Does he mean that literally? After all, it follows logically from that sentence that if you don't believe these words, then you don't believe *in* Christ. One could use what Nephi says to argue that only Latter-day Saints are Christians. Does that make sense? How or why not?

Verse 12: Of whom is Nephi speaking in this verse? In other words, to whom does "many of us, if not all" refer?

Verse 14: To what does "words of the Jews" refer? How does one respect those words? Could an anti-Semite respect the words of the Jews? (Reread 2 Nephi 29:4–5.)

Verse 15: What has Nephi sealed on earth? How are we to understand that sealing power? Are there other times when we've seen it used?

Lesson 12
Jacob 1–4

Jacob 1

Verses 2–4: What things did Jacob tell Nephi he should write about? Why that and not the history of his people? Later Mormon includes more of what we would call history rather than making it a record of sacred things only. Why?

Verse 7: What does Jacob's use of *persuade* suggest? What does it mean "to partake of the goodness of God"? How do we partake, in other words, share in that goodness?

If Jacob is talking about something like being converted, how is this description apt?

What does it mean to "enter into his rest"? Jacob probably knows the phrase "his rest" from Isaiah 11:10. Does that scripture shed any light on what he means?

Verse 8: Jacob seems to say there are only two choices: we can "rebel against God" and "provoke him to anger," or we can "believe in Christ, and view his death, and suffer his cross and bear the shame of the world." (Compare 2 Nephi 2.) Why are there only those two choices? What does it mean to believe in Christ? How do we "view his death"? How do we "suffer his cross"? How do we "bear the shame of the world"? How is viewing Christ's death, suffering his cross, and bearing the shame of the world the opposite of rebelling against God?

Verse 9: At this point in the Book of Mormon it's been about fifty-five years since the Nephites landed in the New World. About how old would Nephi have been?

Why doesn't Jacob tell us the name of the man anointed to be king?

Verse 10: What might it mean that Nephi has "wielded the sword of Laban" to defend his people? When might that have happened?

How do you imagine that Nephi "labored all his days for their welfare"?

Verses 13–14: What do these verses tell us about the designations *Lamanite* and *Nephite* in the Book of Mormon? Are they political divisions? Are these divisions always used in the same way throughout the Book of Mormon? What does this description of these divisions show us about how we are to understand the terms?

Verses 15–16: What does Jacob imply when he says that the Nephites began to "indulge themselves *somewhat* in wicked practices" (verse 15)? Does Jacob 2:5 throw any light on this?

What does this verse tell us about the polygamy of David and Solomon?

In verse 16, Jacob gives two additional reasons for his sermon. Do you see anything in these verses that applies to us?

Verse 17–18: Why do you think Jacob taught them in the temple? Why does he describe his calling and consecration as a priest and teacher as an "errand from the Lord"? What does it mean to be *consecrated* a priest?

Verse 19: What does it mean to magnify an office? Perhaps seeing how the word *magnify* is used in the scriptures will help us understand. The KJV translation of the Old Testament uses *magnify* thirty-four times in several ways: it speaks of magnifying the Lord's name (e.g., 2 Samuel 7:26); it speaks of the Lord magnifying one of his servants (e.g., 2 Chronicles 1:1); and it speaks of those who magnify themselves against the Lord (e.g., Psalm 55:12). As far as I can tell, however, it never speaks of magnifying an office. (The closest it comes is in 2 Chronicles 31:18, where it says the priest sanctified themselves in their office.)

The KJV translation of the New Testament uses *magnify* six times, in five cases as the Old Testament does. In Romans 11:13, however, Paul speaks of magnifying his office. Here *magnify* can also be translated "praise" or "honor." When used to refer to the resurrection, the Greek verb that Paul uses here means "to clothe in splendor." The noun form of the word means "glory" and refers specifically to God's glory.

The Book of Mormon uses the term *magnify* only five times, three times as the Old Testament does and twice in terms of magnifying one's office. (Every use occurs before the coming of Christ.) Jacob is the only Book of Mormon writer to use *magnify* in connection with magnifying one's office (Jacob 1:19 and 2:2). However, the Doctrine and Covenants differs from the other scriptures in that it uses *magnify* only in connection with magnifying one's office.

What do you make of those differences in usage?

99

Jacob 2

Verse 4: When Jacob says "as yet, ye have been obedient unto the word of the Lord," does that contradict what he said in verses 15–16 of chapter 1 or what he says in verse 5 of this chapter?

Verse 5: Why do you think he describes the Lord as "the all-powerful Creator of heaven and earth"? What does that description of the Lord emphasize? How is that emphasis appropriate to the circumstances in which he is preaching?

What does it mean to "labor in sin"? Does anything in this verse help us understand why Jacob used *somewhat* in talking about their sins (Jacob 1:15–16)?

Verses 6–10: What bothers Jacob about what he is going to say? Why does he shrink with shame (verse 6) when he seems not to have done anything wrong, and why should his soul be burdened (verse 9)?

What does Jacob think is the usual purpose of preaching the word of God (verse 8)? Considering the circumstances, what might these verses tell us about calling people to repentance? What does verse 10 tell us about Jacob's understanding of his task?

Verse 13: What does Jacob point to as the problem of riches? How do we avoid that problem?

Verse 16–17: What is pride of the heart (verse 16)? Is it a different kind of pride, or is this just another way to speak of what we usually describe as pride?

How does listening to the Lord's commands keep us from pride? How does pride destroy our souls?

What does it mean to think of our brothers and sisters like ourselves (verse 17)? What does it mean to be familiar with all? Can you think of specific ways in which you can do this?

What does the word *substance* mean literally? In this usage, what does it mean? Given the meaning of the word *substance*, what does it mean to be free with it? How are we already rich? In what specific ways can we make others rich like ourselves?

Verses 18–19: How do we seek the kingdom of God?

What does it mean to "obtain a hope in Christ"? How do we obtain that hope?

If we can't answer those questions, Jacob seems to say, we have no business seeking riches.

Notice what Jacob says: (1) After we obtain a hope in Christ, we will obtain riches if we seek them. (2) If we seek riches after we have obtained a hope in Christ, then we will do so in order to do good. He doesn't say we *should* do so to do good. Why not? Does Deuteronomy 8:18 help us understand better what Jacob is teaching?

Verses 20–21: Jacob doesn't just say that pride is bad; he says it is an abomination. Why?

Notice that he brings in the description of God as Creator again, as in verse 5. How is that relevant to his message? Why does Jacob say we were created?

Verses 24–30: How do these verses apply to us?

Why did Jacob deliver this part of the message second, and the part about pride and seeking for riches first?

Verses 31–34: What has prompted the message Jacob is giving? How do we cause the daughters of Zion to mourn and have sorrow today? In verse 32, is the term *men* being used generically, or does it refer to male human beings?

Verse 35: Why is what the Nephites have done worse than what the Lamanites did? (What did the Lamanites do?) As you think about this question, remember how Jacob tells us that he distinguishes Lamanites from Nephites (Jacob 1:13–14).

Jacob 3

Verse 1: Has Jacob saved "the word which healeth the wounded soul" (Jacob 2:8) for now?

What does it mean to be pure in heart?

Verse 2: What does it mean to lift up our heads?

What does it mean to "receive the pleasing word of God"?

What does it mean to "feast upon his love"? How is that related to feasting on the word (2 Nephi 31:20; 32:3)?

What does it mean to have our minds firm?

Verse 3–8: How might these verses apply to us? What do they teach us about chastity?

Why are the Lamanites better off than the Nephites?

What might verse 7 tell us about our own situation? What does Jacob mean when he says "their skins will be whiter than yours, when ye shall be brought with them before the throne of God" (verse 8)? Why does he fear that will be true?

Does this verse tell us that a white skin indicates righteousness? How do we make sense of this verse without inferring that Jacob condones racism?

Verse 9: Why did the Nephites look down on the Lamanites? Why was that wrong? What does Jacob say they should do instead? When he commands them to "remember your own filthiness, and remember that their filthiness came because of their fathers," what is he saying about the origin of the Nephites' filthiness? Isn't he telling them something that today we believe would be harmful, telling them to think badly of themselves?

Verse 10: What consequence of their sins does Jacob warn them of? How does that apply to us?

Jacob 4

Verses 1–3: Why does Jacob tell us of the difficulty of writing on the plates and that the Book of Mormon writers can write only a little?

Who are the "beloved brethren" to whom Jacob refers in verse 3?

How does he want us to think of those whom he writes about?

Verse 4–5: Once again we are told the purpose of the Book of Mormon. Why is it important for us to know that the Nephites and the prophets before them knew of Christ?

Why do the Nephites keep the law of Moses? What does it mean to say that the law points our souls to God? We are no long required to keep the law of Moses, but does our law also point our souls to God? If the law points us toward God, what gets us to him?

Verse 6: How does this verse answer the questions I asked about in verses 4–5? How did Jacob and those like him get the faith that he describes here?

Verse 7: Why is it important that his listeners remember their weaknesses? What might that say to us about our weaknesses and problems?

Verses 8–9: This seems to be a short psalm of praise. What is its point, and how does it fit in with the discussion that came before? How does it lead into the following discussion?

Verse 10: How do we try to counsel the Lord? How do we take counsel from him?

This verse begins with "Wherefore . . . ," indicating that it follows from the previous verses. How is that so?

Verse 11: Does this verse answer the question asked earlier about obtaining a hope in Christ (Jacob 2:18–29)?

What does it mean to be reconciled through the Atonement? How do we do that?

What does it mean to be presented as the "first-fruits"?

Verse 12: What is Jacob's point here? What possible objection is he replying to?

Verse 13: Why is this advice or explanation about prophecy appropriate here as part of his explanation of the gospel?

Verses 14–17: Of what is Jacob warning the Nephites? How can we apply this warning to ourselves?

Lesson 13
Jacob 5–7

We will concentrate on chapter 5, the longest chapter in the Book of Mormon. However, because chapters 4 and 5 were one chapter in the first edition of the Book of Mormon, and Jacob 4:15–18 is essential to understanding the allegory, I suggest that you read both chapters as part of the lesson.

Rather than the usual verse-by-verse list of thought questions, here are two outlines of the chapter followed by a few general thought questions on chapter 5 and then several questions on chapters 6–7.

Outline 1

Jacob 4:15–16: The stumbling stone is also the only possible foundation.

Verses 17–18: If someone has rejected the only stone that could be their foundation, how can it become that foundation? (Compare Romans 11.)

Jacob 5:3: The master finds the olive tree (the house of Israel) in "decay."

Verses 4–5: The master prunes it, digs about it, and nourishes it, hoping it will send out new shoots.

Verse 6: It sends out new shoots, but the top dies.

Verses 7: In an effort to save the tree, the master commands his servant to bring wild olive branches to be grafted in, and he says the old branches will be burned.

Verse 8: The master says he will take the new shoots and graft them in somewhere else. What matters most is that the root of the old tree is preserved.

Verse 11: The master has the old grafted tree dug about, pruned, and nourished, saying he has grafted in the new branches in an attempt to save the root.

Verses 13–14: The master takes the new shoots to secret places in the garden and plants them to preserve them and their fruit.

Verse 17: The tree into which the wild branches were grafted bears good fruit, fruit like the natural fruit. The tree has been saved.

Verses 20–25: The master and the servant visit the transplanted new shoots. Two have been placed in poor spots in the garden but have produced good fruit. One has been placed in a good spot but has produced mixed fruit: some branches bear good fruit, some don't.

Verse 26: The master commands the servant to cut off the branches that do not bear good fruit and to burn them.

Verse 27–28: The servant dissuades him. They dig about and nourish all the trees in the vineyard.

Verses 30–32: When they return to the original, grafted tree, they discover that it bears a lot of fruit, none of it good.

Verses 38–40: When they check the transplanted trees, they discover that they too all bear bad fruit. The good branch of the tree that brought forth mixed fruit has withered away.

Verse 48: The servant suggests that the trees have gone bad because the tops have been allowed to "overcome" the roots.

Verses 49–51: The master says, "Let's cut all of them down and burn them," but the servant asks him to wait and he agrees.

Verses 52–56: In order to save the roots, the master and the servant remove the worst of the branches of the old, grafted tree and graft the natural branches back in. Then they graft branches from the old tree onto the transplanted trees.

Verse 62: The master orders that the trees be dug about and nourished one more, final time.

Verse 65: As the trees grow, the master commands that the workers are to gradually remove the worst branches.

Verses 73–74: With the worst branches gradually removed and the growth of the tops kept in line with the root system, the trees begin to produce good fruit again, each of them equal to the other.

Verses 77–76: The Lord of the vineyard gathers fruit for a long time from these trees but suggests that some of the branches will eventually go bad again. He says that when that happens, he will preserve the good and put the bad "in its own place." In the end, however, he will burn the entire vineyard.

Outline 2

I.

    a. The stumbling stone and the foundation stone are the same.

    b. How can a stumbling stone become a foundation stone?

II.

    a. The olive tree is found in decay.

    b. It is nourished but produces only a few new shoots; the old part remains decayed.

    c. The wild is grafted in; the new shoots are transplanted.

III.

    a. The old tree bears good fruit; of three transplants, three produce good fruit and one produces some of each.

    b. The master is dissuaded from destroying the bad branches on the one transplanted tree.

IV.

    a. Later all the trees are producing bad fruit, and the good branches of the one previously mixed tree has withered away. The cause: the tops grew faster than the roots could bear.

b. The servant dissuades the master from destroying the entire garden.

V.

a. They cross-graft the trees.

b. They nourish the trees and gradually remove the worst branches.

c. All of the trees begin to produce good fruit.

VI.

Some will produce bad fruit in the future; those branches that do will be removed.

VII.

At the end the whole garden will be burned.

Overall questions: Jacob 5

1. Why do the scriptures use allegories and metaphors? What might that say about how we should think about the scriptures? Might it say anything about how we should think? Does the fact that a prophet uses metaphors suggest that the things that he teaches might all be "only" metaphorical? Why not? Should we, perhaps, teach our children more about metaphor and allegory than we usually do? Should we, perhaps, learn to use them more than we usually do?

2. Who or what do each of the elements of the allegory represent? Verse 3 identifies the original tree. What does the wild tree represent? What about the master? The servant? The grafting of the wild branches into the old tree? The transplanting of the old branches? Pruning, digging about, and nourishing? The good fruit? The bad fruit?

3. What does each event in the story stand for? Does this allegory have one meaning, or one way of being understood? If so, why is it given as an allegory? Why not just tell us the point? If not, what are some of the things it teaches us?

4. In two different places the servant dissuades the vineyard master from carrying out his plans for destruction, once with bad results, once with good. What might this teach us? About ourselves? About prophets? About the Lord?

5. Why was the allegory of Zenos important to the Nephites?

6. Why is it important to us?

7. Why is the *olive* tree used in this allegory?

8. What other trees are important scriptural symbols? The trees in the Garden of Eden? The tree of life in Lehi's dream? The tree that grows from the seed planted in our hearts (Alma 32:37)? The cross? Any others? Why is a tree such an appropriate symbol? Does the use of the tree as a symbol in each of these places connect the others in some way or ways? How?

Jacob 6

How is the prophecy of this chapter related to the allegory? Why does Jacob first read/record the allegory, then give a prophecy of his own that has a similar message, if not the same one? To whom is Jacob speaking, those who are of the house of Israel (the Church), or those who are not? How is that significant?

Verses 4–5: How are these two verses related to each other? One way to think about that is to ask what to make of the word *wherefore* at the beginning of verse 5.

Verses 11–12: Jacob commands the people to repent, and then he commands them to be wise. Do these mean the same thing? What kind of wisdom is repentance? Is the wisdom of repentance prudential: we will avoid our guilt if we do? Or is it something else? Is repentance, the mighty change of heart, itself a kind of wisdom?

Jacob 7

Why does this story follow the allegory of the olive tree? What is the thematic connection?

Verses 1, 4: Do these verses suggest that perhaps Sherem was an outsider, someone who did not come from among Jacob's people and was not a native speaker of their language?

THE BOOK OF MORMON MADE HARDER: SCRIPTURE STUDY QUESTIONS

Lesson 14
Enos, Jarom, Omni, Words of Mormon

We will concentrate on Enos 1:1–18 and several verses in Omni.

Enos

As you read through Enos, notice what an accomplished writer he is. Though the scriptures are filled with good writing, few scriptural writers write as well as he.

Verses 1–2: This sentence is odd. It begins with a thought, "I, Enos, knowing my father that he was a just man," then moves to an example of his father's justice (namely that he taught Enos his language and also taught him "in the nurture and admonition of the Lord"). Then it takes up the theme of the rest of the book: Enos's wrestle before the Lord and its results. The first part begins the sentence as if Enos intended to tell us something about what he did because he knew his father was just; then he seems to get sidetracked. Can you explain what is going on here?

Why does Enos mention that his father taught him his language? Surely all parents teach their children their language. What point is Enos making?

What does it mean that Enos's father taught him in the "nurture and admonition of the Lord"? What does *nurture* mean? What would the Lord's nurture be? How would

113

one teach it to someone? What does *admonition* mean? Is it perhaps being used here as a synonym for *nurture*? The same phrase appears in Ephesians 6:4, where it means something like "discipline and instruction." Does it have the same meaning here?

In verse 2, why does Enos describe his experience as a wrestle with God? Does he perhaps have Jacob's wrestle with the Lord (or one of his messengers) in mind (see also Genesis 32:24–26)?

Verse 3: Can you think of specific things in Jacob's teaching to which Enos may be referring when he writes about the words he had often heard his father speak?

What does "eternal life" mean in this context? The phrase is used eighty-eight times in scripture, but it is never used in the Old Testament. On the other hand, on a percentage basis it occurs twice as often in the New Testament as in the Book of Mormon (though the Book of Mormon uses are almost all before Christ's coming—Old Testament times), and about twice as often in the Doctrine and Covenants as in the New Testament. What do you make of those differences in usage?

Though the words *joy* and *saints* are frequently referred to in scripture, this is the only place where the phrase "the joy of the saints" occurs. What do you think it means?

Verses 4–5: What does Enos mean when he says his soul hungered? What caused his soul to hunger? For what did it hunger?

What is supplication? What has it to do with his hunger of soul?

Verse 6: Enos says here that his guilt was swept away, but he didn't mention guilt before. Instead he talked about remembering what he had heard about eternal life and the joy of the saints. Why does guilt come up here?

Verses 7–8: Enos asks, "How?" and the Lord replies, "Because . . ." How can *because* answer a how question? What does it mean to "go to"? (Compare Genesis 11:7.) What is the Lord commanding Enos?

What does it mean to be whole?

When the Lord says that Enos has "never before" seen or heard Christ, does that suggest that he now has?

Verse 9: What do we learn from Enos's reaction to receiving forgiveness? To whom do his thoughts turn?

Verse 10: How is the Lord's promise an answer to Enos's prayer? This is the same promise that has been given all along. How is it an answer to his concerns for their welfare?

Verse 11: In verse 4, he prayed for his own soul; in verse 9, he prayed for his family (presumably the Nephites); now he prays for the Lamanites. Is it a series of steps or a progression of some kind? Why does he call the Lamanites "my brethren"?

Verses 12–13: Notice the difference between what happens in response to his concern for the Lamanites and what happened in response to his concern for the Nephites. When he asked about the Nephites, the original promise was repeated to him. When he asks about the Lamanites, the Lord tells him he can have whatever he desires for them. Why the difference? Why does the Lord grant Enos "according to [his] desires" in this case?

Why does Enos imagine the possibility about which he is concerned—that the Nephites will be destroyed and the Lamanites will not? What do you think might motivate that particular concern?

Verse 14: How does his description of the Lamanites compare with his description of them as his brethren? What do we see about Enos in these things?

What might the Lamanites have meant when they threatened to destroy the traditions of the Nephites' fathers? What specific fathers would they have had in mind at this date?

Verses 13–18: Notice that Enos is quite concerned (as are Jarom and Omni after him) that the records be preserved. Why? Why is it important that their concern be recorded in the Book of Mormon? What does it mean to us?

Omni

Why do Omni, Amaron, Chemish, and Abinadom write so little on the plates? And why would Omni confess in the plates his wickedness? Why mention it?

Verse 11: What does this verse tell us about the Nephite people at the time of Abinadom?

Verses 12–22: What do these verses show us about the Book of Mormon and Book of Mormon peoples?

Verse 25: Amaleki exhorts us to believe in four things: in prophesying and revelations, in the ministering of angels, in the gift of tongues, and in the gift of interpretation. Then he adds to those specific things that we should believe in all good things. What is the significance of the particular things he mentions? Why mention those four things rather than some others? In other words, when we choose examples of something, those examples often reveal much about what we are thinking, how we see the matter we are thinking about, and how we want those we are addressing to understand our point.

What do these examples tell us about Amaleki and his message?

Verse 26: How do we come to Christ? How do we partake of his salvation? Are coming to him and partaking of his salvation one thing or two?

Does "the power of his redemption" mean something different than "his redemption"? How do we partake of the power of his redemption?

Is "partake of his salvation, and the power of his redemption" parallel to "offer your whole souls as an offering unto him, and continue in fasting and praying, and endure to the end"?

In the context of this verse, what does it mean to be saved? From what are we saved?

Verses 28–30: What do these verses tell us about the Book of Mormon and Book of Mormon peoples?

Lesson 15
Mosiah 1–3

Mosiah 1

Verse 2: Notice that once again a Book of Mormon writer mentions a father teaching his children in "all the language of his fathers." The theme is a relatively important one. What might it mean to *us*?

Verse 3: The phrase "he also taught them" indicates that the language and prophecies the writer has in mind in verse 2 may be the language and prophecies of the Book of Mormon writers who preceded him. If so, it may indicate that teaching them about the language of the brass plates was an additional thing he did. Thus, "The language of their fathers was the language of the brass plates rather than the language they spoke" may not be a sufficient answer to the questions above. What else could *language* mean here?

Without the scriptures we cannot know the mysteries of God. What is a mystery? If we can assume that the scriptures contain those mysteries, what are they?

Verse 5: Verse 4 identified the scriptures with Lehi's memory: without them he couldn't have remembered, so they functioned as his memory. Here we see that without that memory his people would have "dwindled," and we see the implication that the problem of the Lamanites was a loss of memory. Instead of memory they had the "traditions of their fathers." As many scriptures indicate, remembering—the Lord remembering us and we remembering our sins and remembering him—is an important theme of the scriptures, especially the Book of Mormon. The word *remember* originally meant something like "call to mind again," but it may also have to do with re-memorializing and even re-membering (putting back together, making whole again). How do we remember the Lord? Do we use the scriptures and scripture study to remember?

Verse 6: These sayings and records are true. Is this claim a rejoinder to the Lamanite claims about the records?

What does it mean for something to be true? The most obvious answer is something like "it corresponds to reality," but that meaning is too narrow for the ways we use *true*. It doesn't, for example, explain what it means to say that the Church is true. There are, however, other significant meanings of *true*. Here, for example, we see the word *surety* used as a synonym for *true*: "trustworthiness" and "security," as well as "certainty." Other meanings include "honest" and "without deviation," and even "revealed," "disclosed," or "remembered." Do these other possible meanings of *true* add insight to our understanding of what it means to say that the Book of Mormon (or the Church or something else) is true?

Verses 7–12: King Benjamin says that he wants to do two things: give the people a ruler and give them a name. Since he is about to die, it is fairly clear why he wants to do the former, but why would he want to do the latter? What is the significance?

How does his sermon about Christ and the Atonement, the central part of his message, fit with his desires to give the people a ruler and a name? Why doesn't he mention that as one of his desires?

Verse 16: Why does King Benjamin give his son the sword of Laban and the Liahona? Of what might they be symbolic?

Mosiah 2

Verses 3–4: It has been more than four hundred years since Lehi left Jerusalem. That is like going to the temple to offer thanks now for something that happened in 1600. Why do the people come to the temple to offer thanks for that?

Verses 5–6: Why does the writer give us such detailed information about how the people pitched their tents? It must be important—after all, the original writer thought it important enough to engrave it on gold plates, and Mormon thought it important enough to include it in his abridgment when he could easily have left it out. Why do you think it was given to us?

Verse 9: Benjamin says he didn't have his people come so they could trifle with his words. What does that mean? Do we have that attitude when we listen to someone? Have you ever trifled with a talk? On the other side of the coin, when we speak, do we trifle with those who've come to hear us? Or when we call a meeting, do we trifle with the time of those who come?

Benjamin says he has had them come so they can hear and understand, so they can learn the mysteries. Can you make a list of the mysteries that he teaches?

Verse 11: Why does Benjamin remind them that he too suffers infirmities of body and mind?

Why does he rehearse how he came to be king?

Verses 12–15: Why do the things Benjamin lists allow him to have a clear conscience? What do they show?

Verse 17: This verse contains one of the most popular quotations from the Book of Mormon, but it contains a linguistic oddity: Why does it say that "when ye are in the service of your fellow beings ye are *only* in the service of your God"? What does that word *only* mean here?

Verses 17–19: Notice how Benjamin shifts from his service to thanks to God by focusing on service and kingship: If you owe me thanks for the service I've wrought as king, just think of the thanks you owe the Heavenly King.

Verses 20–21: Notice the things we might do for God and what God might do for us:

What he gives		What we might return
creation	life	thanks with our whole soul
keeping	movement	praise with our whole soul
preservation	agency	service with our whole soul
rejoicing	continual	
peace	support	
the loan of breath		

Even if we return everything we can, it is obvious that we will continue to be indebted. As Benjamin says, we will remain unprofitable servants.

What does it mean to say that the Father has kept us? That he has preserved us? How has he caused us to rejoice?

Why is peace a gift from God? (Does that mean, then, that we should expect not to have continual peace?)

Why does Benjamin say that the Father lends us breath?

What does it mean that he supports us from moment to moment?

What is a profitable employee (servant)? What does it mean to say that we are unprofitable servants even when we do everything in our power to thank and praise and serve God?

Verse 22: Notice that obedience is what he requires in return for what he gives, not what he requires in order for us to get what he gives. Benjamin is not teaching that we earn what the Lord gives, but he is also not teaching that we don't have to do anything. How can obedience be our response to the Lord's gift?

Verse 23: We owe him our lives. Is this a repetition of what Benjamin said in verses 20 and 21?

Verse 24: Here Benjamin repeats verse 22, with an addition: We are required to be obedient, and if we are, we are immediately blessed and so are still in debt. What do you make of that addition?

Benjamin speaks of the Lord blessing us, and he also says the Lord pays us, but blessings and payments aren't the same, since the former is something given and the latter is something owed. Why does he mix the language this way? Are we blessed or paid for our obedience?

For another good discussion of the impossibility of boasting, see Romans 3 and 4. In fact, King Benjamin's sermon and Romans are good scriptural texts to read side by side, each one illuminating the other. They are an excellent example of how the Book of Mormon helps us read and understand the Bible, and vice versa.

Verse 25: In what sense do our bodies belong to the Creator? What does that mean to us?

Verse 28: In Mosiah 1:11, Benjamin said that his people had been diligent in keeping the commandments. Now he says he must rid his garments of their blood before he dies. Why is that necessary if they have been good people?

Verses 32–33: I suspect the contentions Benjamin has in mind are like the contentions between the Lamanites and Nephites. But how might this verse apply to us? What kinds of contentions are we susceptible to?

Verses 34–35: They have been taught about the results of contention and that they are indebted to Heavenly Father and must give him everything they have and everything they are. They have also been taught the contents of the brass plates and the teachings of the Nephite prophets. Why does Benjamin mention these particular things? The first is relatively apparent; contention is an obvious problem for the Book of Mormon people. But why does Benjamin remind them that they have been taught the contents of the plates and the teachings of their prophets? And why does he remind them that they have been taught that they owe everything to God?

What does it mean to give God everything we are?

Verses 36–41: Why does Benjamin remind them of what happens to those who rebel as well as what happens to those who are faithful?

Mosiah 3

Verse 1: What do you think moves Benjamin to make the transition to the topic of this chapter, Christ's coming in the flesh? Is there something in what he has just been discussing that points in that direction? In other words, what's the connection?

Verse 3: In what other incident does an angel speak of his message as "glad tidings of great joy" or something similar? Are there any parallels between the other case and this one?

Verse 4: What do you suppose Benjamin had been praying for in order to receive this answer?

Verse 5: Consider the name of the Lord used here: "The Lord Omnipotent who reigneth, who was, and is from all eternity to all eternity." First, why does the angel use such a long name? Why not just say "the Lord"? Second, what is the significance of that name? How is it related to the Lord's coming to dwell in a tabernacle of clay?

Verses 5–6: Look at the list of activities described, and then think about the Gospels, particularly the synoptic Gospels (Matthew, Mark, and Luke). Why is there such an emphasis on these miracles?

125

Verse 7: What is the significance of this list of the things Christ suffered? What does it tell us?

Verse 8: Notice again a contrast that Benjamin makes, the contrast between another lengthy name of the Lord and the name of His mother. What might the purpose of this contrast be?

Verse 9: What does "he cometh unto his own" mean? What salvation is Benjamin speaking of? Salvation from what?

Rather than attach some of the mysterious connotations to faith that are sometimes attached and that, as a result, often leave us thinking that we don't know what faith is or that we don't have it, it might be helpful to remember that the word *faith* means, more than perhaps anything else, "trust." Why is it that salvation comes through trusting the Savior? To what is Benjamin referring when he says "even after all this"?

Verse 10: To what is he referring when he says "all these things"? How do those things make a righteous judgment?

Verse 12: Why does Benjamin say that salvation comes only to those who repent and have faith? Since they are necessary, why doesn't he mention works or ordinances?

Verse 14: What does it mean to be stiff-necked? What does it mean to say that the law of Moses was given because the people were stiff-necked? What is it about the law of Moses that makes it appropriate for such a people?

Verse 15: Benjamin says that the Lord showed the Israelites many signs, wonders, types, and shadows. What are each of these, particularly types and shadows?

Verse 16: Why does Benjamin introduce the discussion of little children here?

Verse 17: Is there any significance to the name of the Lord used here? Does it relate to the content of the verse in some way?

Verse 18: Notice the contrast between little children and adults. Does that help explain verse 16? Given what has been said about little children in the previous verses, what does it mean to become as a little child? Notice again Benjamin's emphasis on belief. We usually emphasize actions. Why doesn't he?

Verse 19: There is sometimes a lot of discussion of the phrase "natural man." It is used outside latter-day scripture only once, in 1 Corinthians 2:14. In latter-day scripture it is used only three other times, and it isn't clear that it means the same thing each time: Alma 26:21; D&C 67:12; and Moses 1:14.

In 1 Corinthians, where it is used in a way similar to its use here, it could also be translated "unspiritual man." The word translated "natural" or "unspiritual" describes the life of this world. Does the 1 Corinthians use of the term help us understand the meaning here?

Notice the verb *yields* and the noun *enticings*. Benjamin describes the Holy Ghost's entreaties as if we have to resist them in order to not receive them. We often think of sin as easy and life by the Spirit as difficult, but Benjamin's language says something quite different. How can that be? How do we put off the natural man?

127

Notice the comparison to children again. It is fairly obvious what it means to be submissive to the Lord, to be humble, and to be full of love, but what does it mean to be meek—gentle—in relation to him? What about patient? How could we be anything but patient with the Lord? Can you think of specific ways in which one might not be meek with him, or ways in which one might not be patient?

Why does the list begin and end with submission? Why the repetition? This verse uses *saint* in the singular, the only time in scripture it is so used. It is plural every other time. Why is it plural except here? Why is it singular here? How does one become a saint?

Verse 21: How do you understand the word *only* here? Does it mean "except," as in some older usages?

Verses 24–27: This is the first time Benjamin has mentioned works in this sermon. How do they fit in? What is the relation between belief and faith on the one hand and works on the other?

Lesson 16
Mosiah 4–6

In addition to the normal questions, I also provide an outline of chapter 4 in appendix 1.

Mosiah 4

Verse 1: What is the fear of the Lord? Are King Benjamin's people afraid that the punishments he has described in verses 25–27 of chapter 3 will come upon them? How so if they are the diligent people Benjamin said they were in Mosiah 1:11?

Verse 2: How can those who have been diligent in keeping the commandments say these things of themselves, namely, that they are carnal and less than the dust of the earth? Today we would say such people have a poor self-image, but Mosiah doesn't seem to be telling us that the people were wrong to think of themselves this way. How do you explain this?

What do they ask for? How does that explain the question above?

How is what they ask for related to being diligent in keeping the commandments?

Is there any significance to the description they give of Christ at the end of the verse?

Verse 3: Notice what we have in the story we've seen so far: a diligent people who are filled with the fear of God and are humbled, and who then ask for mercy and for-giveness and receive those blessings. What might that say to us about our own salvation?

Might the joy described here have something to do with the "joy of the saints" mentioned by Enos? How does the experience of Benjamin's people compare and contrast with Enos's experience?

Verse 5: Benjamin is emboldened by his people's response. But rather than congratulating them on their repentance, he rubs it in: The knowledge of God's goodness has made you realize your worthless and fallen state. Why does he do this? Why not speak kind words to them? Why encourage the "negative attitude" and "bad self-image" that they seem to have? (Or does this whole sermon begin to make us wonder about the truthfulness of what we are told about the importance of a positive self-image?)

Verses 6–7: The things we need to come to know if we want salvation:

> God's goodness
>
> his matchless power
>
> his wisdom
>
> his patience
>
> his long-suffering
>
> the Atonement, which he prepared in the beginning in order to bring salvation

The things we must do in response:

trust the Lord (i.e., have faith)

be diligent in keeping the commandments

continue in the faith to the end of mortality

What is the relation between these two lists? How does the first one prepare us for the latter? Why do we need to know the things on the first list?

Verse 8: Notice that there are no other requirements for salvation than the three listed. But what about repentance? Ordinances? Did Benjamin leave them off the list, or are they included somehow?

Verses 9–10: These verses repeat what was just said in verses 6–8, but in different terms: what we must believe and do in order to receive salvation.

We must believe:

in God; that he exists

that he is the Creator

that he has all wisdom

that he has all power

that we don't understand all that he can

that we must repent and forsake our sins

that we must humble ourselves before God

We must:

ask for forgiveness

do the things corresponding to what we believe

What is the significance of each of the things we must believe? Why must we believe each of those things in order to be saved? What must we do that corresponds to each of the things we must believe? For example, what must we do that corresponds to believing in God and that he exists? What must we do that corresponds to believing that he is the Creator with all wisdom and power?

Verse 11: Once again, Benjamin repeats what he has been saying in different words. Why is this threefold repetition necessary?

Notice that he equates "coming to a knowledge of God's glory" with "knowing his goodness, tasting his love, and receiving a remission of sins." How are those the same things? (The word *glory* means "praise" or "praiseworthiness.")

Why does he say "retain in remembrance" rather than "remember"? What does the first add to our understanding?

If we've come to a knowledge of God's glory, Benjamin says, he wants us to remember God's goodness and our own nothingness, and also his goodness and long-suffering to us unworthy creations, and he wants us to humble ourselves "to the depths" and call on the Lord and remain steadfast in faith in what is to come. Why do we need to remember both the Father's goodness and our own nothingness?

Why do we need to remember his goodness and long-suffering, especially in relation to our unworthiness?

Is Benjamin a "negative" person?

What does it mean to be humbled to the depths? (Haven't we seen an example in this chapter?) Why is that necessary?

What is it that "is to come, which was spoken by the mouth of the angel"? (Remember the beginning verses of chapter 3.) In whom or what must our faith remain steadfast?

Verse 12: Notice that what follows, presumably through verse 16, is contingent on what has come before; it is contingent on remembering God's goodness and our own nothingness, humbling ourselves, calling on God, and remaining faithful.

We often cite the following verses as if they were commandments, but the beginning of this verse makes it plain that they are blessings that follow from receiving a remission of our sins. On the other hand, aren't commandments blessings?

Verses 12–16: If we do the things Benjamin has described, we will:

> always rejoice (even in the midst of difficulty?)
>
> be filled with the love of God (is this his love for us or our love for him?)
>
> always retain a remission of sins
>
> grow in a knowledge of the Creator's glory (which is the same as the knowledge of what is just and true!)
>
> not have a mind to injure one another, but to live peaceably and render to each his due (what is that due?)

not allow our children to go hungry or naked or to transgress the commandments (what does this say about child rearing?)

> or to fight and quarrel with each other and serve the devil

> but we will teach them to "walk in the ways of truth and soberness" (what are those ways? what does it mean for our children to be sober?)

> and to love one another

> and to serve one another

succor those who need succor

administer our substance to those who need it (what does the word *substance* mean?)

not allow the beggar to beg in vain (given the number of beggars in the world and the limitations of our resources, how do we do this?)

This list is important, for in it Benjamin has given us a test we can use to judge whether we are doing what it takes to receive salvation. The logic of what he says looks like this:

> If you are doing what it takes to receive salvation, then you will also be doing these things.

> So if you aren't also doing these things, then you aren't doing what it takes to receive salvation.

> > (An analogous argument would be: If you are a millionaire, you can afford a fifty-cent ice cream

cone. So if you can't afford a fifty-cent ice cream cone, you aren't a millionaire.)

What's interesting is that it doesn't follow from what he says that if you *are* doing these things you are doing what it takes to receive salvation. That invalid argument would look like this:

> If you are doing what it takes to receive salvation, then you will also be doing these things.

> So if you are also doing these things, you are doing what it takes to receive salvation.

>> (An analogous argument would be: If you are a millionaire, you can afford a fifty-cent ice cream cone. So if you can afford a fifty-cent ice cream cone, you are a millionaire. Obviously that isn't right, so neither is the hypothetical argument.)

Why does Mosiah give us a test for when we aren't doing what it takes to receive salvation, but no test for when we are doing what it takes?

What does "master of sin" mean? When Benjamin equates being the master of sin with being the evil spirit spoken of by the fathers, an enemy to all righteousness, what does he teach us?

What does it mean to be an enemy to *all* righteousness? How is that possible?

Verse 16: To whom does the word *beggar* refer in this and following verses? Is it the same as "those that stand in need your succor"?

Verse 17: In what ways do we say this?

Verse 18: Why would saying this about a beggar mean that we have no interest in the kingdom of God?

Verse 19: Is the answer to the question about verse 18 that if we say that about a beggar, we say it about ourselves and we condemn ourselves in saying it?

Verses 20–21: We must impart of our substance because the Father imparts of his. What does *substance* mean in this case? Why use that word rather than *wealth* or something similar?

Verses 17–23, 26: Of all the things on the list, why does Benjamin give so much emphasis to this particular one?

Verse 24: At what point can we deny the beggar because we cannot give to him? How little can we have?

Verse 25: Can we say, "I give not because I have not" in our hearts but be wrong? Can we deceive ourselves about how much we have to give? What does it mean that if we don't say this in our hearts we are condemned "because we covet that which [we] have not received"? What is it that we have not received but covet?

Verse 26: Notice the qualifier on our administrations to the needy: "according to their wants." What does that mean in practical terms? As home and visiting teachers? As people approached by various charitable organizations? As people approached on the street by a beggar?

Verse 27: All these things must be done in order. All what things? To what does this admonition refer—to caring for the needy? To other things as well?

What does it mean to do these things "in wisdom and order"? How do we decide what way of dealing with the needy is in wisdom and order? When we are told that we must not run faster than we have the strength, is Benjamin giving us a way out after such a strong sermon about service? In what must we be diligent? What prize is it that we can win?

Verse 28: How is this admonition related to those which have come before? Particularly to the admonition about beggars?

Verse 29–30: The fact that no list could be made of all the ways one could sin shows why no law, except the law of the Spirit, could suffice for salvation.

How do we watch our thoughts and deeds? Must we be continually looking over our shoulders for fear we have done something wrong?

How would the Nephites "continue in the faith of what [they had] heard concerning the coming of [the] Lord"? What does that mean? How would it apply to us? What does the admonition to remember entail?

Mosiah 5

Verse 2: Earlier we saw that the people were so many that they couldn't all hear King Benjamin. In fact, he had a transcription of his sermon sent around so all could hear his words (2:8). That makes it difficult to believe that they all answered his question at the same time. (Presumably, they

137

heard the question at different times.) So what might it mean to say that "they all cried with one voice"?

When the people say they have no more disposition to do evil, but to do good continually, are they saying anything about the natural man mentioned in 3:19? What does it mean not to have a disposition to do evil? Have you ever had that experience? Does this mean that the people never did evil again? Does it mean that they never desired to do evil again?

During Joseph Smith's day, *disposition* meant "arrangement" as well as "natural state of mind." The latter meaning is obviously relevant to the people's description of themselves—they no longer tend to do evil naturally (without thinking about it)—but might the first meaning also be informative?

Notice too that the writer doesn't describe the change that occurred as something they *did,* but as something that happened to them because they accepted the testimony of the Holy Spirit: the Spirit of the Lord Omnipotent wrought a mighty change in their hearts. They had faith, but their faith didn't change their hearts; the Holy Spirit did. Does that say anything about repentance? About overcoming our own evil dispositions?

Verse 3: They say they could prophesy of all things if it were expedient. What does it mean to prophesy of all things? Why is that important? What does it mean to prophesy, beyond foretelling the future?

Verse 4: To what does "this great knowledge" refer? Why is it important that faith has taught them?

Verse 5: At what times do we enter into a similar covenant, to do the will of God and to be obedient to his commandments?

In Mosiah 1:11 the writer pointed out that the people had been diligent in keeping the Lord's commandments. Now we see that a mighty change has occurred and that they covenant to keep his commandments. What happened? What's the difference between their previous obedience and this that they now covenant to? What might we learn from this change that has occurred, a change from one kind of obedience to another?

Verse 6: What does King Benjamin mean when he says this is a righteous covenant?

Verse 7: The covenant they have made makes them Christ's children. Does this suggest anything about our reference to the Savior as our "Elder Brother"? What does it mean to be spiritually begotten of Christ? What does it mean to be born of him? Is there a difference between being begotten of him and born of him?

Verse 8: Why does Benjamin call Christ a "head"?

What does it mean to be free?

Lehi says we all have agency, so in what way are these people now free that they weren't before?

King Benjamin's grammar makes being free and receiving salvation parallel. In what sense or senses do they mean the same thing?

What does it mean to take the name of Christ? How do we do that? When do we do it? (What does it mean to take that name in vain?) Since Benjamin is speaking to the members of the Church, how is this different from what they did when they were baptized?

Benjamin says his people who have entered into the covenant should take Christ's name on themselves *so that* they will be obedient to the end of the lives. How does taking his name on ourselves make us obedient? What is Benjamin saying?

Verse 9: Are the children of Christ the only ones who will know the name by which they are called, as this seems to imply?

Verse 10: Why do we have to be called by some name or other? What other name or names might we be called by? What does it mean to be called by one of these other names?

Verse 11: We are accustomed to hearing that our names will be blotted from the Lord's records if we transgress and do not repent, but what Benjamin says here is unusual. What does it mean to have Christ's name blotted out of our hearts?

Oddly, the discussion of having our names blotted out occurs mostly in the Old Testament. (See Deuteronomy 9:14; 29:20; 2 Kings 14:27; and Psalm 109:13, as well as Alma 5:57; D&C 85:5, 11). In the New Testament, the only discussions are discussions of those whose names will not be blotted out (Revelation 3:5; 19:12, 16).

In the latter-day scriptures, the only discussion of blotting out names is this one and an earlier instance (1:12).

Do you have any idea why this is primarily an Old Testament theme? In contrast, having one's name written in the book of life can be found in Malachi 3:16; Luke 10:20; Revelation 2:17; 13:8; 17:8; 21:12; Alma 5:58; 3 Nephi 24:16; and D&C 76:68.

Verse 12: What does it mean to have the Savior's name written in our hearts?

Verse 13: Why is the Lord compared to a master here? Why must we serve him? What does that say about the necessity of obedience? In other words, does this explain why obedience is a requirement of salvation?

Verse 14: We cannot even claim our own bodies (2:25), so we necessarily belong to someone, the being by whose name we are called. What does the image used in this verse say about our relation to our master?

Verse 15: What does it mean to be steadfast and immovable? Steadfast in what? Immovable with respect to what?

What does *abound* mean?

What does it mean to be sealed Christ's? How is it that being steadfast and immovable as well as abounding in good works make it possible for us to be sealed Christ's?

What does the word *salvation* mean in this context? What is eternal life?

What does it mean that we have them through the Creator's wisdom, power, justice, and mercy?

Why does the writer mention that the Father is the Creator? What has that to do with the subject of this verse?

Mosiah 6

Verse 1: Why did Benjamin record the names of all those who entered the covenant?

Verse 3: What does the word *consecrated* mean? Why would a king be consecrated?

What does "stirred up" mean in this context? Why did the people need to be stirred up to remember the covenant?

Isn't the experience they had, the changing of their hearts, a permanent experience? (How long did its results last?)

See appendix 1 for an outline of Mosiah 4.

Lesson 17
Mosiah 7–11

Chapters 7–10 are, for the most part, the story of Ammon, the man who went back to the land of Lehi-Nephi (originally called the land of Nephi) to find out what had become of an earlier group that had returned. If you were to pick two major themes from these chapters, what would they be? What passages would you use to show those themes?

Why do you think the Book of Mormon writers gave us this part of the book? We can easily see why we need the clearly doctrinal portions, like Benjamin's sermon. But why do we need the story part of the book?

There is a great deal of moving about in the Book of Mormon, especially in these chapters. These scriptures may help you figure out the migrations.

2 Nephi 1:5

Omni 1:12–30

Mosiah 7:1–6

Mosiah 8:7–11

Mosiah 18:34–35

Mosiah 22:11–16

Mosiah 24:3–25

Ether 1:1–2

Ether 12:1

To keep the material in this lesson to a usable amount, I will focus my questions on chapter 11.

Mosiah 11

Verse 1: Why do you think the scriptures use the metaphor of walking on a path or road (a way) for being obedient?

If something about his background might account for Noah's wickedness, what can you imagine it might be?

Verse 2: How does the description of Noah at the beginning of the verse contrast with Mosiah 5:2?

As you read from here through verse 11, think about how Noah and Solomon compare. How are they the same? How are they different? Do you think the writer makes that comparison intentionally? If so, why?

Verses 3–6: Notice the contrast between Noah and Benjamin. Is this comparison intentional or only our inference as readers? What does it show us?

Verse 7: How does this verse explain idolatry? How does idolatry result from flattery?

In our days, what might the cultural equivalent of King Noah's priests be? How do they flatter us to idolatry?

Verse 12: What's the point of this tower? Why does the writer tell us about it? How does it contrast with Benjamin's tower?

Verses 18–19: How does Noah's attitude about war compare with Moroni's? Could Noah say, as did Moroni, that he and his soldiers are fighting for religion, freedom, peace, their wives, and their children (Alma 46:12)? Why or why not? If he could say something like this, how does he differ from Moroni? How do we avoid being like Noah?

Verse 20: Notice how Abinadi seems to come out of nowhere. He has been among them, but no mention is made of his family or of anything else about him. Why not? Why give him such a dramatic entrance?

What Old Testament prophets might Abinadi compare to? Hosea? Amos? Others? What are the circumstances in which those prophets appear, and how are they like these circumstances?

Why does the Lord use the word *visit* to describe bringing his anger to the Nephites? Isn't that a strange word to use in such circumstances? It might help to look in an etymological dictionary—like the *Oxford English Dictionary*—or in a copy of the 1828 Webster's to see what meanings *visit* had when the Book of Mormon was written.

Verse 21: What is the answer to the problem that Noah's people are having with the Lamanites?

Verse 22: What does the Lord mean when he says he is jealous? Is that only metaphorical, or does he feel jealousy? Is there another alternative?

Verse 25: What does the phrase "repent in sackcloth and ashes" mean to Abinadi? Does it mean the same thing that it means in the Old Testament? Why might you think so? What might be an equivalent phrase for us, given the different way that we mourn today?

Verse 27: Does King Noah's question about Abinadi tell us something in answer to the question above about Abinadi's

145

sudden appearance? How can we make sense of Noah's question about the Lord? Can you think of how someone today might say something with the same meaning?

Verse 28: Noah says Abinadi will raise contentions among the people, implying that there is a relative absence of contention now. In other words, except for the attacks of the Lamanites (whom they've just put to rout), things are going pretty well for the Nephites right now.

Why do you think the Lord sends Abinadi at a time when, in Noah's eyes and probably in the eyes of his people, everything is going so well? Do you think they will believe what Abinadi says about their destruction, having just rejoiced in their victory over the Lamanites?

Lesson 18
Mosiah 12–17

Mosiah 12

Verse 1: Why has Abinadi come in disguise if he is going to tell them who he is immediately? Someone reading the Book of Mormon for the first time, not knowing what is coming up, might chuckle at the scene described here. What's going on? What does this verse show us about Abinadi?

Verse 2: Being smitten on the cheek seems pretty mild. We hear something like: "Thus saith the Lord, because you have been so iniquitous, you're going to be slapped on the face." The oddity of this is heightened by the fact that the other consequences are so stark: you will be driven by men and killed; you will be eaten by vultures, dogs, and wild beasts. Can you think of any explanation for this oddity?

Verse 8: Abinadi gives us another of the Book of Mormon's purposes. Why is it important in the latter days for us to know of the wickedness of Noah's people?

Verses 10–12: Why do the people embellish Abinadi's prophecies against Noah? Why do they change the object of his prophecy from the people as a whole to Noah specifically? Were we in a literature class, we might talk about the characterization occurring in this speech. How does

147

the writer characterize these people? Why does he give us this characterization?

Verses 13–14: Notice how the people seem to admit they have been included in the prophecy by including themselves in their excusing.

Verse 15: Why would a group feel it necessary to tell their leader, "We are strong, we shall not come into bondage"? Does their need to bolster their confidence say something about them?

Verse 16: The people tell Noah to do what he thinks is good. Are they afraid to do it themselves? Why?

Verse 17: Notice that Noah isn't willing to decide on his own what would be good to do with Abinadi. Do you sense fear on Noah's part?

Verse 19: The priests question Abinadi to see if they can cross him, hoping to find an accusation against him. Why do they need to do that? The people took him and turned him over to Noah to do with Abinadi as he pleased. Now Noah's priests are looking for something to charge him with. What's going on?

Verses 21–24: How ironic that they should ask him about a scripture concerning prophets and the heralding of God's kingdom on earth. Why do you think they asked him about this particular scripture?

Verse 25: Abinadi has claimed to be a prophet, and they have asked him to explain the words of another, rather difficult prophet. That seems quite a natural thing to do; why does Abinadi condemn them for it?

Verses 26–27: Look carefully at what Abinadi says here:

1. If you have understood these things, you haven't taught them.
2. So you have perverted the way of the Lord.
3. You haven't applied your hearts to understanding.
4. So what have you taught?

What's the connection between 1 and 2, especially given that he says they haven't applied their hearts to understanding? How do 1 and 2 relate to 3 and 4? We would usually speak of applying our minds to understanding. What does it mean to apply our hearts to it?

Verses 29–37: Here Abinadi shows that they've not kept the law of Moses themselves, and neither have they taught it to the people. How is that related to what he said in verse 26 and 27?

Mosiah 13

Verse 1: Do you think this verse shows King Noah to be fearful? Why or why not?

Verse 4: Notice how the parallel grammatical structure creates an "equation" between "the truth" and "the word of God," and between the people's anger and Noah's judgment that Abinadi is mad.

Verse 10: Types and shadows aren't necessarily the same thing. Though the terms aren't used with technical consistency, the type seems usually to be the "original" that the shadow imitates. (Think of a piece of type that leaves an impression, a shadow.) Of what is Abinadi's fate a type? In other words, something in the future imitates his fate. What is it? Of what is it a shadow? In other words, his fate imitates something that has passed. What?

Verse 11: Why does Abinadi read the scriptures to them? What has that to do with the scriptures not being written in their hearts?

Verse 28: Why doesn't salvation come by the law alone?

Verse 29: If a stiff-necked people require a strict law, what would a humble, celestial people require?

When he says they are quick to do iniquity and slow to remember the Lord, does he say anything about why a strict law is required?

Verse 30: The law was given, with its performances and ordinances, to make them remember the Lord. What might that say about our own law?

What does it mean to remember the Lord?

Verse 31: Of what are the performances of the Mosaic law types (patterns)? How are they such types?

Verses 32–35: Here Abinadi gives at least some of the answer to the question just above; he tells them what the law of Moses is a pattern of. But how is it a pattern for the coming of the Savior? How is it a pattern of the redemption? How is it a pattern for Christ's incarnation? How is it a pattern for the resurrection and for the oppression and affliction of Christ? To understand the importance of Abinadi's message to Noah's priests (and its ability to influence

Alma), think of specific ways in which the law of Moses gave the patterns for these things.

Mosiah 14

Abinadi has been telling Noah and his court how the law of Moses is a type of Christ. He concluded that discussion by foretelling Christ's incarnation, his resurrection, and his persecution. How does this quotation of Isaiah 53 expand on those themes? Is it significant that he quotes a section from Isaiah that follows just after the section they asked him to explain (Mosiah 12:21–24)? This prophecy gives many details of Christ's life, details testified to by the Gospels. Why would such detail have been important to the people of Isaiah's day? To Noah's people?

Verse 1: The parallel grammar compares those who believe to those to whom the Lord's arm (his power) has been revealed. How is this so?

Verse 2: Why does Isaiah compare Christ to a newly sprouted plant? To a plant sprouted from dry ground? What things might the dry ground indicate? The image may be one of dry desert growth—scrub brush and sage. Why might the Savior be compared to scrub brush?

Why does Isaiah say that Christ isn't someone we will find attractive? Notice that it isn't the world who won't find him attractive; it is we who will not.

Verse 3: In Isaiah, the word translated "grief" in this and the next verse can also be translated "disease." Why is it important for us to know that Jesus was despised and rejected, that he felt sorrow and was acquainted with grief or disease? Might this follow up on Abinadi's earlier point, that what happens to him is a type and shadow of things to come?

Sometimes we try to answer the question "Why is there suffering?" but we rarely come up with very satisfying answers. Notice, however, that the scriptures don't even ask the question. Instead, as here, they point to Christ, showing that he too suffered, seeming to suggest that if he did we should expect to. (See also Romans 8:17–18, where Paul suggests that those who become the children of Christ must suffer as he did.) How do we square such an approach with our desire to account for suffering?

Verse 4–7: Much of these verses is deeply ironic: The Savior bears our diseases and sorrows, but we count him as one whom God has afflicted. Because we sinned, he was punished; because he suffered, we are healed. Though we have all gone astray, he is punished. What is the point of that irony?

In verse 7, in addition to the obvious reference to his appearance before Pilate, what might it mean that he didn't open his mouth?

In verse 6 we are compared to sheep. In verse 7, the Savior is. But our comparison is negative, and Christ's is positive. What might the use of sheep in both comparisons indicate?

Verse 8: Why does Isaiah tell us that Jesus was taken from prison? Why does Abinadi tell the Nephites? (One translation of this sentence in Isaiah says, "He was taken away by arrest and by trial"; another says, "He was taken away by perverted judgment.")

152

What does the clause "who shall declare his generation?" mean? Some have taken this to ask, "Who will convince [or explain him to] his generation?" What do you think?

Verse 9: Does it make a positive difference if we translate *because* as "although"?

Verse 10: By making himself an offering for sin, the Savior will see his children. Can you explain straightforwardly what this means? What does it mean about becoming a child of God?

This is an important point of focus for Abinadi in chapter 15. With what other scriptures can you connect it? Mosiah 5:7? 1 John 3:2? Others?

Verse 11: Another translation of the beginning of this verse in Isaiah is "By his suffering he shall see joy." Why is that teaching important to us?

What does it mean to say that he will justify many "by his knowledge"? What knowledge does this refer to? Do you think it means knowledge of the factual kind or something more like "acquaintance"? Many languages make this distinction. If you were translating this verse into one of those languages, which way would you translate it?

Verse 12: What does it mean to say he will get a portion with the great and will divide the spoil with the strong?

Mosiah 15

What does the sermon that follows have to do with the Isaiah passage that Abinadi has just read to them?

Verses 2–5: Why does Abinadi give them this explanation of the relation of the Father and the Son?

These verses are fairly difficult. Can you take them apart to see what is being said? For example, it is fairly clear why dwelling in the flesh makes Jesus the Son. But why does subjecting his flesh to the will of the Father make him both Father and Son? (Mosiah 5 may be helpful here.)

More difficult: why does being conceived by the power of God make him the *Father*? And why are they the Eternal Father?

Verses 5–10: Why does Abinadi give this overview of the quotation from Isaiah? Which things does he focus on? Why those?

Verse 11: Notice the progression: (1) If you've heard the words of the prophets, then (2) if you've hearkened to the words of the prophets and believed that Christ will redeem his people and you've looked forward to a remission of your sins, then (3) you are Christ's seed. How does what Abinadi says here compare to what Benjamin said in chapter 4? Similarities? Differences?

Verse 14: Notice that Abinadi returns to the scripture they asked him to explain. Why does he do so now?

Verses 15–18: What does the image of beautiful feet suggest? Why is it repeated? What changes occur from one repetition to the next? Are those changes relevant?

Verse 19: In what senses would all have to perish if it weren't for the redemption that Christ brings?

Verses 21–25: Compare this description of the first resurrection to that in the Doctrine and Covenants (e.g., sections 63 and 76). What are the similarities? What do you make of the differences?

Verse 26: To whom is Abinadi speaking when he says "ye ought to tremble"?

Verse 27: The end of this verse seems to identify the Lord with justice: he can't deny himself; he can't deny the claim of justice. Why is it that he would deny himself if he gave salvation to those who willfully rebelled against his commandments? (And haven't any of us who have been given the commandments, and ever disobeyed them, willfully rebelled?)

Verses 28–31: What is Abinadi prophesying?

Mosiah 16

Verses 1–5: Notice how Abinadi has been alternating between a description of those who rebel and a description of those who are saved. Here he focuses on those who rebel. Why do you think he alternates in this way? Why not discuss one completely first and then the other?

Verses 6–8: Why is the message of the resurrection such an important part of Abinadi's message to Noah's people?

Verse 12: How does this verse describe the situation of Abinadi's audience?

Mosiah 17

Verses 5–6: Are Abinadi's three days in prison a shadow of Christ's death?

Verse 7: Noah was willing to kill Alma immediately (verse 3), but it takes him and his priests three days to come up with a pretext for killing Abinadi. What do you make of that difference?

Verse 8: One of the most common accusations made against prophets is blasphemy, the substance of the accusation made here against Abinadi. Why do you think that is so?

Verse 9: Notice that Abinadi may have known from the beginning that this would happen.

Verses 11–12: We often think of Noah as a powerful ruler, but here we see him as a "wimp." It becomes clear here that he hasn't ever really been in charge. The priests rule through him: The original accusation was that of blasphemy, but when Abinadi answered that with his testimony, Noah was ready to drop everything. Then the priests charge Abinadi with speaking evil of the king—the original charge they made against him (12:10–14). That charge makes Noah mad once again, and he has Abinadi executed. There can be little doubt that the priests know how to manipulate Noah for their own purposes.

Verse 15: Of what is Abinadi prophesying in this verse?

Verses 16–17: How does this relate to Abinadi's quotation of Isaiah 53?

Verses 18–19: In what ways is Abinadi's death a type of Noah's and the priests' future? Is it a type of the final future of those who rebel against God?

Verse 20: In what sense wouldn't Abinadi deny the *commandments*? He wouldn't deny his testimony or the truthfulness of the prophecies, but what does it mean to say that he wouldn't deny the commandments?

Lesson 19
Mosiah 18–24

Mosiah 18

Verse 1: Many of the conversion stories in the Book of Mormon are more detailed and more dramatic than this brief description of Alma's repentance. (Compare Enos's story and Alma the Younger's, for example.) Why might this story be told so briefly?

Verses 1–2: What doctrinal teachings has Alma learned from Abinadi's sermons?

Verses 3–7: Alma hides by day and, evidently, preaches at night. Though he preaches in secret, a good number of people hear his teaching. Yet the king's men cannot find him. What might this say about the relation of the king to the people?

Verses 6–7: Those who believed Alma went to the waters of Mormon to hear him. Evidently the teachings he gave in secret were fairly limited in scope. What might he have taught that motivated people to go to the waters of baptism to hear about repentance, redemption, and faith?

Verses 8–9: Notice the qualifications that Alma lists for baptism:

    1. That they desire to come into the fold of God

2. That they desire to be called God's people

3. That they be willing to bear one another's burdens that they might be light; that is, that they might mourn with those who mourn and comfort those who need comfort

4. That they do these things so that they can stand as witnesses of God in all times and places until they die

    a. so they may be redeemed and numbered in the first resurrection and

    b. so they may have eternal life

The first two qualifications are explained fairly fully in King Benjamin's sermon (though Alma couldn't yet know about those explanations). The fourth obviously parallels what we have just seen Abinadi do. 4a and 4b (which may be the same thing) are obviously necessary to preaching repentance; we've seen them before. The third, however, is new in the Book of Mormon, though it anticipates what will be preached later. What are we to make of this new idea and its placement here in the Book of Mormon?

Verse 10: Alma baptizes them so they can covenant to serve and obey the Lord and so the Lord can pour out his Spirit on them. Why can't/won't the Lord pour out his Spirit on them if they aren't baptized?

Verses 21–29: Notice that these verses discussing the commandments that Alma gave the people begin with the commandment to be one and end with a description of that unity. The theme of unity acts as parenthesis around the commandments. What might that tell us about our obedience and worship?

Mosiah 19

Verse 17: What do the scriptures mean when they say that a person is just? Does *just* mean the same as *righteous*? For comparison, look at the scriptures that use the phrase "just man": Genesis 6:9; Proverbs 9:9; 20:7; 24:16; Ecclesiastes 7:15, 20; Matthew 1:19; 27:19; Mark 6:20; Acts 10:22; Enos 1:1; Omni 1:25; Mosiah 2:4; 19:17; Alma 63:2; 3 Nephi 3:12; 8:1; D&C 129:6, 7; Moses 8:27.

Verse 24: What do you make of the odd use of the word *ceremony*? To what does it refer?

Mosiah 20

What does this chapter teach us about the Lamanites?

Mosiah 21

Verses 2–12: What's the difference between these people who fight for their freedom so unsuccessfully and the people of General Moroni's time who fight for their freedom successfully?

Mosiah 23

Verses 7–8: How do you explain Alma's teaching here? On the one hand, he says if they had just men for kings, it would be good to have a king, implying that having a king can be a good thing. On the other hand, he tells them they shouldn't have a king, because they have been commanded that no one should think himself superior to another. Is it possible to have a king who doesn't think himself superior to his subjects? What would it take?

Verses 21–23: Notice the introduction that the writer gives to the Lamanites' capture of the land of Helam. The Lord was chastening and trying his people, but those who trust the Lord will be delivered (for the Lord is the only one who can save). What's the difference between this attitude and that which assumes that the bad things that happen to us are punishment from the Lord?

Mosiah 24

Verses 14–15: Does this have anything to do with the covenant of baptism described in Mosiah 18:9?

Lesson 20
Mosiah 25–28; Alma 36

To help keep track of the chronology, Arthur Bassett has constructed this approximate chronology. The dates in bold are those that he feels are probably most accurate, based on information in the Book of Mormon itself. Of course, all dates are BC rather than AD.

200 The Zeniff colony leaves the land of Zarahemla and moves back to the land of Nephi.

173 Alma is born after the colony has lived twenty-seven years in Nephi.

160 Noah becomes the king. Alma is thirteen years old.

154 Mosiah is born in the land of Zarahemla. Alma is nineteen.

150 Abinadi appears in the land of Nephi. Alma is twenty-three, "a young man" (Mosiah 17:2), and Mosiah is four.

148 Martyrdom of Abinadi. Alma is twenty-five, and Mosiah is six.

147 Alma moves to the Waters of Mormon (he is twenty-six, and Mosiah is seven) and then to Helam, where he and his colony are later taken into captivity

by the priests of Noah and the Lamanites, under the direction of Amulon, one of Noah's original priests.

124 Mosiah becomes the king in Zarahemla. He is thirty, and Alma is forty-nine.

121 Benjamin dies; Ammon sets out on his mission to Nephi. Limhi returns to Zarahemla some unspecified time later. Mosiah is thirty-three, and Alma is fifty-two.

120 Alma returns to Zarahemla. Mosiah is thirty-four, and Alma is fifty-three.

120–100 Rebellion in the land of Zarahemla, culminating in the conversion of Alma the Younger and the sons of Mosiah. Alma ages from fifty-three to seventy-three, and Mosiah ages from thirty-four to fifty-four.

92 The sons of Mosiah leave for a twenty-year mission to the Lamanites. Mosiah is sixty-two; Alma is eighty-one.

91 Mosiah and Alma the Elder die. Alma the Younger becomes the first chief judge. Mosiah dies at the age of sixty-three and Alma the Elder at the age of eighty-two.

Mosiah 25

Verses 1–3: To which groups do "people of Nephi" and "people of Zarahemla" refer? Why is it important for us to know that the Nephites were a minority, a smaller group than the people of Zarahemla, and that the two groups together were much smaller than the Lamanites? What might account for those relative differences in size?

Verses 5–11: How do you account for the see-saw of emotions that we see here? What effect do you think that see-saw would have?

Verse 19: (See also Mosiah 26:8.) How can a king decide who has authority over the church? What does your answer to that question tell us about Mosiah and Alma's society?

Verse 22: What is the point of the remark that the groups of believers were called churches?

Mosiah 26

Verse 1: Why is it so important for the young people to understand King Benjamin's words? Is there something about that specific sermon that is essential to them?

We are given two reasons that the young people could not understand the sermon: they were young when Benjamin gave it, and they didn't believe the tradition of their fathers. The implication is that because they were young they couldn't understand the sermon, so the alternative was to learn what it meant from the tradition of their parents, which didn't happen.

What does the word *tradition* mean? What tradition could their parents have given them that would have taught them what Benjamin meant? Can we teach our children the meaning of Benjamin's sermon by our tradition? How?

Verse 3: Notice that in order to understand the scriptures we must believe.

Verse 4: Flattery is often mentioned by the Book of Mormon in connection with people being deceived into leaving the church. How does that happen? What kind of flattery is involved?

Verses 10–12: Why do Alma and Mosiah each seem to shirk judging the people who have been brought before them?

Verse 17: What does it mean that Alma's people shall be the Lord's people? How does this tie in with King Benjamin's sermon? Does it help explain why that sermon was so important? How is it important to us?

Verse 20: Three things occur in this verse: the Lord calls Alma his servant, the Lord covenants that Alma will have eternal life, and the Lord says that Alma will serve him. (This rhetorical pattern, a cousin of chiasmus, is called inclusion.) How are these things connected to one another?

Why is the covenant sandwiched between the descriptions of Alma as a servant? What does the arrangement tell us?

What is a covenant? (It is more than a contract or mutual promise.) What does this covenant mean? What does it mean to have eternal life?

Verse 29: Alma asked what to do about the transgressors in verses 13–14. Not until verse 29 does he receive an answer. Before giving Alma the answer to his prayer, the Lord blesses Alma, reaffirms the covenant relation with him, and tells Alma about the Atonement and the final judgment. Why that long interlude between Alma's question and the Lord's answer?

Verse 31: This verse suggests that we are to take the word of the person who tells us that he or she has repented. Why?

Mosiah 27

Verse 3: Not only are the nonmembers forbidden to persecute the members, but the members are forbidden to persecute one another. How might members do that? How might we persecute each other today?

The members are also told that there should be equality among all men. What does *equality* mean in this instance? In what or in what way are people supposed to be equal? Equality is grammatically parallel to the absence of persecution. Does that tell us something about what each means?

Verse 4: Does this explain at least some of what it means to not persecute and to be equal?

Verse 8: This verse says that Alma was idolatrous. What does that mean? Does Mosiah 28:4 explain this remark?

Notice that there is no description in the Book of Mormon of what we usually think of as idol worship. Does that mean that the Nephites didn't have a problem with idol worship or just that it isn't mentioned? Why might it not be mentioned?

Alma leads people away by flattery, something mentioned frequently in the Book of Mormon in this connection. What kind of flattery might he be using? How would flattery get people to follow him in sin? Where might we see such flattery in our own lives?

Verse 10: Why do Alma the Younger and the sons of Mosiah do what they do secretly? Why does it say that the king had forbidden what they are doing? It is against the law to persecute the saints, but is it against the law to flatter

167

people into unbelief? Or might there be some connection between flattery and persecution? What might that be?

Verse 11: What do we learn from being told that they were rebelling against God? What are the connotations of that word? What is the significance of the way the angel appears to them: "as it were in a cloud" and "as it were with a voice of thunder"? What are we to envision? Is any connection being made to other appearances of heavenly beings, either by comparison or by contrast?

Verse 13: The angel has appeared to all five of them. Why does he address only Alma? If the only thing that can overthrow the church is the transgression of the members, Alma has been on the right path for his purposes, persuading people to become sinners.

Verse 14: Alma the Elder has prayed that his son might come to know the truth. What does this mean? Surely his father has taught him. And we know from verse 11 that he was rebelling, but you can't rebel against something if you don't know what it is. What is it Alma the elder wants him to know that he doesn't yet know? Whatever it is, it is something he learns in this experience.

Verse 16: Did the angel come to save Alma the Younger and the sons of Mosiah? Notice that the angel uses the type of Israel in captivity to Egypt and then freed by God's power, and he applies that type to Alma the Younger's life: remember when you were in captivity and the great things that the Lord has done for you in freeing you from bondage.

Why is that type so important for Alma the Younger? In what ways it is important to our understanding of the gospel? To our understanding of our own lives?

Verse 21: Alma the Elder uses his son as a testimony of God's power. Notice that he calls people to see "what the Lord had done for his son." At this point, what had the Lord done besides frighten him into unconsciousness?

The angel commanded Alma the Younger to stop destroying the church, even if he himself wanted to be destroyed. He said nothing to him or to the sons of Mosiah about being converted. How can his father be so confident that he will be saved?

Verse 23: Notice that "after two days and two nights" means the same as "on the third day." What is the significance of rising on the third day? What does it mean to be of good comfort? What does the word *comfort* mean in this context?

Verse 24: What does it mean to repent? What does the word *redeemed* mean? What does it mean to be redeemed by the Lord? What does it mean to be born of the Spirit?

Verse 25: Notice that "born of God," "changed from their carnal and fallen state, to a state of righteousness," "redeemed of God," and "becoming his sons and daughters" are parallel. How does this compare to what King Benjamin taught about becoming sons and daughters of God (Mosiah 5:7; see also Romans 8:14)?

What do the scriptures tell us it means to be a son or daughter of God? How is that related to the doctrine that we are the literal spiritual offspring of God?

Why is the word *changed*—in the phrase "changed from their carnal and fallen state, to a state of righteousness"—passive?

Verse 26: What does the word *creature* mean? (Look at the first five letters of the word to see its etymology.) What does it mean to become a new creature? Does being a new creature help explain the use of the passive voice (verse 25)?

Verse 28: What does it mean to repent "nigh unto death"? What does it mean to be snatched from an everlasting burning? (D&C 19:6–12 may be relevant here.)

Verse 29: What is gall? What is "the gall of bitterness"?

What does it mean to be racked?

What does he mean when he says, "I am snatched"? Why does he put that in the present tense rather than the past?

Verse 35: They explained the prophecies and scriptures to all who would hear them. What might this say about their childhood training? Had they been taught in their youth? If so, why didn't they understand the prophecies and scriptures before? What made the difference? (Mosiah 26:3 seems relevant here.)

What difference would explain why Alma the Younger went through such a horrible experience and the sons of Mosiah don't seem to have? Both he and they seem equally converted. Why would he have to experience such torment and not they?

As you think about the story of Alma's conversion, think about the difference between his experience before an angel and Laman and Lemuel's experience before one. Why do we have such a dramatic difference between the results of the two?

Mosiah 28

Verse 3–4: Verse 4 says the feelings described in verse 3 are given by the Spirit of the Lord. Would the Spirit give anyone the same feelings? (If so, the absence of such feelings indicates the absence of the Spirit.) Alma the Younger had endured endless torment (Mosiah 27:29), but there is no indication that the sons of Mosiah had, even though they did suffer. What might give them the feelings described in verse 3?

Verse 18: Reading of a group of people who were destroyed might sober us or even make us sad, but it usually wouldn't make us "mourn exceedingly." Why do you think Mosiah's people reacted in this way? What kind of knowledge did they get that caused them to rejoice?

Alma 36

Verse 2: What is the significance of what Alma asks Helaman to remember? (Compare Mosiah 27:16.)

Verse 3: Why do you think Alma bears this particular testimony to Helaman: "whosoever shall put their trust in God shall be supported in their trials, and their troubles, and their afflictions, and shall be lifted up at the last day"? Why this rather than something else?

Verses 6–30: Appendix 2 has a side-by-side comparison of the three accounts of Alma the Younger's conversion. Compare the three and ask yourself how to explain the differences between them. What does each version do that the others do not?

Verse 14: Why do you think Alma describes what he had done as murder? (Compare Alma 5:23 and Matthew 10:28. What does it mean to destroy both soul, i.e., spirit, *and* body in hell?)

Verses 18–19: Why does Alma's cry in verse 18 bring the results in verse 19? How is this connected to King Benjamin's teaching in Mosiah 4?

Is it significant that Benjamin delivered that address to a people who were diligent in keeping the commandments but that it also seems to apply to someone like Alma who has openly rebelled against those commandments?

Verse 19: Since Alma is here telling us about the pains he experienced, what can he mean when he says, "I could remember my pains no more"?

Verse 22: Why does Alma have a vision of *Lehi* at this point?

Verse 28: Is this verse parallel to verse 2? Why would Alma begin and end the account of his conversion by reminding Helaman of this scriptural type?

Verse 30: How are verses 28–29 (and, therefore, also verse 3) a type for what Alma says in this verse?

See appendix 2 for an outline of Alma the Younger's conversion.

Lesson 21

Mosiah 29; Alma 1–4

Mosiah 29

Verses 7–9: Aaron has just been converted in a miraculous manner, and he is obviously serious about his conversion. His mission is evidence of that. Nevertheless, here we see Mosiah worried that making Aaron king might destroy Aaron. Does he lack confidence in his son? If so, why? If not, how do you explain Mosiah's remarks?

Verse 12ff.: What is necessary in order to have a king? Are the judges that Mosiah suggests as rulers the same or similar to the judges of ancient Israel, or is this a different system of government? How would you decide that question?

Verse 13: Mosiah tells us that the problem with kings is that sometimes they are unjust. How does having judges instead of kings ameliorate this problem? (Compare verses 28–29.)

Verse 16: In the Old Testament the king is often understood as a shadow of the Messiah, one for whom the Savior is the type. Is Mosiah suggesting here that, because of our iniquity, that parallel doesn't work?

Verse 25: Does this verse tell us that the judges were elected democratically, or does it mean something else? What evidence can you give for your conclusion?

Verse 26: Given the Nephite experience so far, the record they have of Israel before Lehi left, and what they have just read in the book of Ether, how can Mosiah say this? All the evidence seems to indicate that it is quite common for the majority to desire what is wrong, doesn't it?

Verse 27: Does this verse answer the question I asked about verse 26? How are we to understand these verses as they apply to us today?

Verse 31: Israelites also had this belief, that the wickedness of a king causes the wickedness of a nation. It was the flip side of the belief that a king typifies the Messiah. What bearing does this belief have on our understanding of government?

Why might the ancient Israelites and King Mosiah have believed that a wicked king caused a wicked people? We don't usually believe that a wicked CEO in a company is necessarily a bad leader for the company. Why would a wicked national leader necessarily be a bad leader for the country? In other words, how do the two kinds of leadership differ, if they do?

Verse 32: To what inequality is Mosiah referring?

Verses 33–34: Is Mosiah arguing that it is too difficult to be king, even for a righteous person, so no one should ask someone to be king? Why would that argument be different for a king than for any other leader?

Verse 38: Two things seem to have most impressed Mosiah's people to give up their desire for a king: they wanted each person to have an equal chance, and they wanted each person to answer for his or her own sins. What kinds of things has Mosiah been talking about that would have led them to the conclusion that each should have an equal chance at something?

For what do you think they want each person to have an equal chance?

How is their desire to have each person answer for his or her own sins a response to Mosiah's teaching? Why wouldn't each person be responsible under a king? Is this, perhaps, a reflection of the Israelite understanding of the king (see verse 31)?

Verse 42: Does this tell us that Alma held two offices or that the office of chief judge and that of high priest were the same, in the same way that for us the president of the United States and the commander in chief of the armed forces are the same?

Verse 43: Alma judged righteously and there was peace throughout the land. Is that a cause and effect relation? If so, how so?

Alma 1

Verses 3–4: What are Nehor's doctrines? For what appears to be more of them, see Alma 15:15 and 21:6–8.

Verse 12: To what group does "this people" refer?

Is Alma saying that this is the first case of priestcraft since Lehi's colony arrived? Why would priestcraft result in the destruction of the people? Do we have priestcraft among us today? Outside the Church? In it?

Verses 13–14: What is Alma's justification for the death penalty?

What does the last part of verse 14 mean: "[the law] has been acknowledged by this people; therefore this people must abide by the law"? How do we acknowledge our laws?

Verse 15: Why do you think ancient peoples felt it was important for a criminal given the death penalty not only to die but to suffer an ignominious death?

Verses 19–22: The nonmembers persecuted the members "with all manner of words." On the other hand, there was a strict law that forbade the members from persecuting others or each other. What was the result? (Be sure also to look at verse 24.) What lesson is in this for us?

Verses 25–27: What are the three things that distinguish this church?

Verses 29–30: Why do you think the writer felt it so important to record these two verses?

Alma 2

Verse 10: Amlici commands his people to go to war so that he can subjugate them. How does going to war do that? Do you know of contemporary examples of someone using a declaration of war to subjugate his people? What lesson is there in this for us?

Verse 30: What is significant about Alma's prayer? How does his intent differ from that of Amlici?

Alma 3

Verses 14–18: How do these verses understand the mark put on the Lamanites and others? How do you reconcile these verses with verses such as 2 Nephi 5:21–24? How do you reconcile the fact that in verses 14–16 the Lord says he will put a mark on certain groups of people and verse 18 tells us that the people put the mark on themselves?

Alma 4

Verses 6–8: What do you make of the fact that wearing costly apparel is the sign of Nephite pride? To what could we compare this in our own day?

The word *heresy* originally referred to something that created divisions in the church, whether it was a belief, a practice, social divisions, or something else. What does verse 8 tell us created divisions among the Nephites? What sorts of things are comparable today?

Verses 12–13: What kind of inequality begins to come among the people? What causes it? How is that inequality related to the sins we saw described in verses 6 and 8?

Verse 19: What does the last part of this verse suggest we must do if we wish to see peace in the world? How is this related to Alma's teaching in Mosiah 18:9? Does Alma imply that other things are unnecessary?

This verse suggests that testimony has a saving power not only in heavenly things but also in temporal things. How can that be?

Lesson 22
Alma 5–7

In these chapters we have two magnificent sermons by Alma the Younger, more than enough material for several Sunday School lessons. These study questions will focus on chapter 5, with a few things also from chapter 7.

Alma 5

To whom is the address in chapter 5 given? How is it particularly relevant to their situation? To whom is the sermon in chapter 7 given? How is it particularly relevant to their situation?

In this sermon Alma asks forty-five questions. Why do you think he uses questions to structure what he says?

Verses 1–7: Alma begins as he seems to begin each of his sermons, with a reference to the type of bondage and deliverance. (Verse 6 captures both parts of the type: have you remembered the captivity of your fathers and their deliverance?) Sometimes the specific instance of that type is Moses and Israel in Egypt. In this case it is Noah and the people of Nephi. Why do you think the type, bondage and deliverance, has such power for Alma the Younger? Is it or ought it to be an important type for us?

Verse 10: Alma announces his theme, the conditions of salvation. Compare this sermon to King Benjamin's sermon in Mosiah 4. How are they different? How are they the same?

Verses 10–12: To what cause of salvation does Alma first refer? Why is that particular cause so important? What does it mean to him? To us?

Verse 12: Verse 11 tells us that Alma the Elder heard and believed the words of Abinadi. What does this verse describe as the result? Why does Alma the Younger say that the mighty change was something that happened to his father rather than something that he did?

Verse 13: Why is it enough to say that the people "humbled themselves and put their trust in the true and living God" and "were faithful until the end" to explain their salvation?

Why doesn't Alma include such things as baptism and the gift of the Holy Ghost, or keeping the commandments, in his description of salvation?

Verses 14 and 19: What does "receive his image in your countenances" mean? Does it have anything to do with Genesis 1:27: "God created man in his own image, in the image of God created he him; male and female created he them"?

If we have already been created in the image of God, how can Alma ask whether those in Zarahemla have received that image?

How is Alma's teaching related to the teaching of 1 John 3:2: "Beloved, now are we the sons of God, and it doth not yet appear what we shall be: but we know that, when he shall appear, we shall be like him; for we shall see him as he is"?

Just how close the connection is between Hebrew and the language of the Nephites is a matter of nothing but conjecture. Normally we would expect a good deal of language change in the five hundred years since Lehi's family arrived in the New World. However, if Hebrew is the priestly language of the plates rather than the everyday language of the Nephites, it may not have changed very much. If so, we can draw some tentative conclusions about Book of Mormon language from what we know about Hebrew.

Perhaps the first thing to notice is that in Hebrew the word for face (*pannim*) is plural rather than singular. What implications might that have for how Hebrews and perhaps Nephites too understood the face?

Another important thing about the Hebrew word for face is that it often stands for the person as a whole. (See, for example, Deuteronomy 28:50; Job 29:24; Proverbs 7:13; and Jeremiah 5:3.) Does that suggest anything about what Alma is saying here?

Verses 14–15: Are the questions that Alma asks in these verses different questions, or are they different ways of asking the same question?

Verse 16: What would it take for us to imagine that we hear God calling us blessed and calling us to him? If every person sins, what does it take for our works to be the works of righteousness?

Verse 21: Compare what Alma says here about salvation with what he said about it in verses 10–13. Here he says that to be saved we must have our garments washed white in the blood of the Redeemer. Earlier he says that we must have our hearts changed, humble ourselves, trust God, and remain faithful. How are those two descriptions of salvation related?

Verse 23: Alma seems to use murder as the type of all sin. Why is it appropriate to do so?

Verse 26: Why is experiencing the change of heart described as singing "the song of redeeming love"? What does the question of this verse suggest is Alma's concern for the people of Zarahemla? How is it an appropriate question for us?

Verses 27–30: Does it make sense to understand these questions as tests we can use to answer the question "Am I clean?"

Verse 27: Is Alma using humility and having one's garments washed clean as parallel concepts in this verse? If not, why does he particularly mention humility?

Verse 28: What does it mean to be stripped of pride? Why are we unprepared to meet God if we are not stripped of pride?

Verse 29: What might Alma mean here by *envy*? How does envy prevent us from being in the presence of God?

Verse 30: What mockery or persecution within the church might Alma have in mind? (Compare Alma 1:22–24; how did the contention with those *outside* the church lead to excommunications?)

Verse 32: Who are the workers of iniquity? Is iniquity different from sin?

Why does the verse end with "for the Lord God hath spoken it"?

Verse 33: Is it significant that the Lord doesn't demand but offers an invitation? Why do we have to repent in order for him to receive us?

Verses 34–36: From where do the images that Alma uses in these verses come? What do those scriptures have to do with Alma's message?

Verses 40–41: What does it mean to be a child of the devil? Does that tell us anything about what it means to be a child of God and the Good Shepherd?

Verse 42: The scriptures sometimes speak, as Alma does here, of the wages of sin. (See, for example, Romans 6:23.) Why don't they speak of the wages of righteousness?

Verses 43–44: Does verse 44 tell us what it means to speak plainly—to testify—or does Alma speak plainly *because* he has been called to testify?

Verse 46: To what does the phrase "these things" here and in verse 45 refer? Is its antecedent in verse 44?

How does Alma's testimony that he has fasted and prayed many days to know these things square with the story of conversion, in which he seems to have gained a testimony quickly and without fasting and prayer?

Verse 47: What particular words of the fathers does Alma have in mind? Does the context answer that question?

Verses 53–55: What are the sins of the people of Zarahemla? Are our sins today the same, or do we have different problems?

Verse 57: How do we come out from the wicked? How do we avoid touching their unclean things? Does coming out from among them and not touching their unclean things mean that we dissociate ourselves from them? If so, how can we do missionary work among them? Indeed, how can we even live in any society where it is possible to come in contact with wicked persons as well as good ones? If coming out from the wicked doesn't require us to dissociate ourselves from them, how do we separate ourselves?

What is the result of Alma's sermon? (See Alma 6:1–4.)

Alma 7

Verses 3–6: In these verses Alma makes it clear that he hopes the Gideonites are different than the people in Zarahemla were. Are they?

Verses 7, 9–12: Does Alma's message to the Gideonites differ from his message to those of Zarahemla?

Verse 12 teaches a doctrine that is hidden from most of the rest of the world, that Christ suffered so he will know how to succor his people. What does *succor* mean? How does Christ succor us?

Verse 14: This verse commands the Gideonites to be baptized not only so they may be washed of their sins, but also so they may have faith in Christ. How does baptism make faith in Christ possible?

Verse 22: If the Gideonites were living righteously, why did they have to be awakened to a sense of their duty to God?

As Alma uses the phrase here, what is "the holy order of God"? Is that different from "the order of the church" in Alma 8:1? Is he using the word *order* here in the same way he used it in Alma 5:49?

Verse 23: How does what Alma says here correlate with what he told those of Zarahemla in Alma 5:6, 13–15, 27–30, and 53–55? How does it correlate with Mosiah 4? What themes recur in each of these sermons about salvation?

Verse 24: Alma says, "If you have faith, hope, and charity, then you will always do good works." Do faith, hope, and charity guarantee good works? If so, how? Can we do good works without them? If not, why not?

Lesson 23
Alma 8–12

The *Gospel Doctrine Teacher's Manual* gives this overview of the material in the lesson:

A. Alma 8–9. After preaching in Melek, Alma calls the people of Ammonihah to repentance, but they reject him. He leaves but is commanded by an angel to return. Alma is received by Amulek, and both are commanded to preach in Ammonihah.

B. Alma 10. Amulek preaches to the people of Ammonihah and describes his conversion. The people are astonished that there is another witness to Alma's teachings. Amulek contends with unrighteous lawyers and judges.

C. Alma 11. Amulek contends with Zeezrom and testifies of the coming of Christ, the judgment of the wicked, and the plan of redemption.

D. Alma 12. Alma further explains Amulek's words, warning against hard-heartedness and wickedness and testifying of the fall and the plan of redemption.

To keep the study materials to a usable length, I will concentrate on chapters 11 and 12, with brief questions for chapters 8–10. Perhaps the above outline will help keep things in context.

Alma 8

Verse 1: What does "order of the church" mean? Alma is said to have established it also in Zarahemla. There he did so by ordaining priests and elders (surprising that they didn't already have them), baptizing repentant converts, and excommunicating unrepentant members (Alma 6:1–4). What kind of order does that suggest?

Verse 10: Alma communes with angels from time to time. Why, then, does he also have to "*wrestle* with God in prayer" (italics added)?

Alma 9

Verses 8–11: Prophets in the Book of Mormon often begin their calls to repentance by reminding the people of what the Lord has done for their ancestors (e.g., Alma the Younger did this in his sermon in Alma 5). Why?

Were a modern prophet delivering a sermon like this, to what might he refer to remind us of what the Lord has done?

Verse 17: Alma says that someday the Lamanites will learn the truth and, therefore, of the falsity of their fathers' traditions. To what traditions is he referring? Does this mean that Native Americans will give up their cultural traditions when they are converted? Why or why not?

Verses 19–24: Why would the Lord prefer to have all the Nephites destroyed rather than allow them to continue in sin after he has blessed them? To unbelievers the Lord may sound petulant, like a "martyr-mother" who says, "Since you are ungrateful after all I've done for you, I'll show you." How would you explain this to someone who saw these verses that way?

Verse 26: How does this description of the Savior square with verses 19–24?

Alma 10

Verses 1–6: Does this fit with the pattern of preaching we have seen Alma use? (See the questions for Alma 8:9–11.)

Verse 12: In what sense has more than one person testified of the things that the people of Ammonihah are accused of? Alma accused them and mentioned things to come, but Amulek didn't.

Verses 13–15, 27, 32: Might these verses say anything to us about our own day?

Alma 11

Verses 4–19: Why do you think the Book of Mormon includes these monetary units? Why are they put here in the middle of the story of Alma and Amulek's preaching? Why do you think the compilers of the Book of Mormon chose to include them? What purpose might this account of money serve in the latter days?

Verse 21: What does "devices of the devil" mean?

Verse 22: Why might Zeezrom begin with such an obvious and insulting temptation? Why not begin with something more subtle?

Verse 25: For what sin does Amulek say Zeezrom will be destroyed? For tempting him?

Verse 34: What does it mean to save the people in their sins?

Verse 37: This verse speaks of something that God *cannot* do. How does it explain that limitation on his power?

Verse 38ff.: Notice how Zeezrom's one question brings a long, detailed response from Amulek. Why does Amulek answer as he does? Why not give Zeezrom a shorter, more simple answer?

Verses 38–39: What does it mean to say that Christ is the Eternal Father? What does it mean to say that he is the beginning and the end? What does it mean to say that he is the first and the last? Given our understanding of the eternal nature of spirits, how do you make sense of these statements about God?

Verses 42–45: Why does Alma tell them of the redemption of the body? How does this function in his call to repentance?

Alma 12

Verse 1: Zeezrom has become conscious of his guilt. What in particular might have brought about that consciousness?

In what sense is Alma "unfolding the scriptures"?

Verses 3–6: Satan laid a trap for Zeezrom by getting Zeezrom to lay a trap for Alma. How is Satan's trap similar to Zeezrom's?

Verse 8: How has Zeezrom changed? (How can you tell?)

Verse 9: What is a mystery of God? *Mystery* and *mysteries* are used seventy times in the English scriptures: Matthew 13:11; Mark 4:11; Luke 8:10; Romans 11:25; 16:25; 1 Corinthians 2:7; 4:1; 13:2; 14:2; 15:51; Ephesians 1:9; 3:3, 4, 9; 5:32; 6:19; Colossians 1:26, 27; 2:2; 4:3; 2 Thessalonians 2:7; 1 Timothy 3:9, 16; Revelation 1:20; 10:7; 17:5, 7; 1 Nephi 1:1; 2:16; 10:19; Jacob 4:8, 18; Mosiah 1:3, 5; 2:9; 8:19; Alma 10:5; 12:9, 10, 11; 26:22; 30:28; 37:4, 11, 21; 40:3; Helaman 16:21; D&C 6:7, 11; 8:11; 10:64; 11:7; 19:8, 10; 28:7; 35:18; 38:13; 42:61, 65; 43:13; 63:23; 64:5; 71:1; 76:7, 114; 77:6; 84:19; 90:14; 97:5; and 107:19.

The most common synonym for *mystery* is *secret*. If many know the mysteries of God, how are they a secret? Notice that these words occur *much* more often in Restoration scriptures than in the Bible. Why do you think that is?

Verses 9–15: Here Alma indirectly explains why he told Zeezrom about temporal death and the resurrection. What is his explanation? What does it have to do with the mysteries of God?

Verse 9: What does "they shall not impart only according to the portion of his word which he doth grant unto the children of men, according to the heed and diligence which they give unto him" mean in contemporary, ordinary English?

Verses 12–13: Verse 12 says we are brought to be judged of our works. Then verse 13 says that our hearts are judged to see whether they contain the word. What does the judgment of our hearts have to do with the judgment of our works? What does it mean to have the word in our hearts?

Verse 16: What does it mean to die in sin? Does the word *in* carry any particular weight?

Verses 17–18: Why is it a punishment to continue to live in our sins? How does this square with the discussion of everlasting punishment in Doctrine and Covenants 19? Do you think Alma knew of the explanation we see in the D&C?

Verses 20–21: Do you think Antionah's questions are sincere? Why or why not?

Verse 24: What does it mean to say that life is probationary? Is the word being used as it is when we speak of criminals on probation? If so, is the implication that we have already been convicted?

Alma teaches here that life is the time given us to repent. How do we avoid a belief in original sin given these teachings?

Verses 26–27: These verses seem to answer the immediately previous questions. How?

Verse 31: Why is *Gods* capitalized in this verse? Usually it is capitalized only when it is used as the name of Deity, not when it is used to refer to an office or position. In what ways are we like Gods? Why is that significant?

Verses 32–34: Both verses 31 and 32 begin in the same way, with "Wherefore . . ." in one case and "Therefore . . ." in the other, but the two mean the same. That suggests that they logically follow from verse 30. How so? What things has the Lord done to make it possible for us to return to him?

Verse 37: What does "the rest of God" mean? How do we enter into it? Consider reading chapter 13 with this lesson. Is it a chapter on "the rest of God"?

Lesson 24
Alma 13–16

In this lesson I will concentrate on chapter 13.

Alma 13

Verse 1: Alma has just concluded a sermon on repentance and the plan of salvation. Now he asks his listeners to recall when those commandments were given. Why does he ask them to look *forward* to that time?

Why does Alma think it necessary to conclude his sermon about repentance and redemption with a lesson on priesthood? Some have argued that the "holy order" referred to here is neither the Aaronic priesthood nor the Melchizedek priesthood, but *temple* priesthood. Do you think that is possible? Why or why not?

Verse 2: How does the manner of ordaining priests teach people how to look forward to Christ for redemption?

Verse 3: This verse consists of one sentence, but its grammar is fairly complex. Can you decide what the sentence says? For example, does it say those ordained were called and prepared in the premortal existence because of their faith and good works? Or does it say that they were prepared in the premortal existence and then called in this life because of their faith and good works? Are there other possible interpretations?

What does it mean that their holy calling was "prepared with, and according to" a preparatory redemption? What is a preparatory redemption?

Verse 4: What does it mean to be hard-hearted? To be blind of mind?

Verses 1–4: One summary of these verses might be "The Lord God ordained priests who have become what we are blessed to become." Is that a reasonable summary? (Certainly it leaves things out, but does it capture an important theme in the verses?) If it is not a reasonable summary, why not?

Verse 5: If those called to be high priests were originally on the same standing as their brethren, does that mean that all were "called [to be priests] and prepared from the foundation of the world according to the foreknowledge of God" (verse 3)? If not, what does it mean?

Verse 6: Those who have this priesthood are to teach the Lord's commandments. In what ways do they do that? What does it mean to enter into the Lord's rest?

Verses 7–8: On the one hand, the high priesthood is said to have been prepared from the foundations of the world, which seems to indicate a particular point in time. On the other hand, the verse says that the high priesthood is "without beginning." Which of these do you think is metaphorical? Why? Notice, too, that Alma says the calling and the ordinance (of ordination?) as well as the priesthood are without beginning or end. What does that mean?

Verse 9: What does it mean to say that the Son of God is "full of grace, equity, and truth"? We often see the phrase "full of grace and truth" used to describe him. (See, for example, John 1:14; D&C 66:12; 93:11; Moses 1:32.) But Alma expands that phrase, here as well as in Alma 5:48 (where he says, "grace, mercy, and truth") and Alma 9:26 (where he uses the same phrase that he uses here). How might you explain the fact that Alma expands that descriptive phrase? What might his additions teach us?

Verses 10–12: Do these verses mean that all who receive the high priesthood are sanctified? Why or why not? Who can be sanctified? How?

Alma says those who have been purified cannot look on sin except with abhorrence. What does that mean? Does it have anything to do with Mosiah 5:2? If a pure person abhors sin, how does he or she feel about those in sin?

Does the last part of verse 12 perhaps tell us something about what it means to enter into the Lord's rest? (See the end of verse 13 also.) Does it equate being made pure with entering into his rest? If so, why is being made pure called "rest"? From what would purity be a rest?

Verse 16: To what ordinances is Alma referring when he says "these ordinances" in the beginning of the verse? The only one he's referred to recently is that of ordination. Is that what he means? We have to know what ordinances Alma is referring to in order to understand the point he is making.

"These ordinances" were given so people could look forward to Christ. How do those ordinances do that?

Alma says that "it" is a type of the Son of God's order and intends that to explain how the people look forward to

Christ. To what does the word *it* refer? How does what it refers to help them look forward to a remission of sins?

Verses 17–19: If Melchizedek was such a great spiritual leader, why do the scriptures say so little about him? Even with modern-day revelation, we know relatively little about him. What lesson might we learn about our own lives from this?

Verses 20: Against what is Alma warning them in this verse? Can we connect the sermon that follows this verse with his sermon on the priesthood?

Consider the message that follows in light of Alma's warning against wresting the scriptures.

Verse 21: What is the day of salvation? When is it? In what sense or senses is it drawing nigh?

Verse 22: What does it mean that the day of salvation was being declared to all nations by angels when Alma was speaking? How is the announcement of the day of salvation something to be greeted with joy rather than fear?

Verse 23: What does it mean that the glad tidings of the Lord are made known to us in "plain terms"? We've seen a number of relatively difficult passages in the Book of Mormon, including some in this chapter.

Verse 25: Though the Savior has already come, do we need to prepare people's hearts to receive the news of his coming? If so, how do we do that?

Verse 27: Do you think Alma has entered into the Lord's rest? If so, how is it that he can still feel pain and anxiety?

How are those compatible with rest? (Does the Lord feel pain and anxiety?)

Verses 28–29: Instead of procrastinating the day of our repentance, we should:

> humble ourselves
>
> watch and pray continually that we may not be tempted beyond our capacity
>
> be led by the Holy Spirit
>
> be humble, meek (gentle), submissive, patient, full of love and long-suffering
>
> have faith on the Lord
>
> have hope for eternal life
>
> have the love of God in our hearts

How do we humble ourselves? What does it mean that we should pray not to be tempted beyond our power to resist? I thought we couldn't be tempted beyond that power. How are we led by the Spirit? How do we show the attributes in the list (humility, meekness, etc.)? How do we show our faith or trust in the Lord? Why do we have to have a hope for eternal life? What does it mean to have that hope? How do we have God's love in our hearts? What shows that we do?

Lesson 25
Alma 17–22

Though this lesson contains sermons by prophets, they aren't its focus. Instead, it is primarily an account of part of the mission of the sons of Mosiah, particularly the missions of Ammon and, to a lesser degree, Aaron. This account makes a good story, with its tale of Ammon's service to Lamoni and his battle with those who wanted to steal Lamoni's herd. We often use that story as an illustration of things such as faithful service or doing missionary work by service. Are those the reasons that the story of Ammon and Lamoni is included in the Book of Mormon? How does this story as a whole and that of Aaron and the other sons of Mosiah fit in the context of the Book of Mormon, and what are that book's purposes for the story? How do the missionary approaches of Ammon and Aaron compare and contrast?

Alma 17

Verse 3: What does this verse suggest about what it means to preach "with power and authority of God"?

Verse 11: As I understand it, here the Lord tells us that to be an instrument in God's hand is (1) to establish his word and (2) to suffer patiently, and it says that to suffer patiently is to be a good example "in Christ." What does it mean to *establish* the word of God? Why *establish* rather than *teach*?

Why does being an instrument require patient suffering? What does "patient suffering in Christ" or "good example in Christ" mean? How would that differ from mere patient suffering or good example?

Verse 18: This verse suggests that administering to someone and imparting the word of God to them mean the same thing. Why do you think the verse uses the verb *administer* rather than *minister*? Webster's 1828 dictionary gives this definition of *administer*: "to contribute; to bring aid or supplies; to add something." Its definition of *minister* is "to attend and serve; to perform service in any office, sacred or secular." Does either of those definitions help us understand this verse better?

Verse 25ff.: Ammon becomes a servant of the king. Is Christ the type that Ammon's work shows here? Does this suggest something about what it means to be a Christian?

Alma 18

Verses 1–4: What does Lamoni understand God to be?

Why are the people who are reporting Ammon's deeds to the king less sure that he is the Great Spirit than Lamoni is?

Verses 10–11: For Lamoni, what is the most important proof that Ammon is the Great Spirit?

Verses 17, 21: Ammon says, "I will do whatever you ask, if it is right." Lamoni responds, "I will give you anything you desire." What is happening?

Verse 20: Why does Lamoni refer to those who've been stealing his flocks as "my brethren"?

Verse 22: What is the thing that Ammon desires of Lamoni and that Lamoni is bound to give Ammon, given what Lamoni said in verse 21?

Verses 36–39: In verses 23–35, Ammon establishes that Lamoni believes in an all-knowing God, and Ammon testifies that he has been sent by that God to teach the people. Then, beginning with Adam, he lays before Lamoni "the records and the holy scriptures" and the history of the descendants of Lehi. Finally, Ammon teaches the plan of salvation. The outline of his method looks like this:

(1) Establish that there is an all-knowing God.

(2) Remind Lamoni of the sacred history of his people.

(3) Teach the plan of salvation.

Why is the first step necessary? How would we do that today? Why is a review of sacred history the second step of Ammon's preaching? What would be comparable for us today? Are the first two steps necessary to the third? Why?

How is Ammon's sermon to Lamoni related to King Benjamin's sermon in Mosiah 4?

Alma 19

Verses 1–7: Ammon knows what has happened to Lamoni. Why does he wait so long to act?

Verses 12–13: Why do you think King Lamoni was given the privilege of seeing the Redeemer in vision?

Verses 29–30: Of what significance is it that this miracle is done by a servant woman, Abish, rather than by Ammon?

Verse 33: What does it mean to have one's heart changed and to have no more desire to do evil? (Compare Mosiah 5:2.) Is this an experience that people have today? If so, when? If not, why not?

Alma 20

Verses 10, 13: What explains the animosity of the Lamanites toward the Nephites? Is their accusation based in fact? Why would conversion to the gospel be the only possible remedy for the accusation?

Alma 21

Verses 1–12: What argument do the Amalekites make against Aaron? Can you state that argument in contemporary terms? How does Aaron respond? Can you state his response in contemporary terms?

Verses 19–23: What reforms did Lamoni make on his return home? Why those reforms in particular?

Alma 22

Verse 3: What is troubling Lamoni's father? Why would that trouble him? What does that suggest about our own social and legal obligations?

Verses 7–14: How does Aaron's sermon to Lamoni's father differ from Ammon's sermon to Lamoni (Alma 18:23–39)? Can you explain the difference?

Verse 14: What does it mean to say that no human being can merit anything of himself?

Verse 15: How does Lamoni's father understand what it means to be born again? Can you explain what this means in practical, concrete terms?

Verse 18: What does "I will give away all my sins" mean? Why use *give away* rather than *forsake*, for example?

Lesson 26
Alma 23–29

At the heart of this material we have the story of the Anti-Nephi-Lehies, converts of the sons of Mosiah. That story has a great deal to teach us today, but it may not be what we expect, whether we read it as a story of pacifism or as something else.

Alma 23

Verses 2–3: The king of the Lamanites has been converted, and he decrees protection for the missionaries. He does so in order that "the word of God might have no obstruction" (which seems to be the same as going "forth throughout all the land") and so that people will obey the commandments ("that they ought not to murder," etc.). He also does so in order "that his people might be convinced concerning the wicked traditions of their fathers, and that they might be convinced that they were all brethren." Are being convinced that the traditions of their fathers are wicked and being convinced that they are all brethren two things or one? If two, how are they related?

Do we have wicked traditions that we have inherited? If so, can you think of some examples? Do those traditions interfere with our ability to see others as our brothers and sisters?

Verse 6: What can we make of the fact that none of these Lamanite converts ever fell away? Does that say something about them? About the missionaries who taught them? Neither? Both? Is it just a fact with no other significance? If that, why is it mentioned in the scriptures?

Verse 7: Why are their weapons of war called "weapons of rebellion"? Against whom were they rebelling? The Nephites? They warred against them, but would that be called rebellion?

As we have it, this verse equates being righteous with laying down their weapons. Why? Is Alma 26:32 relevant?

Verses 8–15: In some cities and regions all, or almost all, of the inhabitants are converted; and in others none, or almost none, are converted. What would account for these differences?

Verse 16: Why do you think a new name would be so important to these converts? Do you have any ideas as to why they might have chosen the name that they did? Your guess would be as good as anyone else's.

In *Commentary on the Book of Mormon*, Reynolds and Sjodahl suggest that the word *anti* seems to have meant "hill" or "region of hills." Many Book of Mormon scholars have suggested that the "Nephi-Lehi" part of the name refers to the lands of Nephi and Lehi rather than to their descendants. However, Hugh Nibley tells us that the Indo-European root is relevant: "to imitate" or "face-to-face" (though he doesn't explain why the Indo-European root rather than the Semitic root is relevant; see *Teachings of the Book of Mormon,* Semester 2, 404–5). On that evidence, "Anti-

Nephi-Lehies" could mean "those who imitate Nephi and Lehi," or it could mean "those who bring together the Nephite and Lehite traditions." Kent P. Jackson suggests that the name means "descendants of Lehi who are not descendants of Nephi" (*Studies in Scripture,* 7:337).

Note that this name doesn't stick; they are later referred to as "the people of Ammon." Why do you think they were called that rather than "the people of the sons of Mosiah"? (See Alma 27:26.)

Alma 24

Verses 12–13: Why does King Anti-Nephi-Lehi command that the people should not take up arms against the Lamanites who were about to attack? If they were to take up their swords again, it would be in self-defense. So why does he worry that if they were to do so, the Atonement might not apply to them any longer? Does the Anti-Nephi-Lehi experience tell us anything about our own repentance?

Verse 15: How does the king explain the symbolism of hiding away their swords?

Verse 18: What is the significance of this testimony? What does bearing this testimony require if it is to continue to be a true testimony?

Verse 21: Why do the Anti-Nephi-Lehies go out to meet the Lamanites? Wouldn't it have been better to wait for them to arrive? The covenant that they made didn't require that they offer themselves for slaughter, did it?

Verses 23–24: What does this experience teach us about our own relations with others?

Verses 28–30: Why is it significant that none of the Nehors were converted? Mormon, the editor, interrupts the narrative here to write in his own voice: "And thus we can plainly discern." How is Mormon's observation important to us?

Alma 25

Verse 1: Why do the unconverted Lamanites leave off killing the Anti-Nephi-Lehies and turn on the Nephites?

Verses 15–16: The sacrifices of the law of Moses were a type of Christ's sacrifice, of course, but how was the law a type of his *coming*? Is there a connection between the covenant that the Anti-Nephi-Lehies have made and their understanding of the law of Moses?

Alma 26

Verses 1–9: We usually think of blessings as good things that come to us. Why is it a blessing (verse 2) to be an instrument in God's hands (verse 3)? Does that suggest that perhaps we should reconsider how we think about blessings?

Verse 10: What in Ammon's exulting might have made Aaron think that Ammon had begun to boast? Why is Aaron so concerned about that possibility? Is Mosiah 4:5–11 relevant?

Verses 11–12, 16: Why does Ammon call what he has been doing both boasting (verse 12) and rejoicing (verses 11 and 16)?

Verse 17: What does Ammon find amazing about the gospel? How does that apply to him personally? To the Anti-Nephi-Lehies? To us?

Verse 22: What mysteries does Ammon have in mind? Has he been speaking of them in the previous verses, such as verse 17?

Verse 35: Is Ammon using hyperbole here? If not, how can this be true?

Alma 29

Verses 1–2: What does Alma desire?

Verses 3–4: Why is his desire sinful? Is *sinful* too strong a word, or does Alma really mean what that word connotes? If Alma isn't using hyperbole when he calls his desire sinful, what in our own experience might be comparable?

How do we avoid such sin?

What does it mean to say that the Lord grants "unto men according to their desire"? Does that suggest anything about the nature of reward and punishment in the gospel?

Verse 5: How does this verse qualify what Alma taught in verse 4?

Verse 6: Alma speaks here of his desires and what he should desire. How is that related to what he has just said about desire?

Verse 9: How is what Alma says here related to Moses 1:39?

Verse 10: How is Alma's missionary experience related to his own history?

Verses 11–12: How is Alma's missionary experience related to the experience of his ancestors? Is there a common theme in these three events: the conversion of the Lamanites, Alma's conversion, and the history of Alma's ancestors?

Verse 16: What is Alma talking about here? If we were traditional Christians who believe that the body is an impediment to spiritual experience rather than something necessary for becoming like our Father, this verse would be easy to explain. How do we explain it as latter-day saints?

Lesson 27
Alma 30–31

Anyone who has been a member of the LDS Church for a while is familiar with the story of Korihor—sufficiently familiar that we may read it too quickly. When we read quickly, we tend to skim over the text and "see" in it what is already in our heads rather than what it says. So take time to read through this story slowly, looking for places where it says things that you do not expect it to say. Those are places where you are likely to learn something new.

Since Alma 31 fits naturally with Alma 32–35 (lesson 28), I'm going to include it in those lesson materials rather than here.

Alma 30

Verses 6–12: The narrator interrupts his story about Korihor coming to the land of Zarahemla with five verses explaining that there was no law governing people's belief because any such law would have broken the divine commandment against inequality. Why does he place that discussion of law where he does, in the middle of his introduction of Korihor?

How would forbidding some beliefs be contrary to the divine law of equality? What does it mean to be "on equal grounds"? What grounds does the writer have in mind? What is equality in them? Haven't we already seen answers to these questions in earlier chapters?

Verses 13, 15: What is Korihor's argument for his claim that we cannot know that there will be a Christ?

Why do you think the Book of Mormon uses the word *Christ* (derived from Greek) rather than the word *Messiah* (derived from Hebrew) when they both mean the same thing and the Nephite language was originally Hebrew?

Verse 14: What is the implication of describing prophecies as "foolish traditions of your fathers"?

Verse 16: Korihor says that their anticipation of forgiveness is "the effect of a frenzied [i.e., mad] mind." What does he mean by that phrase? Of what is he accusing them?

Verse 17: Korihor teaches that we fare "in this life according the management of the creature," that we prosper according to our genius ("strength of mind" in Webster's 1828 dictionary) and conquer according to our strength. How would we say the same thing in today's language?

Where do we find people teaching Korihor's doctrine? Do we ever find it in church classes?

Given the way that Korihor says what he does, he seems to think that if we prosper according to our genius and conquer according to our strength, then there can be no Atonement. Is that a reasonable conclusion? In other words, is the Atonement incompatible with prospering by our minds and overcoming in strength? What alternative is there to that kind of prospering and conquering?

Whose genius and power can we rely on if not our own? Does this have anything to do with the question of grace and works? Which is Korihor preaching?

Verse 18: Korihor seems to connect his advice that people go ahead and commit crimes to his teaching that there is no life after death. The argument is something like this: (1) If there's no life after death, then there's no punishment for sin. (2) If there's no punishment for sin, then we ought to do whatever we wish, for there is, in fact, no sin. (3) There is no life after death. (4) So we ought to do whatever we wish, for there is, in fact, no sin. Latter-day Saints disagree with his third assumption, that there is no life after death. But do we agree with the other assumptions? It isn't difficult to find people who do not believe in life after death but who nevertheless live good, moral lives. What would they disagree with in Korihor's argument?

Verse 20: In what sense were the people of Ammon wiser than the Nephites?

Did the people of Ammon behave in accordance with the law described in verses 7 through 11? Are tying Korihor up and taking him before the high priest and then (in verse 21; see also verse 29) deporting him from the country in accord with the law described in those verses?

Verses 23, 27–28: Here Korihor adds an element to his explanation of religion. What is it? Why might he think that explanation could work among the Nephites and the people of Ammon?

Verse 28: Korihor says that the people dare "not make use of that which is their own" for fear of the priests. Something has to have been happening that Korihor could interpret in that way. To what might he be referring?

Verse 29: Why do Giddonah and the chief judge refuse to respond to Korihor?

Verses 33–35: Why does Alma respond only to the accusation that he and the other priests glut themselves on the labors of the people?

Verses 39–41: Alma turns the tables on Korihor, saying in effect, "What evidence do you have that there is no God? I have all things as a testimony that there is, and so do you." Is Alma making what philosophers call a cosmological argument (the existence of the world is evidence for God's existence)? If not, what is he doing?

Verse 42: Is Korihor backing down a little here, or is he merely saying the same thing he said in verse 15—namely, that he believes only what can be seen?

Verse 44: Alma tells Korihor that he has had "signs enough." Then he refers to three classes of signs: the testimonies of the prophets, the scriptures, and the natural world. He uses the phrase "all things" when he refers to the natural world. Does that show that he was using the phrase in the same way in verse 15? Why does he order these three in the way that he does?

Verse 48: Is Korihor beginning to backpedal here? Compare what he says in this verse to what he said at the end of verse 28. Is he changing his tune or not? What does he mean when he says, "I do not deny the existence of a God, but . . ."?

Verses 52–53: Can we believe Korihor's story, or should we be suspicious of it? What does he mean when he says that he always knew there was a God but the devil deceived him? Korihor says, "An angel told me there is no God." But if an angel told him that, then that is evidence that there is a God, while if there is no God, then there probably wouldn't be an angel to tell him that there isn't. What is going on in Korihor's speech?

He says that he taught Satan's words so long that, in the end, he believed they were true. How does that happen to us?

Verse 55: How did Korihor get into this situation, in which he will return to his apostasy and his activities as an anti-Christ unless he is cursed? I doubt that any of those reading this book are anti-Christs. I doubt that many or any of us know someone who is the kind of anti-Christ we find in Korihor. So why is it important for us to know his story? It is tempting to ask what it tells us about other people, but it is more important to ask what it tells us about ourselves.

Verse 60: Mormon stops to editorialize, to tell us the conclusion he draws from this story. How was that conclusion relevant to his time? How is it relevant to ours?

Lesson 28
Alma 32–35

In the first edition of the Book of Mormon, Alma 30–35 are one chapter (chapter 16). They can be outlined like this:

Korihor (30)

The Zoramites (31–32a; 35)

> The poor in spirit (32a)

> Faith and the Atonement (32b–34)

Separation of the Ammonites from Jershon (35)

This suggests that we should read these stories as a piece, as a story about how Alma deals with different forms of apostasy. Alma's sermon in chapters 32 and 33, with Amulek's response to Alma's sermon, is the conclusion or climax of the story. Notice that the division between chapters 32 and 33 occurs in the middle of the sermon, breaking it up artificially. The result is that we tend to treat the two parts of the sermon as distinct things, but we shouldn't. Notice also that Amulek's sermon is a commentary on Alma's, particularly in the beginning. Amulek tells us what Alma's sermon was about. But we seldom read Alma's sermon as Amulek does. That should give us pause.

Background

Remember what we have seen in our recent readings: The great battle with the Lamanites (Alma 28); Alma's encounter with Korihor (Alma 30); Alma hears of the apostasy of the Zoramites (Alma 31), and fearing that the Zoramites will enter into a covenant with the Lamanites and come against the Nephites in war (Alma 31:4), he decides to go with others on a mission to convert the Zoramites because "the preaching of the word had a great tendency to lead the people to do that which was just—yea, it had had more powerful effect upon the minds of the people than the sword" (Alma 31:5); Alma prays for the success of his mission (Alma 31:26–35).

Too often we read Alma's sermon out of context, truncating it and looking only at Alma 32:26–43 (if that much), ignoring that his sermon is a response to his encounter with the Zoramites and that it continues on into chapter 34 and is followed by a second sermon, a second testimony, by Amulek. The result is sometimes that we use it for our purposes, not mindful of what Alma is teaching. These notes will be longer than usual, but I will cover all of chapters 32–33, with references to chapter 34.

Alma 32

Verses 1–3: What are the various ways in which these people are poor? One is, obviously, monetarily: "they were cast out of the synagogues because of the coarseness of their apparel"; we can presume that they couldn't afford the fine clothing necessary for worship. However, when Alma speaks of being "poor as to things of the world," he means something else. What does he mean?

What does he mean by "poor in heart"?

Verse 5: The man who comes to Alma tells him that "they are despised of all men." Is he exaggerating? If so, why would he do so?

What might the phrase "our God" suggest? Is the man skeptical that his God is also Alma's, or is he appealing to what he and Alma have in common?

As you read what follows, ask yourself what kind of worship the questioner and his comrades were asking to take part in. (See Alma 31:12–18, 23.)

Verse 7: It is odd to feel joy in the suffering of another. In fact, it is often a kind of denial: it's all right that we suffer here because this world isn't anything anyway. But Latter-day Saints believe that this world is something, just as we believe that our bodies are important. So even while we look to eternal reward, we ought not to dismiss this world, or the suffering of this world, as nothing. So what are we to make of Alma's joy?

Alma says that they are prepared to hear the word. Then later, when Amulek speaks, he says that Alma spoke to them "to prepare [their] minds" (34:3). If Alma's sermon was merely preparatory, what did it prepare them for? Amulek's sermon? Something else?

Verses 7–11: Alma identifies the man's question: "What shall we do?—for we are cast out of our synagogues?" He responds with two rhetorical questions. How do those questions answer their question? Why isn't this the end of Alma's sermon?

What beliefs were characteristic of the Zoramites? (See Alma 31:24–28; 31:29). Would those beliefs have been influential with the poor among the Zoramites?

Verse 12a:[1] What does Alma think they should have been asking him?

As you read the rest of Alma's sermon, ask yourself how he is teaching them wisdom and why humility is necessary to learn it.

Verses 12–13: Are we blessed if we are humbled against our wills? Why would we be given mercy if our humility was imposed on us?

Verses 14–15: If even those who are humbled against their wills are blessed, why is it better to humble oneself?

Verse 17: Surely Alma is thinking of Korihor here. Why would that comparison be useful to the Zoramites?

Verse 18: We use the word *faith* in a few senses: sometimes to mean "fidelity" but most often to mean "trust" or "belief in the face of uncertainty." Alma seems here to ignore the fact that the word can have multiple senses. Why might he do that?

Verses 19–20: Alma asks them to decide whether the person who knows and doesn't do is worse than the person who only believes and doesn't do. Why must they decide? Doesn't he tell them the answer in the last clause of verse 20?

Verse 21: Alma recognizes that he has gotten off topic (verses 19–20), and he returns to the topic of faith. Why does he contrast faith and perfect knowledge rather than just faith and knowledge?

---

1. "12a" is a way of referring to the first part of verse 12. So "12b" would refer to the second half.

What does the word *perfect* mean as Alma is using it here?

In philosophy we often use the metaphor of vision to talk about knowledge: to know something is to see it; to be true is to be visible. Is Alma thinking in the same way or in another way?

Verses 22–23: Why does Alma think it important to remind them of these things early in his sermon?

How is what he says here relevant to his own experience?

Was Alma's experience with the angel enough to give him knowledge? (Compare Alma 5:45–46.)

What does the word *confound* mean as it is used here?

Verses 24–25: Alma gets off topic again. In verse 21 he told us that he was going to discuss faith. What do you think caused him to return to (1) the question of what they could do about being cast out of the synagogue and (2) the topic of their humility?

Interlude (Alma 34)

Before reading Alma's teachings to the Zoramite poor, it might be helpful to read Alma 34:1–5, Amulek's description of what Alma did.

Verses 1–2: What does Amulek remind them about their background? Why is that important?

Verse 3: Why does Amulek understand Alma's sermon as preparatory, and why does he focus on Alma's exhortation to faith and patience? Would you have noticed that exhortation in Alma's sermon if Amulek hadn't brought it out? Why or why not?

Verses 4–5: How does Amulek understand the experiment that Alma is going to propose?

How can the great question be whether there is a Christ if the only thing they asked was how to get back into the congregation of the Zoramites? If their real question was whether there is a Christ, even if they didn't know it, what does that tell us about how we should understand Alma's sermon?

Back to Alma 32

Verse 26: Does *surety* here mean "certainty" or "security"? How might the differences in those meanings change our understanding of the verse? Is there any connection between those meanings and faith as trust, on the one hand, and epistemic uncertainty, on the other?

Verse 27: Webster's 1828 dictionary says that *faculty* meant "1) that power of the mind or intellect which enables it to receive, revive, or modify perceptions; 2) the power of doing anything; 6) power, authority; 9) privilege." Which meaning do you think is at work here? Why does Alma make desire the moving, most important force in this verse? Alma speaks of exercising faith, making faith an action. What does it mean to say that faith is something we *do*? Is that a way that faith contrasts with knowledge? Is knowledge an act?

Verse 28: Is it significant that Alma has shifted from his word (verse 27) to *the* word?

Alma uses the phrase "the word" considerably more than any other Book of Mormon prophet (over fifty times), and he uses it to refer to something other than the word of God only three times (Alma 19:9; 41:13, 15). To what does that phrase refer? (Compare Alma 16:16 and 33:22.)

Notice also how Amulek describes Alma's teaching in Alma 34:6. As you read the rest of the first part of Alma's sermon, the part about the seed and its results, keep in mind that he has begun by telling us specifically what the seed is.

Alma uses the passive voice to talk about the seed being planted in our hearts. Who does Alma understand to be doing the planting? Does this have anything to do with verse 22?

Alma uses the terms *good* and *true* as equivalents when he speaks of the seed. We usually use *true* and *accurate* as equivalents. What do you make of his usage?

How would Korihor have understood *true*? (Compare Alma 30:13–16.) What difference does that make?

At the end of the verse, Alma gives three characteristics of the good seed: it enlarges the soul, it enlightens the understanding, and it is delicious. Presumably these are parallel, three ways of saying the same thing. However, consider the metaphors he uses. What does it mean for a soul to be enlarged? If a soul gets larger, what else does it encompass?

Literally speaking, what does it mean for the understanding to be enlightened? What enlightens it?

Why would Alma describe the word as delicious? What does that suggest? Why does he say that the soul *begins* to be enlarged, the understanding *begins* to be enlightened, and the seed *begins* to be delicious?

How does one cast out the seed? What does that suggest about unbelief?

225

When Alma says "it will begin to swell within your breasts," is *your* singular or plural?

Verses 29–30: Is Alma still using the word *faith* to mean an act, something one can do? What do we learn about the seed if we don't cast it out?

Verses 31–32: The word *sure* means not only "without a doubt," but "secure, safe." Which of those meanings do you think is most important here?

Verse 33: Here Alma speaks of planting the seed rather than letting it be planted. Why do you think he may have changed his metaphor? What does it mean to know that the word—the seed—is good?

Verse 34: What knowledge is perfect?

Alma uses parallelism here: "Your understanding doth begin to be enlightened, and your mind doth begin to expand." How might the first half of this parallel help us understand what it means for our minds to expand?

Verse 35: Why might Alma have felt the need to address the question of whether the word is real?

Earlier (verses 28 and 34) Alma spoke of the word enlightening our understanding. Is this a continuation of that point?

Notice how consistent Alma is in identifying the true, the real, and the good. If we think in his terms, we would understand "the facts" to be what they are because they are what is good; we would understand that the good determines what is real. How would we see the world differently if we saw it in Alma's terms?

What does it mean to taste light? Why does Alma keep returning to metaphors of taste?

Verse 36: Why do we need to continue to exercise faith once we know that the word is good?

Verses 37–38: If the seed is the word, what tree do you think Alma has in mind as the tree that grows from the seed that was planted? (Compare Revelation 2:7; 22:2.)

Notice that this is the first time that Alma has said that the seed is that of a tree. Is that significant to understanding how his listeners would have heard what he was teaching?

Verse 36 said that we need to continue to exercise faith. Is that how we nourish the tree?

Is it significant that we will say, "Let *us* nourish it" (italics added)?

What is the fruit of the tree?

Is *ye* in verse 38 singular or plural? What does the verse mean if it is singular? If it is plural?

If Alma had referred to the heat of the sun in verse 37, to what might he have been referring? Does it mean the same thing in verse 38?

Can what causes the tree to grow in our lives also kill it? How?

Verse 39: We already know that the seed is good (verse 33), so we can't blame the death of the tree on the seed. What are the other possible explanations?

What does "your ground is barren" mean?

Verse 40: Alma tells us what tree's seed was planted. Compare what Lehi (1 Nephi 8:10–12; see also 2 Nephi 2:15) and Nephi (1 Nephi 11:8–9 and the interpretation of the tree given in the rest of that chapter; see also 1 Nephi 15:22) say about the tree of life. What does Genesis tell us about the tree of life (2:9; 3:22)? Do Proverbs 3:18; 11:30; 15:4; and Revelation 2:7; 22:2, 14 shed light on the tree of life?

Alma has spoken of the tree of life before (Alma 5:34, 62; 12:21–26). Do those earlier discussions shed light on what he is saying here?

The Book of Mormon never refers to the tree of knowledge, only to the tree of life. Why?

Compare Nephi's description of the fruit of the tree of life (1 Nephi 8:10–12) with Eve's description of the tree of knowledge (Genesis 3:6; Moses 4:12). Does that suggest an answer?

Verses 41–43: Why does faith require both diligence and patience? In the end, what is the point of the experiment on the word? What does Amulek identify as the point (Alma 34:3)?

Alma began with desire (verse 27); now he ends this part of his sermon with the satisfaction of desire. Has desire been a major theme of his discussion? If not, why begin and end with it? If so, why doesn't the word appear more often in the body of the sermon?

Alma 33

Verse 1: What do the Zoramites desire? Have they understood what Alma has taught them? What is your evidence for your answer?

Verse 2: Does Alma answer the question that the people have just asked? Which question does he answer? It is as if they ask, "What shall we do about being cast out of our synagogues?" and he responds with a discussion of how to be nourished by the word of God. So then they ask how to obtain that fruit, the word of God, and he responds by answering their first question. What is going on? Why does he refer them to the scriptures?

Verse 3: Alma equates prayer and worship. Why?

Verses 4–10: Why is Zenos's prayer particularly appropriate to the Zoramites? Notice the movement of Zenos's prayer: wilderness → enemies → fields → house → closet → congregations → enemies. Is that a progression of some kind, perhaps from individual in the wilderness in the beginning to the congregation at the end? Why are enemies mentioned twice?

The first five in the series (wilderness → enemies → fields → house → closet) are separated from the last two (congregations → enemies) by verse 8 and its reference to God's mercy. Does that suggest that we should treat the two groups distinctly in trying to understand the meaning of these verses?

How would you characterize each group?

Why does the explicit reference to mercy occur at the center of the prayer rather than at the end?

Verse 11: How do Alma's concerns and the concerns of the Zoramites come together in this verse?

Verses 12–14: Why has Alma waited until this point in his sermon to appeal to the authority of scripture?

It is obvious from the way that Alma speaks with the Zoramites that they had the scriptures, though clearly they must not have accepted all of their teachings. What does that add to our understanding of the experiment that Alma has proposed to them?

Verses 15–17: Why did the people kill Zenock? How is *would* used in "the people would not understand"? What does that word tell us?

Verses 18–19: Why does Alma pile up the witnesses of Christ?

How does his sermon compare, at this point, to his refutation of Korihor (Alma 30:40–44, especially verse 44)?

Verse 20: Why is this lesson important for Alma's audience? What Alma says is very strong: ultimately those who do not believe the message of Jesus Christ do not believe because they refuse to believe. Does this have anything to do with his teaching from chapter 32 that goodness and truth are the same?

Verses 21–22: In the previous chapter, Alma used the metaphor of the seed. Now he uses the metaphor of looking around. What does this metaphor teach us about coming to know the truth—in other words, the good?

Verse 23: Alma returns to his metaphor of the seed, taking his audience back to the beginning of his sermon. Why does he feel the need to take them back to the beginning?

Why does God make our burdens light rather than remove them?

Lesson 29
Alma 36–39

Alma 35:15–16 explains Alma's motivation for counseling his sons, Helaman, Shiblon, and Corianton: he grieved for the hardness of the hearts of the people to whom he and others had been sent as missionaries. (See Alma 31:6–7.) How does that explain what he says, especially since one of his sons, Helaman, was not part of that mission?

Alma 36

Verses 1–2: Why does Alma begin by asking Helaman to remember the captivity of their fathers? What captivity do you think he has in mind? (Compare Mosiah 27:16.)

Verse 3: Alma tells Helaman the principle he wishes him to learn. Why is this principle so important that it required gathering his sons together and giving them these individual admonitions?

Verses 6–30: At the end of the study materials for lesson 10, I have provided a side-by-side comparison of the three accounts of Alma the Younger's conversion. Compare them and explain the differences between them. What does each version do that the others do not?

Verse 14: Why do you think that Alma describes what he had done as murder?

Compare Alma 5:23 and Matthew 10:28—what does it mean to destroy both soul (i.e., spirit) *and* body in hell?

Verses 18–19: Why does Alma's cry in verse 18 bring the results in verse 19? How is this connected to King Benjamin's teaching in Mosiah 4? Is it significant that Benjamin delivered that address to a people who were diligent in keeping the commandments but that it also seems to apply to someone like Alma, who has openly rebelled against those commandments?

Verse 19: Since Alma is here telling us about the pains he experienced, what can he mean when he says, "I could remember my pains no more"?

Verse 22: Why does Alma have a vision of *Lehi* at this point?

Verse 28: Is this verse parallel to verse 2? Why would Alma begin and end the account of his conversion by reminding Helaman of this scriptural type?

Verse 30: How are verses 28–29 (and therefore also verse 3) a type for what Alma says in this verse?

Alma 37

Verses 1–4: In chapter 36, Alma described his own salvation, then that of the Israelites, then that of the Lehites. Now he follows those stories with a command for Helaman to keep the records. How does recounting these stories of salvation lead to that command?

Verse 5: Of what is this verse a prophecy? As used here, what does *brightness* mean?

Verses 6–7: Why might Alma have thought it necessary to tell Helaman this?

Verses 8–9: What does it mean to enlarge a people's memory? How has doing so convinced people of the error of their ways? Why were the records essential to the conversion work that Ammon and the other missionaries did? How do we enlarge our memory?

Verses 10–12: Does Alma understand what the ultimate purpose of the Book of Mormon will be? If not, why not? What might your answer to that question suggest about our understanding of things?

Verses 21–22: What twenty-four plates is Alma referring to? (See Mosiah 8:9.) Why are those plates so important to the Nephites? How is that the same as, or different from, the way in which the Book of Mormon is important to us?

Verse 25: These interpreters have been made available so that God can "bring forth out of darkness unto light all their secret works and their abominations." Why must those things be revealed? Why isn't it enough to reveal the truths of the gospel?

Verses 27–29: If the abominations are to be revealed, why not also the covenants, agreements, signs, and wonders that went with those abominations?

What do verses 25–29 have to do with us today? Anything?

Verses 32–34: Helaman is not supposed to teach his people the secrets on the Jaredite plates (though it appears that he is to teach them about the abominations of the Jaredites). Instead, he is supposed to teach the people to respond to evil by (1) teaching them to hate evil, (2) preaching repentance, (3) teaching them to be humble, (4) teaching them to resist temptation with faith, (5) teaching them to be unwearying in doing good works, (6) and teaching them to be meek. First, are items 2 and 6 the same? If so, why is it repeated? If not, how are they different? More important, what does this say to us about how we are to respond to evil? How, for example, can we be meek and humble *and* hate evil? What form would our hatred take? How are good works a response to evil?

Verses 35–37: These verses are beautiful and often quoted. Why does Alma seem to equate wisdom with learning to keep the commandments (verse 35)?

Why do you think he followed "keep the commandments" with "cry unto God for all thy support"? Is Alma using hyperbole when he says "let all thy thoughts be directed unto the Lord," or is there some way that this is really possible? If there is, what is it?

What are the affections of our hearts? What does it mean to place our affections on the Lord?

Verses 43–46: Alma sees the world and its history in terms of types and shadows. How does that help him understand the work of the Lord? Do we understand the world in the same way? Can we? How?

Alma 38

Verse 4: What does this verse suggest about our knowledge of the history of the descendants of Lehi?

Verses 6–8: Why do you think Alma explains his conversion so briefly to Shiblon but explained it at length to Helaman?

Verse 9: How does Alma's conversion story show us that we can be saved only in and through Christ?

Verses 10–14: Do you think that Alma gives this counsel to Shiblon because he knows what things tempt Shiblon? What kind of intemperance do you think Shiblon might find tempting? Are there any suggestions in these verses?

Why must we bridle our passions in order to be filled with love? What does it mean to bridle the passions? All passions or particular ones? If particular ones, which ones?

Why is it important to acknowledge our unworthiness before God at all times? How do we do so?

Alma 39

Verses 2–4: What sins is Corianton guilty of? I suggest that you make a list of the sins that Alma mentions.

Does Alma say that Corianton has been guilty of unchastity?

Verse 5: Notice that when Alma speaks of the severity of Corianton's sins, he says "*these* sins." To what is he referring, to Corianton's sin with regard to Isabel (verse 3) or to that sin and his pride (verses 2–3)?

Verse 6: Is Alma using "deny the Holy Ghost" and "murder against the light" as synonyms in this verse?

See if you can explain the teaching of this verse in your own words. Why did Alma think it necessary to explain this to Corianton? How is it relevant to us?

Verse 7: What does it mean to harrow up a person's soul? When is it good for a soul to be harrowed? Think about what a harrow does. How do we do that to a soul? Who has the right to harrow another's soul?

Verse 9: How is the phrase "lusts of the eyes" significant? (Compare Isaiah 3:16; 2 Peter 2:14; 1 John 2:16; 1 Nephi 16:38; and D&C 56:17; 68:31.) Does this suggest anything about the sin that Alma refers to in verse 3?

Twice Alma tells Corianton to cross himself. What does that mean? Webster's 1828 dictionary of American English had these possibly relevant definitions: "to erase; to cancel"; "to pass from side to side; to pass or move over"; "to thwart; to obstruct; to hinder; to embarrass"; "to counteract; to clash or interfere with; to be inconsistent with"; "to counteract or contravene; to hinder by authority; to stop"; "to contradict"; "to debar or preclude." Do any of these help us think about what Alma is telling Corianton?

Verse 11: What does *vain* mean? What does *foolish* mean? What kinds of vain or foolish things might we be led away by?

In addition to the personal consequences of sin, what are some of the other consequences?

Verses 12–14: What advice does Alma give Corianton? What does it have to do with the sins he has committed? Does this advice help us understand better the list that Alma made earlier (verses 1–3)? How will this advice help Corianton overcome those sins?

Lesson 30

Alma 40–42

Why is the lengthy discussion of resurrection in chapters 40–41 addressed to Corianton?

Why does that part of Alma's sermon come before his discussion of the punishment of sin (chapter 42)?

Alma 40

Verses 2–4: Why do you think Alma reiterates what he doesn't know when he tells Corianton about the resurrection?

Verse 5: It seems odd that Alma doesn't care about the facts of the resurrection when we often make such a big deal about it. For him, it is enough to know that the dead will be resurrected. How would you explain that? What might it teach us?

Verse 6: Why must there be a space between death and the resurrection? Why can't it be immediate or almost immediate?

Verses 11–12: How does what Alma says here square with our understanding of the three degrees of glory?

Verse 13: What does the term *outer darkness* mean in other scriptures? (See Matthew 8:12; 22:13; 25:30; and D&C 101:91; 133:73.) To what does it refer here?

Verse 15: Alma says we can think of life in the spirit world as a state of resurrection (even though it isn't the resurrection of the body). In what sense is that life a resurrection? Why is Alma willing to use resurrection to speak of life in the spirit world?

Verse 20: Alma gives his opinion that the righteous will be bodily resurrected at the time of Christ's resurrection. First, why does he mention it as his opinion? Was he right?

Are we as scrupulous in distinguishing our opinions from the truth as Alma was?

Verse 23: What does it mean to be restored? We say that the Church has been restored. Alma says that the spirit will be restored to the body. We talk about ill people being restored to health. What does that word imply?

Alma 41

As you read this chapter, notice that Alma speaks here of restoration rather than the need to pay the price for sin: if we choose evil in this life, the Father allows us to continue to be what we have become through those choices; if we choose good, he allows us to continue to be what we have become through those choices. Given those options, why is an atonement necessary?

Verses 3–6: We see two kinds of restoration: restoration to good and restoration to evil. In what sense is the latter a restoration? In verse 6 "repented of his sins" and "desired righteousness until the end of his days" seem to be parallel. If they are, then we can understand the second as an explanation of the first. Does that make sense? If so, how? Is there a similar connection between works and desires in verse 3?

Verse 10: We often quote, "Wickedness never was happiness." What does it mean in the context of Alma's discussion of restoration?

Verse 11: What does it mean to be in a state of nature? Since the Church does not believe the doctrine of original sin—that we naturally desire to do evil—Alma must be saying something different here. *What* is he saying?

Verses 12–13: How does Alma's use of the word *restoration* help us understand such things as the resurrection and the judgment? Does it give us any insight into the restoration of the Church?

Verses 14–15: What do these verses offer Corianton? Why are they important advice to him? Given what Alma has taught about restoration so far, why isn't it too late for Corianton to be merciful?

Alma 42

As you read this chapter, think about the context of what Alma is saying. How will the teachings of this chapter affect Corianton? How is it motivated by Corianton's particular problems? What does Corianton seem not to have understood in the previous chapter?

Verse 4: Here we seem to see Mormon's interjection: "thus we see." How does the story of Adam and Eve help us see that earth life is a time of probation?

Verse 7: What is the significance of the fact that Adam and Eve were allowed to follow their own will? Is it significant that Alma speaks of their *will* rather than of their *wills*?

Verses 8–9: Verse 8 says "it was not expedient that man should be reclaimed from this temporal death." Then verse 9 says "it was expedient that mankind should be reclaimed from this spiritual death." Can you explain why each is true?

Verse 11: Why would our souls be miserable if they were cut off from the Father?

Verses 13–15: How does Alma's teaching about restoration in the previous chapter fit with this teaching?

Verses 15–16: Here is one way to read what Alma is saying: God has given a law with necessary consequences, and then he takes those consequences on himself if we allow him to do so. Does that make sense? Can you explain what Alma says in another way?

Why can't there be repentance if there isn't a punishment?

Verses 18–19: Is Alma saying that fear of punishment and remorse of conscience are the same? Isn't there a difference? When we fear punishment are we behaving the same as when we feel sorry for having done wrong? Does Alma's discussion here depend on the fact that he is speaking to Corianton?

Verses 27–30: Who can escape having their deeds restored to them? If we are restored to righteousness, to whose righteousness are we restored?

Verse 28: How does this verse fit with Alma's teaching about restoration in chapter 41?

Verse 29: Here we see Alma's principle for harrowing his son's soul. What might this verse say about those who "cannot forgive themselves"?

Verse 30: Does this perhaps clarify why Alma has explained the doctrines of restoration, resurrection, and Atonement to Corianton? What does it seem Corianton has been thinking?

How do we let the justice and mercy of God have full sway in our hearts? What does that mean?

What does it mean to be brought to the dust in humility? (How, for example, does that differ from depression?)

Lesson 31
Alma 43–52

The Book of Mormon was written for us and for our day. What do these chapters have to do with us and our day? What spiritual purpose does this account of Lamanite and Nephite wars serve? Or, instead of having a spiritual purpose in themselves, are they primarily part of the background necessary for what follows?

I will concentrate on Alma 43–48.

Alma 43

Verse 9: What is the difference between the motivation of the Lamanites, Amalekites, and Zoramites, on the one hand, and the Nephites, on the other?

Based on what we see here, what kinds of circumstances justify warfare?

Verses 11–13: What additional circumstance might justify war?

Are the people of Ammon (the Anti-Nephi-Lehies) being fair to the Nephites? Why don't the Nephites demand their help in the battles against the Lamanites?

Verses 16–17: What is the relation of this Moroni to the Moroni who finished the abridgment of the gold plates and buried them? Why might Mormon have named his son Moroni?

Verse 23: Moroni sends spies to watch the movements of the Lamanites and messengers to ask the prophet. Why both? Why not just one or the other?

Verses 29–30: Why does Alma feel he must defend Moroni's use of "stratagem"? What do we learn about the Nephites from this? Does it suggest anything about our own behavior in war? Why or why not?

Verses 45–47: This is the third time Alma has told us the reasons the Nephites are fighting (compare verses 9, 29–30). Why does he emphasize this? What application might what he says have for us?

Verse 54: Why does Moroni stop the battle? What's the point?

Alma 44

Verses 1–7: How does this compare to contemporary diplomacy and peace negotiations? Are there any lessons to be learned?

Verse 5: What does Moroni mean by "rites of worship"? By "the sacred support which we owe to our wives and children"? By "liberty"?

How can liberty bind one to his land and country?

What does Moroni mean when he says that the Nephites have gained power over the Lamanites by their faith, by their religion, by their rites, by their church, by the support they owe their wives and children, by their liberty, and by maintaining the sacred word of God? How did these things give them power over the Lamanites?

Verse 10: Why does Moroni give back the weapons of the Lamanites, knowing that they are going to use them to kill his people?

Verses 15, 19–20: Moroni seems to behave very oddly in these circumstances. He lets them go if they promise to leave him and his people alone! What makes him think he can trust them?

Alma 45

Verses 20–24: These verses show the two things that the Book of Mormon mentions over and over again as bringing about the Nephites' destruction: dissension in the church and riches. What effect did riches have on the Nephites? How did they lead to destruction?

How did dissensions come about among the Nephites? Are there similar dissensions among us? If not, could they happen?

How do riches affect our relations to each other?

Alma 46

Verses 1–7: In what ways was Amalickiah a threat to the Nephites?

Verses 8–10: Mormon seems to be interjecting his commentary in the abridgment at this point. Compare what he says to Doctrine and Covenants 98:9–10. What does this say about our own times? About our responsibilities to government?

Alma 48

Verses 7–10: How did Moroni prepare his people for war?

Verses 11–13, 17–18: What characteristics of Moroni do we see here? What, for example, does it mean to say that he was a man like Ammon?

Verses 14–16, 23–25: What was the Nephite "foreign policy"? How did they know against whom they should defend themselves? Is the Nephite attitude toward war "normal"? How did they manage to have such an attitude? Does what we see here have any implications for our own times?

Lesson 32
Alma 53–63

Alma 53

Verses 10–15: What do we learn about the people of Ammon? What do we learn about Helaman? Why is he afraid they will lose their souls if they defend themselves?

Verse 18: How did Nephite armies differ from today's armies? Do our soldiers have any say as to who their officers are? What might this tell us about the Nephites?

Alma 54 and 55

Compare the letters in these two chapters to those in chapters 60 and 61. What kind of personality do you think Moroni has? For example, does he carry out the threat he makes in verse 12? What kind of person is Ammoron?

Alma 60

Moroni's letter is strong. Do you think he knew Pahoran personally? What in the letter would serve as evidence for your answer?

Verses 14–17: What is the best thing the Nephites could have done to prevent the attacks of the Lamanites?

Verses 18–21: What are the three possible explanations Moroni can think of for Pahoran's failure to help? Why doesn't he think of the actual explanation?

When, in verse 20, Moroni asks, "Have ye forgotten the captivity of our fathers?" who are the fathers to whom he is referring? Is he thinking in terms of types and shadows, of Moses and Israel, for example?

Verse 33: Given the actual reasons for Pahoran's delay, what are we to make of what Moroni says about what the Lord has said? Does this tell us anything about the nature of revelation?

Alma 61

Verses 9, 19–20: What kind of person is Pahoran? What does it take for us to learn to respond to criticism as he has, particularly when the criticism isn't justified?

Alma 62

Verses 48–51: Given what we've seen before in the Book of Mormon, what is surprising about these Nephites?

Verse 50: As before, we see the writer, Moroni, telling us that the Nephites remembered what great things the Lord had done for them. Is this typological thinking? If so, how might we learn to think in the same way, remembering what great things the Lord has done for us and, in that, remembering the sacrifice of Jesus Christ?

Alma 63

Verses 4–10: Why is this material important to the Book of Mormon narrative? Why is it important to us?

Verses 10–11: Why would these departures, rather than Shiblon's impending death, have made it necessary for Shiblon to pass the records to Helaman's son Helaman?

Lesson 33

Helaman 1–5

Helaman 1

Verses 7–8: How do we understand a righteous person like Pahoran the elder having a child who was so unrighteous?

For what did the Nephites condemn Paanchi to death? Why was his crime so terrible that it deserved death?

Verse 11: Why do you suppose these people swore by their Maker? It seems very strange to swear by him that you will cover up murder. What is going on?

Verse 13: Why was it Pacumeni's right to be the next judge? We don't know what kind of government the Nephites had, but we do know that the people had a voice in choosing their leaders. How can someone have the right to an office if the people have a voice? Might their voice not have been definitive?

Verse 18: What causes the eventual defeat of the Nephites? Does this mean anything for us?

Helaman 2

The Gadianton robbers appear for the first time in this chapter. The Old Testament distinguishes between a thief and a robber, a thief being someone from within the community who stole property, a robber being someone from outside of the community and its law—an "outlaw." Robbers came in gangs, plundering and killing. Because robbers were so much more dangerous than were thieves, they were punished much more severely. (For examples of both terms, see Exodus 22:2, 7, 8; Proverbs 6:30; Ezekiel 18:10; Matthew 24:43; John 10:1; 18:40; and Helaman 2:10.) The Book of Mormon seems to use this distinction too, but Book of Mormon robbers go further in their crimes than did Old Testament robbers, not only plundering and murdering in gangs but also plotting to take over the rule of the country.

Verse 4: What was Gadianton's craft? Why is it important that he was expert not only in that craft but also "in many words"?

Verse 5: Why do people seek power and authority? How do they do so?

How does priestcraft (see 2 Nephi 26:29) differ from Gadianton robbery? How is it the same? Which is more important for us to recognize, the similarity or the difference?

When do we see people practicing the kind of robbery that the Gadiantons did?

When do we see people (including ourselves?) practicing priestcraft?

Helaman 3

Verse 1: What little thing do we see here that will bring down the Nephites? Why do pride and contention go together? (Compare Helaman 3:33–34.)

Verse 3: What caused the dissensions mentioned? Does the migration of Lehi's family (and others) parallel this migration, or is this a group of dissidents leaving?

Verses 22–23: Is the decrease in contention perhaps related to the fact that Helaman is a righteous man? How does having a righteous leader effect such a change in the people? Anciently it was common to believe that the righteousness of a leader was correlated to the righteousness of the people and that righteousness meant peace and prosperity. Do we believe in such a correlation? Is the righteousness of our leaders today relevant to whether they can lead us well? How?

Verse 24: Helaman says "there was . . . prosperity in the church, insomuch that there were thousands who did join." Does this mean that they joined because the church was prosperous? Isn't that a bad thing? What is prosperity in the church? Does verse 26 answer this question?

Verse 27: What does it mean to call on the name of the Lord? How is the Lord merciful to those who call on his name?

Verses 29–30: What is the word of God? How do we lay hold on it?

What does it mean to say that God's word is quick and powerful?

What is the significance of cutting in two all of the devil's wiles and snares? Explore that metaphor: what is the point of the metaphor as a whole? The sword? The snare? Cutting a snare?

How does the word lead us along the narrow way or course?

When Mormon says that the gulf is prepared to engulf the wicked, is he personifying it (as if to say the gulf is *waiting* to do this), or is he saying it has been prepared to engulf them?

What does it mean to land souls? Why use the word *soul* rather than something else, such as *people*?

What does sitting down with Abraham, Isaac, and Jacob signify? Why them in particular?

What does it mean to go no more out? Out of where? When did we go out the first time?

Verses 33–34: We see here what the Book of Mormon shows us over and over again. If we are to understand its message for us and to avoid the fate of the Nephites, we must think about how we duplicate the pride mentioned here and how we imitate the persecution of our brethren. In what ways might we be guilty of the sins of the Nephites?

Verse 35: How do the righteous among the Nephites handle the persecutions? What might that say to us?

Helaman 4

Verse 1: Once again we see among the Nephites the direct correlation between dissensions in the church and war. What kinds of dissensions do we face today? Are those comparable to the Nephites' dissensions in the church?

Verses 11–12: Here we are told what caused those dissensions. How might we might be guilty of each of these today?

Verse 13: And here we see the result of the wickedness described: the people are left to their own strength. The implication is that when left to our own strength, we discover that our strength isn't sufficient to even save us temporally, much less spiritually. Compare what is said here with what King Benjamin taught.

Verse 14: Lehi was Nephi's father, but Helaman seems to have named his first son Nephi and his second son Lehi. What might this say about how the Nephites think of Lehi and Nephi?

Verse 15: We have been told that the people were rich, but wicked. Now we see that when they repented they prospered. If they were already rich, in what sense might they have prospered? There are hundreds of scriptural references to prospering. It might be interesting to read many of them to get an idea of what the Lord promises the righteous. If you have computer access, you can use the Church's scripture-search program to find them. Go to www.lds.org/scriptures and type the word *prosper* in the search box to see all the uses of that word in the scriptures.

Verse 22: They have trampled under foot the laws of Mosiah. What were those laws? Where do we find them? How do you think they have trampled them under foot?

Verse 23: To "dwindle" is to shrink, to become smaller. Here it seems to be used in opposition to "prosper." What might it mean?

Is the description that follows ("they began to disbelieve in the spirit of prophecy and in the spirit of revelation") something that happened in addition to dwindling, or does it repeat that they dwindled, using different words?

Helaman 5

Verse 2: What does it mean to say that the laws became corrupted?

"They who chose evil were more numerous than they who chose good" and "the laws had become corrupted" are both given as causes of "their ripening for destruction." How are these things related?

Verse 9: Why are King Benjamin's words so important to the people of the Book of Mormon? What value should they have to us? What would show that they have that value in our lives?

Verse 11: What are the conditions of repentance? Where can you find them in the Book of Mormon?

What does it mean that repentance "bringeth unto the power of the Redeemer"? Can you explain the literal meaning of that phrase?

Verse 12: What kinds of ideas might we infer from Helaman's metaphor of a foundation built on rock? Do you see any meaning in the contrast between the Lord as a rock and Satan as a storm?

Verse 14: Notice that Helaman's sons "went forth, keeping the commandments" *because* they remembered what he had said. Does that mean children who don't do what their parents tell them have forgotten? In what sense might that be true?

Verses 17–19: What gave Nephi and Lehi such power in preaching?

Verses 30–31: We often imagine the Lord's voice as a deep, booming voice, but here we see it quite differently. What does the description of his voice as being "of perfect mildness, as if it had been a whisper, and it did pierce even to the very soul" tell us?

Verse 32: What does it mean to say that the kingdom of God is at hand? Does it refer only to Christ's first or second comings? Could it have more than one meaning?

Verse 41: What does it mean to "cry . . . until ye shall have faith"? Do we see anything like this earlier in the Book of Mormon? What would such a cry require?

Verses 46–47: What is the difference in the voice now? Is that difference a difference of the voice itself or a difference in its hearers?

Verse 47: Why does the voice mention that the Savior "was from the foundation of the world?" (Does this use of the word *foundation* have anything to do with the use in verse 12?) *What* was he from the foundation of the world?

Verses 50–52: What do these verses tell us about the Lamanites' wars against the Nephites? What was the root cause of those wars? Was it the personal wickedness of the Lamanites? Might this explain something of how Moroni could wage war against the Lamanites in the way he did?

Does Moroni's way of fighting war teach us anything about our own wars? What?

Lesson 34
Helaman 6–12

Helaman 6

Verse 3: How does the attitude of the members of the church compare here with Moroni's attitude?

Verse 9: Given what we've seen so far in the Book of Mormon, as soon as we read that the Nephites and Lamanites "became exceedingly rich," what do we expect to read about soon? Has Mormon written this to elicit that expectation from us?

Verse 17: Why do they want gain? What does it mean to be lifted up above another? What's wrong with it? How do we lift ourselves above others?

Verse 27: Why is the comparison of the Gadianton robbers to Cain an important one for us? What does it tell us?

Verse 30: What does it mean to say that Satan is the author of all sin? Does that mean I am not the author of any sins? If he is the author of sin, how can I be held responsible?

Verse 37: This verse contains surprises. The first surprise is that the Lamanites hunted down the Gadianton robbers. The second surprise is that we expect to read about how the Lamanites killed them. Instead, however, we read that "they did preach the word of God among the more wicked part of them, insomuch that this band of robbers was utterly destroyed." They destroyed them by preaching to them! Are there situations in our own experience where this might also work? Why didn't it work for Alma the Younger?

Verse 38: When they were seduced, the previously righteous Nephites believed in the works of the Gadiantons, partook of their spoils, and joined them in their secret murders. The last of these is easiest to understand. It means that, whether or not they committed murder themselves, they joined in the oaths that protected the secret murderers. It is also easy to understand what it means to say that the Nephites partook of their spoils. But what does it mean to say that they believed in the Gadiantons' works?

Verse 39: What are the signs of Gadianton rule? Notice the progression of ideas. It seems to move up in increasing violence—trample under feet, smite, tear apart—but then the last of the series is "turn their backs upon." What might that series say to us?

What are the two groups against whom the Gadiantons act?

Helaman 7

Verse 7: Is Nephi being realistic about what it was like at the time of Lehi, or is he thinking about "the good old days"? (How, for example, does this compare to what the earlier Nephi says about life then?—Compare verse 8, where this Nephi says that "in those days" he could have had joy in the righteousness of his brethren.) If he is being realistic, what might this say about how things are at the time he speaks?

What does *entreated* mean? What does it mean to be easy to be entreated?

Why speak of them as "*firm* to keep the commandments"?

Verse 16: Here Nephi speaks of the devil as enticing them. Is there a difference between *entreat* and *entice*? What might that difference signify?

Verse 20: What day is Nephi referring to?

Verse 21: When Nephi says they sin to get gain, to be praised of men, and to get gold and silver, do you think that being praised and getting gold and silver are two ways of getting gain, or is he naming three different reasons for their sins? If he's naming three different reasons, what does it mean to get gain? What are the riches of this world? What are the vain things? What does it mean to have one's heart set on these things?

Verse 23: What does the Lord mean when he says, "I will not show unto the wicked of my strength, to one more than the other"? Can you write out an English sentence that has an equivalent meaning?

Verse 24: Notice that the degree of one's righteousness is a matter of one's knowledge, so that a person with less knowledge could be more righteous than one with more knowledge, even if the one with less knowledge were obedient to fewer commandments. What might this say to us about deciding the righteousness of others? Of ourselves?

Verse 25: In what ways might members of the church have united with Gadianton robbers? Obviously, some might simply have joined. But that seems less likely than that they associated themselves in other ways, ways that allowed them to continue to think of themselves as "good people." What other ways might they have joined themselves? In what ways might we join with today's Gadianton robbers?

Verse 26: Why is pride such a terrible sin? The Book of Mormon condemns pride consistently, but what is wrong with pride?

How do riches cause pride?

Helaman 8

Verse 3: Speaking by the commandments isn't the same as not speaking what is contrary to them. What is the difference? What might the writer be indicating by saying that nothing Nephi said was contrary to the commandments?

Verse 4ff.: How do these judges' motives and methods compare to the motives and methods of the priests of Noah?

Verse 6: What danger is run by those who are prosperous and who have military power?

Verses 11–13: Why would the story of Moses and Israel be such a powerful example for Nephi? Why might the accusation that they deny Moses's words be such a powerful accusation?

Verses 14–15: We don't use the symbol of the cross very much, if at all, but Nephi makes reference to that symbolism here, so it is certainly worth thinking about. What kinds of similarities are there between Christ's crucifixion and the brass serpent on a staff lifted up by Moses? Why, for example, is the serpent used to symbolize Christ rather than Satan? In what senses was Christ lifted up? What might we learn from the symbol of Christ being "lifted up"? What does it mean to "look to" Christ, especially in the context of looking to his crucifixion, the context implied by the metaphor?

Verse 16: To what does the phrase "these things" refer?

Verses 16–22: Why does Nephi mention all these prophets? How will that be convincing? *Who* would be convinced by such evidence?

Verse 24: Nephi says they have received "all things" as a witness that "they" are true. First, what does the word *they* refer to? That is, what is it that they know to be true? Second, how do all things, both in heaven and earth, stand as a witness that they are true?

Helaman 9

Verse 21: What does it mean to be circumcised of heart? What does it mean to be blind? What does it mean to be stiff-necked? In addition to such things as "stubborn" and "inflexible" (things *stiff-necked* has meant for centuries), during the early nineteenth century, when Joseph Smith translated the Book of Mormon, *stiff-necked* was used to describe a horse that wouldn't obey the rein. Against what is Nephi warning his people?

Against what does he warn us? Can you be specific about that warning? In other words, in what specific ways might we be uncircumcised, blind, or stiff-necked?

Verse 41: In the last chapter we saw that the Nephites remembered Moses and seemed to honor him. However, given the remark they make here, how well did they understand the gospel?

Helaman 10

Verses 4–5: What does it mean to declare the word with unwearyingness? Does that mean Nephi didn't get tired? He also has "not sought [his] own life." What does that mean?

Verse 5: Why won't Nephi ask that which is contrary to the Lord's will?

Verse 6: Why might the Lord begin as he does, saying, "Thou art Nephi, and I am God"?

Verse 7: We usually think of the sealing power in connection with such things as eternal marriage. Here we see that it goes beyond that. Can you explain how and what that might mean to us?

Verses 10–14: What does it mean to say that God smites people? Literally, *smite* means "hit." How do we explain what seems here to be vengefulness on the part of the Lord, as if he is saying, "Do what I say, or else"? Is destruction something the Lord brings on the wicked, or is it something he will save them from if they repent? Whatever your answer, how do you justify this portrayal of God?

Helaman 11

Verse 7: What does this verse tell us about Nephite righteousness? If we are righteous because we have been humbled by circumstances and finally see the need for the Lord, how righteous are we?

Verses 9–17: If Nephi has already been given the authority that whatever he says will come to pass, why does he pray to the Lord here, asking that the famine be stopped? Why not just command it to stop?

Verse 19: If Lehi wasn't a whit behind Nephi in righteousness, can we assume that he too had the sealing power? If not, why not? In either case, why don't we hear more about Lehi?

Verses 22–23: What points of doctrine do you think they might have disputed? Is there anything we've read or that you know is coming up that might suggest an answer to this question?

Verse 24: Notice that Helaman distinguishes between the Lamanites who are descendants of the Lamanites and those who have taken the name *Lamanite* because they are dissenters. The distinction between Lamanite and Nephite is becoming more and more a political, cultural, and religious distinction rather than a genealogical one.

Verses 26–33: Notice too that though we think of the wars in the Book of Mormon as wars between the Nephites and the Lamanites (and for the most part they are), we see here that the Gadianton robbers are neither Lamanite nor Nephite: both nations send armies out against them, and both nations are under siege from them. Why is this—and the point about verse 24—important to our understanding of the Book of Mormon? How might it help us teach that book more accurately?

Verse 34: In verse 7 they repented because of the famine (which replaced a war); then in verse 23 (four years later) they began to strive with each other again, but Nephi and Lehi were able to bring the strife under control, so there is relatively little strife among them. The next year the Gadianton robbers reorganized themselves and began to attack the people. This verse tells us that the attacks of the Gadianton robbers were because of the people's wickedness. What wickedness do you suppose the verse is referring to?

Verse 36: The eighty-first year ended with the Nephites remembering the Lord because of their afflictions. Now we see that the very next year they began to forget him again. There seems to be less and less time between each period of wickedness and each period of repentance. What's going on?

Helaman 12

Verse 1: The phrase "and thus we see" is one of Mormon's favorite phrases. This verse begins with a variation of it, so it may well be a section written by Mormon—his commentary on what he is reading. The record of the Nephites is titled the Book of Mormon not only because it is Mormon's abridgment, but also because it is his prophetic response to his people's history.

We see that the Lord blesses and prospers those who trust him. In fact, we have seen him bless and prosper those who only "trusted" him because they were forced to it by their suffering. What does this tell us about the Lord?

Verse 2: Do we have ease and prosperity? If so, Mormon seems to feel that what he has seen describes us as well as the people he is reading about. How might this verse apply to us? How has the Lord increased our fields, flocks, and herds? Our silver, gold, and other precious things? How has he spared our lives? How has he delivered us from our enemies? How has he softened their hearts not to declare war against us? How do we harden our hearts? How do we forget the Lord? How do we trample him under our feet? (Think about the power and the horror of that image—we trample our God as a mob might trample someone else, perhaps not even noticing he is there in our rush to get something or somewhere.)

Verses 3–6: Mormon gives his description of the Lord's people, not just of some of those people. Is he just a pessimist because of the hard life he has led, or is what he is saying here prophetic? If the latter, these verses describe us as well as the people of the Book of Mormon. How do such things fit in with the message of the Book of Mormon for the latter days? What do they mean to us? What do they say about us?

Verse 7: When we read verses like this (e.g., Mosiah 4:5, 11) we almost always add, "But . . ." Then we explain all the ways that we aren't nothing. In the scriptures, however, we don't find any such addition. Why not? What are we supposed to learn from this verse and others that say we are nothing?

Verses 8–22: What is the point of these verses? In context, what are they to teach us?

Verses 7–23: Compare what Mormon says here with Mosiah 4:5–16.

Verse 24: What does he mean by God's "great fulness"?

What does the phrase "restored unto grace for grace" mean?

Can there be good works without repentance? Repentance without good works?

Verse 26: How do we square scriptures such as this with those such as Romans 3:12: "There is none that doeth good, no, not one"? That scripture is a quotation of Psalms 14:3 and 53:3 and is a common theme in the scriptures. See, for example, Psalms 14:1; 36:3; 53:1; Ecclesiastes 7:20; Jeremiah 13:23; Romans 3:12; 3 John 1:11; Helaman 12:4; Moroni 10:25; and D&C 33:4; 35:12; 82:6. What makes it possible to do good works?

Lesson 35
Helaman 13–16

Helaman 13

Verse 1ff.: Does the Lord threaten the Nephites through Samuel, telling them to "repent or else"? If so, how do we understand such a threat? How does it differ from bullying? If not, how are we to understand this kind of prophecy?

Verse 5: What does Samuel mean by "the sword of justice"?

Verse 7: What are the glad tidings that the angel brought him and that he hoped the Nephites would receive?

Verse 8: Why does the Lord say he will withdraw from them because of the hardness of their hearts, rather than because of their wickedness?

What does the Lord mean when he says he will take his word from among them? When he says he will suffer them no longer? When he says he will turn the hearts of their brethren against them? (After all, it can't mean he'll send the Lamanites against them since the Lamanites are now righteous.)

Verses 12–14: Why does he emphasize the fact that he is sparing Zarahemla for the righteous' sake?

Verses 18–19: What does it mean to hide one's treasure up to the Lord? What kinds of treasure might Samuel mean?

Notice that the parallel but opposite phrase is "hide up their treasure in the earth." What does that mean? What significance might it have for us? Few of us bury our treasure, but what do we do that is comparable?

Verse 20: In concrete, contemporary terms, what does it mean to have one's heart set upon riches?

Verse 21: He says that they are cursed and their riches are cursed because they have set their hearts on riches. It may be relatively easy to understand how *they* are cursed for having their hearts so set, but how are their *riches* cursed?

Verse 22: Does this verse answer the question above, about verse 20? What does it mean not to remember the Lord in the things with which he has blessed us? What does it mean to remember our riches?

How do pride, boasting, great swelling, and so on, result from remembering our riches and forgetting God, as the verse implies they do?

What does it mean for our hearts to swell with great pride unto boasting and unto great swelling? Why is the phrase so repetitive? About what would we boast? How does pride bring envy?

How does envy bring strife, malice, persecution, murder, and all sorts of iniquities?

Verses 26–28: Perhaps we don't openly deny the prophets as do the people described in verse 26, but are there ways in which we do what is described in verses 27 and 28? What kinds of people does our culture honor—whom do we honor with gold, silver, and fine clothes? What kinds of people flatter us, saying that all is well? In this context, what does "All is well" mean? What other kinds of things do they teach?

Verse 33: They seem to be saying, "If only we had repented, we would still be rich." Is this a portrayal of genuine repentance? If not, why is it part of the record?

Verse 36: Not only have their riches become slippery, but all things have. What does that mean?

Verse 38: In verse 11 he told them that if they would repent, the Lord would turn away his anger. Now he tells them that their destruction is sure, that it is too late. How do you reconcile these—especially when he admonishes them in verse 39 to repent as soon as he says it is too late?

Helaman 14

Verse 1: What might prevent these things from being written?

Verse 2: Why does the prophet give them a sign?

Verse 8: Does this mean that those who believe after having seen the sign will be saved? If so, isn't that unfair to those who haven't seen such signs?

Verse 13: What does it mean to believe *on* the Savior? We usually speak of believing *in* him. Is believing *on* him different, or is that just a difference between the older language of the Book of Mormon and our own language?

Notice that Samuel says "if you believe on Christ, you *will* repent" instead of "if you believe, you *ought* to repent."

Why does he put it that way? Is it possible to believe on Christ and not repent? Why not?

Verse 16: Those cut off from the presence of the Lord are dead, both temporally and spiritually. To be dead temporally means to have a physical body that will die or to already be dead. But what does it mean—here—to be dead spiritually? Here we learn that spiritual death and temporal death come together: we are dead spiritually and temporally because of Adam's fall. So to be human is, at least initially, to be spiritually dead. How is what Samuel says in this verse like what we usually say about spiritual death (we bring it about through sin), and how is it different?

Verse 28: What reason does the angel give for the signs of Christ's birth in the New World?

Verse 29: The second word of the verse is *this*. To what does it refer? In other words, what is this verse explaining?

Verse 30: It is pretty clear that if we die, we do it to ourselves. But what does it mean that whoever does iniquity does it to himself? Didn't Hitler do evil to others rather than to himself? How does our freedom account for the fact that when we do evil we do it to ourselves?

Helaman 15

Verses 1–2: The calamity predicted for the Nephites is clearly a literal one. It may also be a literal one for us if we aren't repentant. But are there also other ways to understand these verses? For example, in what other ways might our houses be desolate if we don't repent?

Verse 4: What does it mean to say that the Lord has hated something? (This isn't the only scripture that says this; the phrase is relatively common, especially in the Old Testament, but also in the New Testament and the Book of Mormon.) How do we square that description of him with the scripture that says he is love?

At the end of the verse Samuel says "for this intent hath the Lord prolonged their days." For what intent? Whose days?

Verse 7: Faith and repentance bring a change of heart in the Lamanites. What is a change of heart? How might our hearts be changed?

Verse 9: Notice that this behavior isn't confined to the Anti-Nephi-Lehies. The other Lamanites appear to have taken up the same covenant, or at least to be motivated by the same fear.

Verses 12–13: What promises have been extended to the Lamanites in the last days? Does verse 13 describe those promises completely?

Helaman 16

Verses 18–19: Notice the irony in their question.

Verse 21: What is the Nephite and Lamanite explanation of why the prophets have come? Compare what they say here to what Korihor said (Alma 30). If you talk to some inactive members of the Church, or to people who aren't members of the Church, you sometimes hear modern variations of the same charge. What explains the frequency of this charge? How can we best refute it?

Lesson 36

3 Nephi 1–7

These notes will concentrate on chapters 5–7 of 3 Nephi.

3 Nephi 5

Verses 8–26: Once again the people have repented after having to defend themselves against an enemy. Why does Mormon insert his commentary here?

Verse 9: Why does he tell us of the existence of other records? Why do we need to know about them?

Verse 10: How would you say this verse in your own words?

Verse 12: Why does Mormon tell us the origin of his name? What was the particular transgression of the Nephites to which Mormon refers? Is there a connection between his name and what happened in that land? Is there a connection between his name and what he has just described?

Verse 13: What does it mean to be a disciple? Might Mormon be using *disciple* as we use *apostle*? What does it mean to have everlasting life?

Verse 14: Who are the holy ones to whom he refers?

Verse 18: We have an idea of what it means for a person to be just, but what does it mean for a record to be just? The most common meaning of *true* is something like "in accordance with the facts," but there are other meanings as well, such as "steadfast," "constant," "reliable," "verified," "straight," and "plumb." Do any of these other meanings give further understanding of what it means for the Book of Mormon to be true?

Verse 20: Mormon said he was making an end in verse 19, but he continues. How might you explain this?

What does it mean to be a *pure* descendant of Lehi? Why do you think Mormon mentions this?

How can knowledge bring salvation? Isn't something more needed? Or, perhaps, is he using *knowledge* differently than we might expect?

Verse 21: How is Mormon using the word *surely*? When we use it, it usually indicates some previous doubt. Is that what he is implying?

What is the point of the comment of this verse? Why is it important to notice that the Lord is blessing the seed of Jacob and that of Joseph?

Verses 23–24: Notice the repetition of *surely*. Does its use in verse 24 suggest something about the way in which it was being used earlier?

Verse 23: Is the knowledge referred to here the same as that mentioned at the end of verse 20?

Verse 25: What covenant has the Lord made with the house of Jacob? Why does the house of Jacob have to know about that covenant?

Verse 26: In this case does the word *then* mean that they will know their Redeemer after they know the covenant the

Lord has made with Israel, or does it mean that they will know their Redeemer *in* knowing that covenant?

3 Nephi 6

Verse 10: The Nephite story starts all over again: riches corrupt them, causing disputes, pride, boasting, and even persecution. Couldn't the Book of Mormon have been shorter with fewer examples of that cycle? Why does Mormon feel compelled to give us so many cases?

Verse 11: In our culture, at least in jokes, we might identify well with how the presence of lawyers in the Book of Mormon land accounts for disputes, pride, boasting, and persecution, but what about the presence of merchants? How is it a problem to have many merchants? Do we need to be concerned about having too many merchants today?

What does it mean to say there were many officers? What would the modern equivalent of Nephite officers be?

Verse 12: Do we distinguish by ranks, according to riches and opportunities for learning? We often pride ourselves on the level of learning in the Church. We also often pride ourselves on the material achievements of the members in general. But in doing so, do we make those with less riches or less opportunity for learning feel uncomfortable? Do we exclude them? Perhaps even more to the point being made here, is our society one that makes it more likely that the poor will be ignorant and that the rich will be learned? If so, what should we do about that?

Verse 13: What is the connection between not returning railing for railing but suffering persecution and affliction, on the one hand, and being humble and penitent before God, on the other?

Verse 14: What is the great inequality that began to be in the land?

3 Nephi 7

Verse 18: What has the daily ministering of angels to do with Nephi's power to convince these bands of people? How does his ministration to them (verse 17) compare to the angel's ministration to him?

Verse 24: Why does the writer need to tell us that those who were converted were baptized? Though true, it is something we might not think to include in a history. What might this say, not only of the prophet's insight into our needs, but also of the situation in his own day?

Lesson 37
3 Nephi 8–11

3 Nephi 8

Verses 1–23: Why might there have been so much destruction in this hemisphere at the time of the crucifixion and so little destruction in the other hemisphere?

3 Nephi 9

Verse 2: When the Lord says that his fair ones have fallen because of their iniquity, is he saying they died because of it, or is he using the word *fallen* in some other sense?

Verses 3–12: Why does he give them this catalogue of destruction?

Verse 13: Of what will he heal those who repent?

Verse 14: What might we make of the fact that the Lord says we must *come* unto him? Why use that metaphor of travel to describe accepting him? Have we gone somewhere? Compare the Lord's invitation here to Nephi's prayer in 2 Nephi 4:33. What image is conveyed?

Verse 15: When Christ announces himself, why does he tell them he was with the Father from the beginning? Isn't that true of all of us? Weren't we also with the Father in the beginning?

What does he mean when he says, "I am in the Father, and the Father in me"? (For related scriptures, see Luke 10:22; John 14:10–11, 31; Mosiah 15:2; 3 Nephi 11:27, 32; 20:35; 27:13; 28:10; and D&C 35:2; 50:43; 93:3.) Compare 2 Samuel 19:43: "We have ten parts in the king, and we have also more right in David than ye." Compare also 2 Samuel 20:1: "We have no part *in* David, neither have we inheritance *in* the son of Jesse" (italics added). The wording in those verses suggests that to be *in* a person was to recognize him as one's lord or king. It was to become one of his people, part of his family as it were. To be in David is to be in covenant relation to him. So for the Father and the Son to be in one another is for them to be in covenant relation, and for us to be in Christ is to be in covenant relation with him.

Verse 16: Though Jesus is willing to receive all who will repent (return to him), his own are not willing to receive him. Who are "his own"? Is he referring to those who are of the house of Israel? To Gentiles adopted into the house? To more than them?

What is the significance of saying that his own have rejected him? Is it significant in more than one way?

Verse 17: We often speak of ourselves as the children of God, but here it says he will give us the power to *become* his children. What is the point he is making? Doesn't our spiritual birth in the premortal existence make us his children already? If so, why must we become them again?

What does the word *redemption* mean? What are some other circumstances in which we speak about redeeming something? Do those give us insight into the meaning of the word in scripture? What has redemption to do with Christ's sacrifice?

Verse 20: We usually think of sacrifice as the act of giving something up. What is it that we give up when we offer the sacrifice of a broken heart and a contrite spirit? On the other hand, the English word *sacrifice* looks like the noun form of the old verb *sacrify*, meaning "to make sacred." Does that suggest anything about what sacrifice might be? What is made sacred when we offer up our sacrifice?

Verse 22: If we come as little children, we will become the children of God. How do we become as little children?

3 Nephi 10

Verse 14: Who is speaking here?

Verses 14–17: Why are the prophets' testimonies of these events important?

3 Nephi 11

Verses 3–6: The voice heard *pierced* the Nephites. Is the use of that word merely a coincidence, or is it connected to Christ's piercing in some way? If the latter, how?

Is it significant that they didn't understand the voice the first two times? If so, what might that inability to understand teach us?

Verses 10–11: How is the particular way in which the Lord introduced himself to the Nephites significant?

What bitter cup did the Father give him? Why does he describe it in those terms here? Is the metaphor he uses important?

How did he glorify the Father by taking the world's sins on himself? The wording here is interesting, for he says, "I . . . have glorified the Father in taking upon me the sins of the world, *in the which* I have suffered the will of the Father in all things from the beginning" (italics added). The words I have italicized seem to refer back to his taking the sins of the world on himself. If they do, then he seems to be saying something like this: "In taking the sins of the world on myself, I have suffered the will of the Father from the beginning." We can also read the phrase as if it refers to "I have glorified the Father": "I have glorified the Father, something I have done by suffering the will of the Father from the beginning." What insights or ideas do you get from these different ways of understanding what Jesus said? Which seems most plausible to you? Can you see another way of understanding what "in the which" refers to?

Why does he say, "I have suffered the will of the Father" rather than "I have done the will of the Father"? Does that difference have any implications for us?

Verses 14–15: What is the significance of this event? Compare it to Thomas's experience in John 20:24–29. Is it possible to see this as, among other things, a symbol of their part in the crucifixion?

Why does the Book of Mormon use the word *thrust* here? For us the word connotes physical force. The entry for *thrust* in Webster's 1828 dictionary suggests that it had the same meaning when the Book of Mormon was translated: "a violent push or driving," "attack, assault." Do we really believe that people were violently putting their hands into Christ's wounds? If not, what is the point of this usage? What does it teach us?

Verse 21: Doesn't Nephi already have power to baptize? If not, why not?

Verses 23, 25: In verse 23, the Lord tells them to baptize in his name. In verse 25, he tells them to baptize in the names of the members of the Godhead. Is there a discrepancy here? How would you respond to someone who thinks there is? Is the teaching of Colossians 2:9 relevant?

Verse 28: The Lord says, "There shall be no disputations among you . . . ; neither shall there be disputations among you concerning the points of my doctrine." Is he forbidding two kinds of disputation? If so, what are they? What does "points of my doctrine" mean? What would be an example of a disputation over a point of his doctrine?

Verses 29–30: Why is this the preface to the part of Christ's sermon on his doctrine? What does this tell us about how to teach the gospel? Does it teach anything more?

Verses 31–36: Verses 31–35 begin and end with a declaration that what occurs between the declarations is the Lord's doctrine: repent and believe in him; those who believe in him and are baptized will be saved and inherit the kingdom of God; those who do not believe and are not baptized will be damned. How can this be the summation of the gospel? For example, why isn't enduring to the end mentioned? What about covenants? We know from latter-day revelation that these things are essential, so why aren't they mentioned here?

In verses 31, 35, and 36, and then again in verses 35–36, the Lord tells us that the Father and the Holy Ghost bear record of him. Presumably, the Holy Ghost bears that record through the spiritual witness that he gives. How does the Father bear record of the Son?

Verses 39–40: The doctrine of Christ taught here is to be our spiritual foundation, and teachings that are more or less than that doctrine have an evil origin. What would be an example of a teaching that is more than that doctrine? Less?

Verse 41: This verse begins with the word *therefore*, suggesting that what it says is the logical consequence of what came before. Is that the best way to understand the word *therefore* here, or is there another way? How might the commandment to teach the things that Christ has said be the logical conclusion to the things he has said?

We have one understanding of what this verse requires of us, but what might it have meant to those listening to him speak?

Lesson 38
3 Nephi 12–15

This is one of the longer sets of notes, but even so I have left a great deal unexplored. There is a great deal of material in these chapters.

3 Nephi 12

Verse 1: Why does Jesus describe those he calls as ministers and servants? What sense does it make to tell people that they should pay attention to their servants? What is going on here?

Verses 1–2: Why are those who have not seen and heard more blessed than those who have?

Verse 3: This begins the parallel version of the Sermon on the Mount. It may help you to read the two versions of the sermon side by side. Sometimes the footnotes in Matthew will also help you understand the version of the sermon we have in 3 Nephi. What is the advantage of having two almost identical accounts in scripture?

When Jesus delivers the sermon as Matthew reports it, the setting is important to our understanding of it. Matthew 4:23 tells us, "Jesus went about all Galilee, teaching in their synagogues, and preaching the gospel of the kingdom." Then Matthew 5–7 tells us the gospel that he preached. As Matthew tells the story, Jesus seems deliberately to give the Sermon on the Mount in a way that compares him to

Moses: he goes up on a mountain and delivers a "new" law for a multitude who are gathered at the base of the mountain waiting for his return.

What is the setting in the Book of Mormon, and how might it make the Nephites understand it differently than did those in Galilee? In Matthew, the Sermon on the Mount is partly a response to the Pharisaic focus on the law of Moses. To what Nephite problem or problems might the sermon in Zarahemla be a response?

Arthur Bassett has pointed out that we can understand verse 3 as a repetition of verse 2, as a kind of summary of the gospel. In that case, it isn't one of the Beatitudes, and the next verses, which are the Beatitudes, have a chiastic pattern with mercy at its center:

A They that *mourn* shall be *comforted* (verse 4)

  B The meek shall *inherit* the earth (verse 5)

    C Those who hunger and thirst for righteousness will be *filled with the Holy Ghost* (verse 6)

      D The merciful will obtain *mercy* (verse 7)

    C' The pure in heart will *see God* (verse 8)

  B' Peacemakers will be the *children of God* (verse 9)

A' Those who are *persecuted* for righteousness will *receive a great reward, the kingdom of heaven* (verses 10–12)

If you think that Bassett's understanding of how these verses are related to each other is plausible, why might the beatitudes center on mercy? Why would mercy be an important lesson for the Nephites? Have recent events made the necessity of mercy clear? Which ones in particular, and how do they do that?

Verse 3: What are other words that mean the same as *blessed*?

What does it mean to be poor in spirit? It cannot mean that one has a spirit that is poor or wanting, so what does it mean? In the King James translation of the Bible (KJV), the phrase "theirs is the kingdom of heaven" translates a Greek phrase that could also be translated "the kingdom of heaven belongs to them." If we understood the phrase that way here, would it give any additional meaning to the verse?

Verse 4: Compare this verse to Isaiah 61:2.

Verse 5: Who are the meek? In verses 39–42, the Savior will give examples of meekness. Note, too, that this verse is a quotation of Psalm 37:11. Why would Jesus quote from the Old Testament so much in this explication of his gospel?

Verse 6: What false understandings of righteousness have the Nephite and Lamanite prophets had to deal with? What does Jesus teach about righteousness? Where, specifically, do you find a Book of Mormon explanation of what it means to be righteous? The word translated "righteousness" in the KJV translation of Matthew could also be translated "justice." Does that also make sense as a way of understanding righteousness here? Why or why not?

Verse 7: What does *mercy* mean? What does it take to be merciful? How are the requirement to be righteous (verse 6) and the requirement to be merciful related to each other?

Verse 8: The word translated "pure" in the KJV could also have been translated "cleansed." Is that relevant? What does it mean to have a pure heart? What does it mean to see God? *Where* do we see God?

Verse 9: Whom do you think Jesus has in mind when he speaks of the peacemakers? (Does this have anything to do with 3 Nephi 11:28?) Do verses 21–26 give us an idea of what he means? What does it mean that the peacemakers *will be called* the children of God? Aren't we already his children? Why might Jesus have associated being a peacemaker with being a child of God?

Verses 11: We can see a division in the sermon at verse 11: the Beatitudes (verses 4–10) give us the general description of the gospel, and the verses that follow expand on that general description.

Verses 13–16: Do verses 13 and 14 teach the same thing, or does each teach something different? Compare 3 Nephi 18:24 to verses 15–16; verse 16 seems to explain the other verses in this group. What does verse 16 teach us about good works?

Verses 17–20: What does it mean to say that Jesus did not come to annul the law? How does verse 19 explain the purpose of law? Does that explain why law cannot save us—why an atonement was required? Verse 20 tells us that obedience is required. How does that fit with the definition of his doctrine that the Savior gave in 3 Nephi 11:31–35, where obedience wasn't mentioned and where the Savior said that nothing more could be added to his doctrine (3 Nephi 11:40)?

Verses 21–26: Jesus seems to me to be giving examples of what he meant when he spoke of peacemakers in verse 9.

Verses 22: Notice that the Book of Mormon and the JST omit "without a cause" (Matthew 5:22 KJV) in verse 22—as do almost all Greek manuscripts. How does that change our understanding of the verse?

In verse 22, the word *raca* means the same thing as the Greek word translated "fool" at the end of the verse. It isn't any stronger than the kinds of things we sometimes say to each other when we are angry, such as "You idiot!" What does Jesus mean, then, when he says (paraphrasing), "Whoever calls his brother a fool is in danger of the community's judgment, but whoever says 'You fool' is in danger of hellfire"? Does it make a difference that the first case is about anger towards a brother and no one is specified in the second? What is the point of verses 21–22?

Verses 23–24: What is Jesus saying about reconciliation? Is it more or less important than worship? Notice that we begin with the prohibition of murder in verse 21, move to the prohibition of anger in verse 22, and find a prohibition of hard feelings in verse 23. We would usually begin with the least serious problem and work our way up to the most serious. Why do you think the Savior reverses the normal order?

Verses 25–26: Can you think of particular adversaries that Jesus might have in mind in verses 25–26? How do these examples apply to us?

Verses 27–28: In Galilee, these verses were directed at the Pharisees and their insistence on the formalities of the

Mosaic law. To whom do you think the verses would apply among the Nephites?

Verses 29–30: Jesus is obviously speaking hyperbolically. What is the point of his hyperbole? Does he here give us a definition of what it means to take up one's cross?

Verses 31–32: The scripture to which Jesus refers (Deuteronomy 24:1) is unclear about the grounds for divorce. It says that a man can put away his wife if he finds something shameful in her ("some uncleanness" in the King James translation). In Galilee this was the basis for a major debate about the grounds for divorce. How might these words have been relevant to the Nephites? How are they relevant to us? It isn't easy to understand the exception that Jesus allows here because in the KJV it isn't clear what Matthew means by the word translated "fornication." The Greek word that Matthew uses literally means "prostitution." How do you understand these verses?

Verses 33–37: The part of the law that Jesus has in mind here seems to be that found in places such as Exodus 20:7, Leviticus 19:12, Numbers 30:3, and Deuteronomy 23:22. How might the teaching in these verses have applied to the Nephites? Can you think of specific problems to which this would have been a response? How does it apply to us?

Verses 38–42: It appears that in the Mosaic law "an eye for an eye" was not a directive as to how much punishment to inflict, but a limitation on the retribution one could seek: if someone puts out your eye, you have no right to demand more than the recompense for that eye.

A more accurate translation of the first part of Matthew 5:39 might be "resist not the one who troubles you [or the one who defies you]." Would that also be a reasonable way to understand the first part of verse 39 here? What do these verses teach us about how we are to respond to physical violence? How does this teaching compare to what we find in D&C 98:16–48? How does it compare to the way that the Book of Mormon prophets dealt with violence?

What do these verses teach us about how we should deal with others in legal contention? The demand of verse 41 is one dictated by Roman law: a Roman soldier could compel others to carry his baggage a mile, so the general topic seems to be something like "the demands of the government." How would the Nephites have understood this verse?

What do these verses teach us about how we should respond to the demands of those who oppress us? Compare verse 42 to Mosiah 4:16–23. What obligation is Jesus giving us in verse 42?

Verses 43–47: The Old Testament teaches that we must love our neighbor. (See Leviticus 19:18.) But nowhere does it teach that we should hate our enemies. How do you think this idea of hating one's enemies became part of the understanding of the commandment to love our neighbors? What particular enemies does verse 44 suggest Jesus had in mind? What reason does verse 45 give for loving our enemies?

What does verse 45 suggest that it means to be one of God's children? Why might these verses have been even more important to the Nephites than they were to the Jews?

293

Verse 48: This verse marks a significant break in the sermon, the culmination to this point. As such, perhaps we should understand it as a restatement of verse 3. Can you think of ways in which those verses mean the same? In the corresponding verse in Matthew, notice the footnote that explains what the word *perfect* means: whole, complete, finished, developed. A better translation of the Matthew verse might be: "Be ye therefore whole, even as your Father in heaven is whole." Does that tell us anything about how to understand this verse?

I believe that Jesus may be quoting or paraphrasing Leviticus 19:2 here: "Ye shall be holy: for I the Lord your God am holy." What does it mean to be holy? The Hebrew word in Leviticus means "sacred" or "set apart." Does that help us understand what it means to be holy? To be whole?

James speaks of the double-minded person (James 1:8). What does it mean to be double minded? In contrast, what does it mean to be whole?

Can we be whole in this life? If not, then why has Jesus commanded us to be whole?

Is wholeness something that pertains only to myself—I must be undivided—or is it something that also pertains to my relation with others, including God—my relations with others must be whole? What would it mean for a relation not to be whole?

How does the Sermon on the Mount teach us to be perfect, or whole? Assuming that the chiasm we saw in verses 4–12 is accurate, does it suggest anything about how we are to be perfect? Is it possible to use the concept of mercy to restate or rethink each of the specific discussions that we saw in verses 11–47? What does mercy have to do with wholeness or perfection?

3 Nephi 13

Verses 1–7: Joseph Smith said, "I have a key by which I understand the scriptures. I enquire, what was the question which drew out the answer, or caused Jesus to utter the parable? . . . To ascertain its meaning, we must dig up the root and ascertain what it was that drew the saying out of Jesus" (*History of the Church*, 5:261–62). Though that is a method of interpreting parables, presumably the same principle applies to other teachings. The corresponding verses in Matthew answered particular questions that the saints in the areas of Jerusalem and Galilee had to deal with. What Nephite questions do they answer? Did these verses mean something different for the Nephites than they did for the Jews?

We probably have no difficulty condemning the behavior described in verses 1–2, but do we have difficulty living the principle taught in verses 3–4? What obstacles do we face in that regard? The teaching in these verses seems, on the surface, to conflict with the teaching in 3 Nephi 5:14–16, but since both are the teachings of the Savior, we must assume that they do not. How would you explain these teachings so that they do not conflict?

Verses 3–4, 5–6: These two proscriptions are parallel. Why do you think that is so? Against what is Jesus warning in them? To whom is he referring when he speaks of "the heathen"?

Verses 8–9: Verse 8 tells us that the Father knows before we ask what we need. Verse 9 says *therefore* we should pray in the manner to be described. Why does the Father's knowledge of our needs mean that we should pray in that way?

Verses 9–13: Compare this version of the Lord's Prayer to the version in Matthew 6:9–13, noting the differences (differences that remain if you compare the Joseph Smith revision of the Bible with the Book of Mormon).

What does it mean to pray that the Father's name will be hallowed, in other words, holy? Why is the phrase "thy kingdom come" missing from this prayer, though we see it in the Matthew version? Why is the prayer for daily bread missing in the Book of Mormon version of the prayer?

How are sins like debts?

What does this verse say about the connection between our relation to others and our salvation?

Why does the Lord speak of the Father *leading* us into temptation in both versions of the prayer?

Paraphrased, verse 13 says "because the kingdom, the power, and the glory belong to thee forever." How does the word *for* ("because") connect the final part of the prayer to the rest? Does it relate only back to the immediately previous verse—forgive us as we forgive our debtors because the kingdom, power, and glory belong to thee forever—or does it relate back to something else?

Verses 14–15: Why does the Savior add this commentary on the prayer? Why is the only part of the prayer on which he comments the part about forgiveness?

Verses 16–18: Notice the parallel between these verses and verses 3–4 and 5–6. What do you make of that parallel? The Lord addresses signs of mourning and repentance that come from the early part of the Old Testament, and he seems to be saying, "You must go beyond these." How would a person go beyond them? Is there anything similar in our own worship? What would it be, and how would we go beyond it?

Verses 19–23: Only righteousness results in anything of lasting value, and what we treasure tells us what we value. What is the Lord teaching here about righteousness? Do these verses help us understand better whom he was speaking of in 3 Nephi 12:6 when he spoke of those who hunger and thirst after righteousness?

Verses 24–34: Verse 24 provides a transition to a new theme: we cannot serve both God and possessions (Mammon). Verses 25–31 give various examples of what that means: we need not take thought for ourselves and our provisions because God will provide.

The Greek translated as "take no thought" in the KJV might be better translated "don't be anxious" or "don't worry." Does that change your understanding of these verses and what Jesus commands?

President John Taylor once taught that these verses do not apply to people generally, but to those who serve in the church through the priesthood (Hyrum M. Smith and Janne M. Sjodahl, *Doctrine and Covenants Commentary,* rev. ed. [Salt Lake City: Deseret Book, 1965], 462–63). How do they apply to them? How does verse 33 explain verses 24–32?

297

What does "Sufficient is the day unto the evil thereof" (verse 34) mean? It isn't a quotation from scripture but seems to be a Jewish proverb of Jesus's time. What could it have meant to the Nephites who probably didn't have the same proverb? What does it mean to us?

3 Nephi 14

Verses 1–5: When are we guilty of the kind of judgment of which Jesus speaks here? Notice that though the Matthew text and the 3 Nephi text are very similar here, they are both quite different from the text in the Joseph Smith Translation. (For some of the differences, see page 802 in your Bible.) How do you explain that?

Verse 6: What is Jesus teaching here? When would we be giving holy things to the dogs or casting our pearls before swine? How do we avoid doing so?

Verses 7–11: The Lord's Prayer in Matthew keeps petition to only one line (daily bread) while the version of 3 Nephi omits it altogether. Here, however, we see that we are commanded to petition for our needs. Is there a contradiction between the Lord's Prayer and these verses? Explain what you think. If the Father already knows our needs (3 Nephi 12:8, 32), why should we petition at all? In verse 11, Jesus calls those to whom he speaks evil. Is he being hyperbolic? Why does he use that term?

Verse 12: This is one version of the Golden Rule. Can a person who is not pure in heart use the Golden Rule as an accurate standard of his conduct? What problem might he encounter using it?

Verses 13–14: Remember that the word *strait* means "narrow": the gate leading to destruction is wide and the road to destruction is spacious, but the gate leading to life—eternal life—is narrow. What does it mean to say that few find the strait gate?

Verses 15–20: We can recognize prophets by their fruits. Notice that verse 19 is a word-for-word repetition of John the Baptist's teaching (Matthew 3:10). Does it make any difference that those in Galilee would probably have recognized that Jesus was speaking of John, while those in Zarahemla almost certainly would not? Why was this teaching particularly important in Jesus's time? How is it important to us today? Where do we encounter false prophets?

Verses 21–23: To whom is Jesus referring when he speaks of those who say "Lord, Lord" to him? Of those who prophesy in his name? Of those who do miracles in his name? Why would some who did these things be excluded from his presence? How can prophesying in Jesus's name and working miracles be iniquitous? Do any of the teachings that have come before this in the sermon answer that question?

Verses 24–27: What does it mean to hear the sayings of Christ and do them? What does it mean to hear them and not do them? As the Lord gives this parable, what do building on rock and building on sand have to do with doing and not doing? How do these verses relate to Deuteronomy 6:4–9? How do they relate to 3 Nephi 14:21–23?

3 Nephi 15

Verse 2: The Nephites respond to this sermon by wondering about the passing of the law of Moses. How was the response in Galilee different? Do those differences tell us anything about the two groups of people?

Verse 8: What specifically is Christ referring to when he says "the law which was given unto Moses"? Are the Ten Commandments part of that law? How do we know what has been fulfilled and what hasn't? What covenant was made that has not been completely fulfilled?

The word *end* has various meanings, including "cessation of existence," "final destination," and "purpose." Which meaning do you think the Lord means when he says "the law . . . hath an end in me"?

Verse 9: What does the Savior mean when he says, "I am the law, and the light"? How is he, a person, the law? How is that different from the law of Moses? What does he mean when he says, "Look unto me"? How do we look unto him? What is the significance of that metaphor?

Verse 11: What does this suggest about whom the Lord has been speaking to up to this point?

Verses 14–24: Why do you think the Father didn't want those in Jerusalem to know about those on these continents or the "other tribes"? He says it is because of iniquity, but how does that explain it? Does this mean that even the apostles did not know? Does verse 18 also describe them?

Lesson 39
3 Nephi 17–19

3 Nephi 17

Verses 1–3: Does the Savior think what he has said is easy to understand? Are the things he has taught "plain and simple"? Why haven't the Nephites understood him well?

In what ways are they weak?

What does it mean to ponder something? What does it mean to ask the Father for understanding?

Verses 5–8: Jesus appears to have been ready to quit for the day. What moves him to continue?

What is the connection between healing the sick and Jesus's ministry? Why do the Gospels, the Book of Mormon, and latter-day revelation consistently connect these two things? How is the scriptural emphasis on his healing ministry related to the sermon that he has just recently given to them?

Verses 12–24: Why is the blessing of the children interrupted by Jesus's prayer? The story implies some connection between the children coming to him and his groaning within himself for Israel. What's the connection?

Is there anything in your own experience to which you might compare what happens in Jesus's prayer? (Though verses 15–17 indicate that it is impossible to tell what Jesus prayed, notice that the end of verse 17 implies that it was a prayer for the people present.)

Why would Mormon think it is important for us to know about this prayer if it is impossible for us to know its contents?

What does Christ mean when, in verse 20, he says his joy is full? What makes it full?

Verses 23–25: What is the import of these verses? What would this vision have meant to the Nephites? What might it mean to us?

3 Nephi 18

Verses 4–5, 9: In what sense or senses were those who ate the bread filled?

Verse 7: Is it significant that he says "ye *do* always remember me" rather than "ye *will* always remember me"?

Verse 10: They are blessed for what they have done. Does this refer to the sacrament? If so, how is taking the sacrament "*fulfilling* my commandments"? What is the connection between obeying the Savior and remembering him?

Verse 11: The language here is slightly odd. How do we do the sacrament *to* those who repent and are baptized? What is the significance of that usage?

Verse 12: To what does the phrase "these things" refer?

Verses 12–13: How would we do more than these things? How would we do less? The Lord ended his first sermon with the same analogy that he uses here. (See 3 Nephi

14:24–27.) Little of what he says to them is repetitious; why does he repeat this particular analogy?

Verses 16, 24: When the scriptures tell us to let our light shine before the world, what do they mean? Compare what Christ says here to 2 Nephi 31:12.

Verse 18: What does it mean to watch and pray lest we enter into temptation?

Verse 22: To what situation in their own lives and history might the Nephites have thought this verse referred? Why does he repeat the injunction so frequently here (see verses 30 and 32)? How is this relevant to us? Are there those whom we cast out of our chapels? Who? How?

Verses 27–31: What is this commandment about? Why does the Savior give it special place by drawing such attention to it?

Verse 33: In this verse, to what does the phrase "these sayings" refer? Do sayings go beyond the commandments, or is *saying* just another word for *commandment*? Why might Christ have used the word *saying* here?

Verse 34: What are the commandments Jesus has given? How are those commandments a response to the disputations that have been among the Nephites? (What disputations have we seen among them?)

Verse 35: What might it mean to say that it is expedient that Jesus go to the Father *for their sakes*?

Verses 38–39: Why do you think that Jesus ascends to heaven in a cloud, obscured from the view of the multitudes?

303

3 Nephi 19

Verses 2–3: Did everyone witness Jesus's appearance?

Verses 11–12: Hadn't the twelve been baptized? If not, why not? If so, why are they baptized again?

Verse 14: Why are this event and that related in 3 Nephi 17:24 so similar? What do those similarities suggest? Do they teach us something?

Verses 18, 22: Jesus was known as Jehovah in the times of the Old Testament. He was prayed to many times by that name. What is different now?

Verses 20–21: How does Jesus's prayer here relate to the context in which it occurs? In other words, why, in this particular context, does he pray that the Holy Ghost will be given to all believers?

Verse 23: Why is this prayer to the Father primarily a prayer for the unity of the believers? What kind of unity does the Savior have in mind here? Is this particularly a response to the Nephites, or should we understand it in a broader context?

What does this mean for us?

Verse 24: What does it mean that "it was given unto them what they should pray"? Are our prayers ever like that? When? If not, should they be, or is this a special case of prayer?

What does it mean that "they were filled with desire"? Desire for what?

Verses 28–29: Compare this prayer to John 17, especially 17:9–10. What does it mean that Jesus doesn't pray for the world? Doesn't he love everyone?

What does it mean that those who have faith have been given to him? If we have faith, in what sense have we been given to him? How do we belong to him?

What does it mean that Jesus will be glorified in those who have been given him? How is he glorified—made more glorious—in us?

Verses 32–34: Did they perhaps receive their endowment? What would justify your answer?

Verses 35–36: What miracles could Jesus show those on the American continents that he couldn't show the Israelites?

Lesson 40
3 Nephi 16, 20–21

3 Nephi 16

Verses 8–10, especially 10: Who are the Gentiles?

Look at each condition given for when these things will happen. What does each mean? What, for example, does it mean in this context to sin against the gospel? What does it mean to reject its fulness? (Are those two things or one?) What does it mean to be lifted up in pride above all nations of the whole earth?

When will the conditions described here occur?

What does Christ mean when he says, "I will bring the fulness of my gospel from among them"? (Why *bring* and not *take*?) We have been told the gospel will never be taken from the earth again. Does that mean we will never lose it? We have been promised that the Church will not be removed from the earth again. So do we have any reason to worry about the fulfillment of this scripture? If so, what reason?

Verses 11–15: What does it mean that when he brings his gospel from the Gentiles, he will give it to the house of Israel? To whom among them? What would it mean for the house of Israel to go among the nations and to tread them down?

3 Nephi 20

Verse 23: How could Moses think to have compared himself to Christ, especially by saying "Christ will be like me"?

Verse 24: When mentioning the prophets after Moses, the scriptures consistently say "the prophets from Samuel and those that follow after him," or something like that. Why do they omit Joshua?

Why is Moses such a central character in Israelite history, so central that time seems to have been reckoned around him—"before Moses" and "after Moses"—much as we measure time around Christ?

Verse 25: What does it mean to say they are the children of the prophets?

Verses 28–29: These verses repeat the warning given in 16:8–10. Why is this warning emphasized?

Verse 38: What does it literally mean that the daughters of Jerusalem have sold themselves for naught? What does it mean figuratively? What does it literally mean that they will be redeemed without money? What does it mean figuratively?

Verse 39: What does it mean that the Lord's people will know his name?

3 Nephi 21

Verse 8: What does it mean that kings will shut their mouths? What will they see that they hadn't been told of? What will they consider that they hadn't heard?

Verses 9–10: Is this a reference to Joseph Smith? If not, to whom does it refer?

Verse 14: What is being prophesied here? Few of us own horses anymore, and I suspect none of us has a chariot.

Verse 16: What are soothsayers? Do we find them among us in any significant numbers? What is this scripture prophesying?

Verse 17: What are our graven images today? What are the works of our hands?

Verse 18: What are the "groves" that will be removed from our cities? In ancient Israel, some pagans worshipped in sacred groves. What might be comparable?

Verse 19: What is priestcraft? Where do we find it among us today? Do we see it outside of religion as well as within? Where?

Verse 25: What does it mean that the power of heaven will come down among them?

Lesson 41
3 Nephi 22–26

3 Nephi 22

Why is this chapter from Isaiah important to the Nephites? To us?

Verse 1: What does this verse mean?

Verse 2: If the tent stakes in this scripture are the stakes of the Church, what is the tent? How is the comparison of Church stakes to tent stakes an apt comparison?

Verses 1–3: These verses clearly are verses of rejoicing. Who is rejoicing and why?

Verses 4–7 (and 1): What does the comparison of the Lord's people to a married woman, and the Lord to her husband, tell us? In what ways has she been barren? How has she been a widow? What does it mean to say that she has been refused? Who has refused her? How will she be redeemed, caused to forget her shame and reproach?

Verses 7–10: What is Jesus describing? How has Israel been forsaken? To what is he referring when he says "this, the waters of Noah unto me"? What do the waters of Noah have to do with covenants?

Verses 11–12: What is the point of this promise? Why would we want pavement of fair colors, foundations of sapphires, and so on?

Verse 13: Does "shall be taught of the Lord" mean "will be taught *by* the Lord" or "will be taught *about* the Lord"?

Verse 14: What does it mean to be established in righteousness?

3 Nephi 23

Verse 1: What are the things we should search? What does it mean to search diligently? How would we search scriptures diligently? (In other words, are we commanded here to read them or to do something more?) For what should we search?

Verse 2: Here Jesus tells them why Isaiah is important. How would you explain what he says here in your own words?

3 Nephi 24

Verse 1ff.: Why would a prophecy of the last days be important to the Nephites?

Verse 5: This is the third time the Savior has made this prophecy during his appearance to the Nephites. Obviously he is emphasizing it. Why such emphasis?

Verse 8ff.: Of all the things the Lord could have taken the time to mention, why does he mention tithing?

Verses 14–15: What complaint does this prophecy depict the people making? Do we make that complaint? How?

Verse 16: How is a book of remembrance an answer to the complaint in 14 and 15? What would you suppose is in that book of remembrance? Does that tell us anything about what we should keep in our books of remembrance? Why is it made "for them that feared the Lord, and that thought upon his name"?

Verse 18: Who is the "you" who will return? Is it Christ? If so, why the shift from the previous verse where he was spoken of in the third person (he) to the second person (you) here? Does it refer instead to Israel? If so, why the shift? (Israel too was spoken of in the third person in the previous verse—"they".)

3 Nephi 25

Verse 1: Since the proud will be burned, it is a good idea to know who is included among them. In what ways might we be proud?

Verse 4: Jesus taught them that the law of Moses was fulfilled in him (though not necessarily everything that had been prophesied). Why then does he repeat a scripture to them that says they should remember the law of Moses? What does this commandment ask them to do?

3 Nephi 26

Verse 1: What might be included in "all things . . . both great and small"?

Verse 2: What scriptures has he given them that they didn't have before?

Verse 3: What does it mean to say that the earth will be wrapped together like a scroll?

Verse 9: How will the things we have, a small part of Jesus's teaching, try our faith? Are there specific things in Jesus's Sermon on the Mount/Sermon at the Temple that try our faith?

Verse 18: Why might the things they heard be unlawful to speak?

Verse 19: What does it mean to have all things common? Can we live this principle now? If so, how? If not, what can we do instead?

Lesson 42

3 Nephi 27–30, 4 Nephi

3 Nephi 27

Verse 6: What does it mean to take Christ's name upon us? (What sermon in the book of Mormon has the most to say about that?) When we are told to endure to the end, what are we to endure?

Verse 7: How do we do all that we do in Christ's name? It is easy to see how we can pray in his name, offer blessings in his name, or perform ordinances in his name, but what about other things? How do I teach my children in his name? How do I execute my profession in his name? How do I shop for groceries in his name? Or should we not take the word *all* quite so literally?

Verse 13ff.: Is the Savior giving a definition of the gospel in these verses? Though at first glance it might appear so, perhaps not. Of course, we don't know what the Nephite word translated "gospel" was, so we don't know any more about its meaning than we can deduce from the English word, but we do know about the English word and about the Greek word used by those who wrote the New Testament.

The English and Greek words both originally meant "to preach the good news." For example, in Matthew 2:10, the phrase translated "I bring you good tidings" could also have been translated "I bring you the gospel." (It is a verb rather than a noun in this verse, but the meaning is the same.) The word *gospel* wasn't used to denote a set of doctrines in New Testament times or in its first uses in English. Only later (perhaps about 1200) did the word come to be identified with the accounts of Christ's ministry (the four Gospels), and only later than that did it come to refer to the doctrinal content of Christian preaching. It seems most likely, therefore, that in the Book of Mormon the word *gospel* has the older meaning: preaching glad tidings. If that's true, we could paraphrase the first part of the verse like this:

> *Behold I have preached my glad tidings to you, and these are the glad tidings I have preached to you . . .*

Notice the first element of the good news: Christ came into the world to do the will of his Father, and he did so because his Father sent him. How is that good news?

We might expect Jesus to say something like, "I came into the world to do the will of my Father in order to make salvation available to all." What is important about the reason he gives for his mission?

Verse 14: The phrase "lifted up" has an obvious literal meaning in reference to the crucifixion. But what else might it say to us? For example, is any analogy intended between Christ being lifted up on the cross and the way in which the Father will lift us up? Does this verse have anything to do with verses that tell us we must take up our cross (e.g., Matthew 16:24; Mark 8:34; 10:21; Luke 9:23;

Galatians 6:12; Jacob 1:8; Alma 39:9; 3 Nephi 12:30; and D&C 23:6; 56:2; 112:14)?

What does the phrase "that I might draw all men unto me" imply? Why use the word *draw*?

Verse 15: What does this verse tell us about what Jesus means when he says he will "draw all men" unto him?

Verse 16: What does it mean to say that those who repent and are baptized will be filled? Does it have to do with having our hunger satisfied? Or are we missing something that is given with repentance and baptism?

Verse 17: How does this verse square with latter-day revelation to the effect that the punishment of the wicked is not eternal burnings? (See D&C 19:6ff.)

Verse 19: Why does Christ use the metaphor of washing our garments in his blood? If you give it any thought at all, it is a fairly gruesome image. What's the point of that image? What does it mean to say they have washed their garments in his blood "because of their faith"?

Verse 20: Is this the only commandment? If not, why does Jesus use such a specific form, *this*?

Notice that the commandment has three parts: "repent . . . and come to me and be baptized." Of what are we to repent? How do we go to him?

Christ gives the purpose of his commandment: "that ye may be sanctified." Does the word *sanctified* here have the same meaning that it has in our contemporary doctrinal discussions? How would you justify your answer?

The Lord says that our sanctification takes place by the Holy Ghost. Does that have something to do with the gift of the Holy Ghost? If so, what? How will being sanctified by the Holy Ghost make it possible for us to stand spotless before him at the last day? What last day is he referring to? The judgment day? The day of a follower's death?

Verse 21: What is his gospel? What is the pleasing message he has delivered? What works do we see Christ do in the scriptures? How do we do those works?

Verse 22: How is "lifted up" being used here?

3 Nephi 28

Verses 1–32: Why does the Book of Mormon tell us this story—including the story of those who ask to come to his kingdom speedily as well as the story of the Three Nephites?

3 Nephi 29

Verse 1: Does "these sayings" refer to what Mormon has just said, to the sermons Christ has just preached among the Nephites, or to the entire Book of Mormon? How would we decide?

In what sense was the covenant the Lord made with the Israelites "already beginning to be fulfilled" when the Book of Mormon was revealed?

Verse 2ff.: How does the book of Mormon serve as a warning to us? How does it serve as a warning to the Gentiles? (Who are the Gentiles?)

4 Nephi

Verse 3: What does it mean that the Nephites had all things in common?

How is it that having all things in common makes them all free?

How does that make them all partakers of the heavenly gift? What is the heavenly gift?

Does this verse mean that those who do not have all things in common are not partakers of the heavenly gift?

Verse 5: What do the great and marvelous works they did have to do with the gospel Jesus preached?

Verse 10: What made these people "fair and delightsome"?

Verse 11: Why is marriage mentioned here?

Verses 15–18: We often say "nobody's perfect," but isn't this a record of a perfect people?

Verse 20: What does the word *Lamanite* mean to the Nephites at this point? What other meanings has it had?

Verses 23–26: What seems to be the cause of the failure of this society? In what ways do we imitate the behavior described here? How can we avoid that behavior?

Verse 36: Is it significant that the Lamanites call those among the Nephites by various names?

Verse 43: The primary meaning of the word *vain* is "useless." In what sense have these people become useless? How is it that love of riches, failure to have things in common, the creation of classes, and so on, make us useless?

THE BOOK OF MORMON MADE HARDER: SCRIPTURE STUDY QUESTIONS

Lesson 43
Mormon 1–6; Moroni 9

Mormon 1

Verse 15: What does Mormon mean when he says he "tasted and knew of the goodness of Jesus"? What might that metaphor say to us?

Verse 16: Notice that Mormon isn't allowed to preach because the people were in rebellion, not because he was only fifteen. We think of Mormon as an incredible fifteen-year-old, but might not this also say something about the potential of our own fifteen-year-olds?

Verse 17: The implication of the beginning of the verse is that Mormon could have left his people, perhaps to go off on his own as Lehi and other prophets have done. It is surprising that leaving is such a real possibility for a fifteen-year-old. How can that be?

Mormon 2

Verse 1: We've seen that Mormon must have been extraordinary, especially when compared with what we expect to see in boys his age. But it is unlikely that we would ask even an extraordinary boy to lead an army. What might this tell us about the Nephites?

Verse 8: How is the word *revolution* being used here? The Lamanites appear to be a separate group rather than a group within the Nephite nation, so *revolution* doesn't seem to mean what we usually mean by it (an internal attempt to overthrow the government).

Verse 12: What kind of rejoicing is Mormon describing? Usually we feel sorrow when we see the kind of suffering and destruction he is seeing, even if those suffering "deserve" what they are getting or are being brought to repentance by their sufferings. (We think something like, "It's too bad it took this to get them to repent.") Is Mormon simply callous, or is something else going on here?

Verse 13: What is the difference between the sorrow of the damned and the sorrow of the repentant? How do we distinguish between the two? (See 2 Corinthians 7:9–11.)

Verse 14: Why do they wish to die but struggle for their lives at the same time?

Verse 15: What does he mean when he says "the day of grace was past with them"? The word *grace* refers to a gift of some sort. What gift is no longer available to them? Why is it a gift? Why is it no longer available—because God now refuses to give it or for some other reason?

Verse 19: To what is he referring when he says he will be lifted up at the last day? How does that contrast with the sorrow he has felt his whole life?

Verse 26: Notice that though Book of Mormon prophets have taken Nephite defeat as a sign of Nephite wickedness, Mormon does not take Nephite victory as a sign of

Nephite righteousness. Does this tell us anything about our own situation?

Mormon 3

Verse 12: What does it mean to say that Mormon loves his people? They are so wicked that he will no longer lead them. *How* can he love them?

What was "without faith"? Mormon's prayer? If so, why was he praying so long for them? Why would a person pray all day long for another, but without faith?

Verses 14–15: What has changed so that Mormon will no longer help them? What do the Nephites now want that they didn't seem to want before? What might that say to us about our attitudes toward our enemies?

Verse 16: What is an "idle witness"?

Verse 17: He begins this verse with the word *therefore*. Is what follows in the rest of the chapter a conclusion from what came before?

Mormon 4

Verse 14: The Old Testament is full of references to idols and warnings against them, but the Book of Mormon has very few—only five that I could find outside this chapter, if you exclude the references in the Isaiah passages (2 Nephi 9:37; Alma 7:6; 17:15; 31:1; and Helaman 6:31). Why do you suppose there are so few references to idols in the Book of Mormon when it is such an important topic in the Old Testament?

323

Mormon 5

Verses 8–9, 11: If these chapters were a movie, it would be "R" rated. Why does Mormon tell us of the carnage he witnessed? (In the next chapter, almost 220,000 people—men, women, and children—are killed in one battle.)

Verse 12: What does Mormon mean when he says "it is known of God that wickedness will not bring them forth unto them"?

Verse 14: How can the Book of Mormon persuade the Jews that Jesus is the Christ?

Verse 16: What does it mean to be "without Christ and God in the world"? Aren't most people without them? Or is Mormon saying something more than we might say if we said that most of those in an area not yet proselytized are without Christ and God in the world?

What does it mean to say that they are driven as chaff? From where? To where?

Verse 17: Is Mormon saying something contradictory here? If Christ was their shepherd, how can they be led by the Father? Is he perhaps speaking of Christ as the Father (compare Mosiah 15:2)?

Mormon 6

Verse 2: Why does Mormon propose a battle?

Verse 17: What does Mormon mean when he calls the Nephites "fair ones"? At this point in Nephite and Lamanite history, it is doubtful he is talking about their skin color.

But given what we have seen, he also can't be talking about their character.

Moroni 9

Moroni seems to have intended the book in his name to be primarily a set of specific instructions for us in the latter days. Why, then, does he stick this chapter, perhaps the most gruesome in the whole Book of Mormon, in the middle of the other chapters?

Verses 25–26: How is Mormon's message in these verses intended to help Moroni? (Does the story of depravity Mormon has just told serve a purpose in relation to these verses?)

Lesson 44
Mormon 7–9

Mormon 7

Verse 1: Notice that Mormon speaks of "the remnant of this people." To whom does *this* refer? To whom was he speaking in chapter 6? We call the remnant "Lamanites," but Mormon seems not to be thinking of them in that way.

Verse 2: Why must the remnant know that they are of the house of Israel?

Verse 3: Notice the number of times this is repeated, each time more fully than the last: here in verse 3 and also in verses 5, 8, and 10. What do you make of that repetition?

Verse 4: Does this verse forbid the remnant from taking up arms to defend the countries in North, Central, and South America in which they live? What does it mean?

Verse 7: What does it mean to be found guiltless before Christ?

Verse 9: The Book of Mormon is written with the intent of helping us believe the Bible. How does it do that? How is it true that if we believe the Bible we will also believe the Book of Mormon? There are, after all, many who claim to believe the Bible who do not believe the Book of Mormon, even when they learn of it. It follows logically from what this verse says that they do not believe the Bible. How can that be?

Mormon 8

Verse 12: Joseph Smith said that the Book of Mormon is the most perfect book on the earth. What, then, does it mean to say that there are imperfections in it? (See also verse 17 and the title page of the book.)

What are the greater things that those who believe the Book of Mormon will know?

Verse 15: What two reasons does Moroni give here for the coming forth of the Book of Mormon?

Verses 18–20: To whom are these verses addressed?

Verses 21–22: To whom are these verses addressed?

Verse 23: Why does Moroni tell them to search the writings of Isaiah? How are they relevant to this context?

Verse 23–25: Who are the saints who have gone before? What covenant did the Lord make with them?

Verse 26: Presumably Moroni is speaking of the Book of Mormon. In the last verse he said it would come forth in a day when people will no longer believe in miracles. That describes many who lived when Joseph received the plates and even more today. Here it says it will come at a time when "the blood of the saints shall cry unto the Lord because of secret combinations and the works of darkness." How does that describe the time when the Book of Mormon was revealed? The blood of which saints? What secret combinations?

Verse 31: What kinds of pollution is Moroni thinking of here? Is it the list that follows, or does it include more than that?

Verse 32: Can you think of an example of this? It is unlikely that a church at the time the Book of Mormon came forth would be so bold as to make this offer explicit. (The Catholic Church had stopped selling indulgences several hundred years before Joseph Smith's day.) How might a church in the nineteenth, twentieth, or twenty-first century say that people's sins will be forgiven for money?

Verse 33: In what ways do people get gain from churches?

How do people transfigure the word of God? Can they do so unintentionally? Do we ever do so, intentionally or unintentionally?

What are "these things" that he promises will be fulfilled?

Verses 35–37: To whom are these verses addressed? To everyone in the last dispensation or only to those at the time of Joseph Smith? To everyone or only to those outside the Church?

What does it mean to walk and to lift ourselves up in the pride of our hearts? What does "fine apparel" mean here? Why is wearing it a problem? How does wearing it lead, as Moroni indicates, to envy, strife, malice, and persecution? Is the wearing of fine apparel a problem for us today? In what circumstances?

Verse 37: What does it mean to love these things more than we love the poor and the needy? How would we tell if we were described by this verse?

Verse 38: To what does "that which will canker" refer? How would that thing canker its possessors?

Verse 39: The beginning of this verse is a little odd. How would we adorn ourselves with what *has* life? What adornment would that be? Does the verse say we shouldn't adorn ourselves with what doesn't have life?

Verse 40: In the Book of Mormon we are accustomed to the phrase "secret combinations." But the phrase "secret *abominations*" is also found in Alma 37:26–27; 3 Nephi 16:10; 30:2; and D&C 117:11. ("Secret combinations" are referred to in 2 Nephi 9:9; 26:22; Alma 37:30–31; Helaman 3:23; 3 Nephi 4:29; 7:6, 9; 4 Nephi 1:42; Mormon 8:27; Ether 8:18–19, 22, 24; 9:1; 11:15; 13:18; 14:8, 10; D&C 42:64; and Moses 5:51.) Is there a difference between the two? If so, what is it?

Mormon 9

Verse 5: What does "nakedness before God" mean?

Verse 8: If we deny continuing revelation, how is it that we don't know Christ's preaching (his gospel)? When might we in the Church be guilty of denying continuing revelation?

Verse 10: Why is it that those who believe in a varying god don't believe in a God of miracles?

Verse 11ff.: What is a miracle? When we think of miracles, we think of such things as healing the sick. Moroni, however, uses the fall and redemption of mankind as his examples. But that is part of the plan, isn't it? How is it a miracle? How might Moroni's discussion of the fall and redemption as miracles help us think differently about miracles?

Verse 20: Are there fewer miracles today than in times past? If so, what does that tell us about ourselves? If we perceive that fewer miracles are done, does that say something of the same sort?

Verse 21: Is this the same promise made to Nephi (in Helaman 10:5)?

Verse 23: What does it mean to be damned?

Verse 25: What does this verse mean? What does it mean that the Savior will confirm his words "even unto the ends of the earth"?

Verse 27: What does it mean to "begin as in times of old"?

We often quote the phrase "work out your own salvation with fear and trembling." What does it mean? The phrase itself occurs in only one other place in scripture, Philippians 2:12. (A related phrase is found in Alma 34:37, and another is found in Ephesians 6:5. The comparison of these verses to the verse in Ephesians may be helpful.) The phrase "fear and trembling" seems to connote the solemn feeling of responsibility we should have before the Father—our recognition of the weight of that responsibility and our fear that we may fail in it. In Philippians, when Paul uses the phrase "your own," he is reminding them that they cannot depend on him to save them, that they must live the Christian life as much when he is gone as when he is present. Does Moroni mean the same thing as Paul, or is he saying something different? If something different, what?

Verse 28: What does it mean to be wise in the days of our probation?

Why do we *strip* ourselves of uncleanness? What might that metaphor suggest? In what sense is uncleanness something that we have put on, an addition to who we are?

How can we ask not to yield to temptation? Can the Lord prevent us from falling prey to temptation?

Verse 29: To what does *this* refer in "if you do this"?

Verse 31: Why does Moroni keep mentioning his imperfections and those of the other writers? What imperfections does he seem to have in mind? Shouldn't he be more self-confident, have a better self-image?

Verse 35: Why do Moroni, Mormon, and the other writers have to rid themselves of the blood of their brothers and sisters? Why would that blood be on them?

Lesson 45
Ether 1–6

The book of Ether is like a Book of Mormon for the people of the Book of Mormon. Why did the children of Lehi need such a book? Does each dispensation have its own "Book of Mormon"? What does seeing that the Book of Mormon people had the Jaredite record teach us? Does it make the story of their fall any more poignant?

Ether 1

Verse 34: Why do you think the brother of Jared isn't mentioned by name? What might account for the omission of the name of such a great prophet?

Verse 43: What promise did Jared's people receive? To whom has this promise been made?

Ether 2

Verse 8: What does it mean to say that the Lord made this promise "in his wrath"?

Verses 9–12: Notice that Moroni begins these verses with one of his father's writing "trademarks": "And now, can we behold . . ." (Usually Mormon says *see* rather than *behold,* but the phrase is essentially the same.) Why do you think Moroni interjects his own thoughts into the book of Ether so often?

Verse 15: The writer (whether Mormon or Ether) calls the brother of Jared's sin of omission—neglecting to pray—an evil. Is he exaggerating for emphasis, or is neglecting to pray an evil thing?

Ether 3

Verse 2ff.: There are two ways to read these verses. We can read Jared as sincere, or we can read him as "buttering up" the Lord. Which do you think is better and why? If Jared is sincere, what does that imply about the doctrinal content of these verses?

Verse 2: What does it mean to say "we are unworthy before thee; because of the fall our natures have become evil continually"? One way of reading this is that we cannot help doing evil; the fall makes us do it. But shouldn't we be excused from what we can't help doing? After all, if we are fallen, it isn't by any act of our own, but a result of what Adam and Eve did. How can we subscribe to what this verse says without concluding that we aren't responsible for our evil desires and, therefore, for our evil deeds if our natures are continually evil because of something we didn't do? Or is there another way of understanding what this means?

Verse 8: Apparently not all the prophets have known that God has a body. It appears, in fact, that before this experience the brother of Jared might not even have known that Christ would come to the earth as a person. Why might that information have been withheld from certain times?

Verse 13: The Lord tells him he is redeemed from the fall *because* he knows that God speaks the truth. Why would that redeem him? What does it mean to be redeemed from the fall?

Because he is redeemed, he is brought back into the Lord's presence. Isn't he already in his presence? He is, after all, speaking with the Lord. (What parallels might one see between the brother of Jared's experience and our experience in the temple?)

Verse 15: The Lord tells Jared that he has never shown himself to a human being. But what about the prophets who preceded the brother of Jared (e.g., Adam, Seth, Enos, Enoch, and Noah)? Hadn't they seen him? Moses 7:4, for example, expressly says that Enoch spoke with God face to face. How do you reconcile Moses 7:4 with this scripture?

Verses 19–20: We often say something like "The brother of Jared couldn't be kept from seeing the Lord because of his faith." Here, however, it says that he couldn't be kept from seeing because of his *knowledge.* What knowledge put him in this position? What kind of knowledge is that? How did he get that knowledge?

Verse 24: Does this verse mean that the Urim and Thummim are made from the stones used by the Jaredites? If so, is there more than one Urim and Thummim, or did the Lord move it from the Jaredites to the Israelites and then back to the Book of Mormon people?

Ether 4

Verse 6: Have the things that the brother of Jared saw "gone forth"? Does that mean the Gentiles have repented and become clean?

Verse 7: Has this verse been fulfilled yet? If not, when will it be fulfilled? What would its fulfillment entail?

Verse 8: How would one contend against the Lord's word?

Those who "deny these things" will also be accursed. To what does "these things" refer? What the brother of Jared learned? His experience? The book of Ether? The Book of Mormon?

Verse 10: We hear that those who won't listen to the Lord's servants won't listen to him. Here, however, that is reversed. Of course, those who won't listen to the master won't listen to the servants; what point is the Lord making here?

Verse 11: To what does "these things of which I have spoken" refer? Is the mark of the truth of those things that they persuade people to do good? If not, what do we make of the remark at the end of the verse? If so, how does that make us rethink what we mean when we speak of the truth? For example, we sometimes justify what we do by saying, "I'm only telling the truth." When we speak that way we must be using *truth* to mean "an accurate portrayal of the fact," rather than "what persuades people to do good."

What difference would it make for us to think of truth as what persuades people to do good? If we thought of it that way, could we also justify portraying the facts *in*accurately, lying?

Verse 12: Jesus says that good comes of none but him. That could mean that what seems to be good, like the work of the Moslem equivalent of the Red Cross, the Red Crescent Society, isn't actually good, or it could mean it comes from Christ. Which seems more reasonable? How might understanding the statement made here about good help us be more understanding and tolerant of those who differ from us?

The Savior makes a distinction between believing his words and believing him. What's the difference?

What does the Book of Mormon mean when it speaks of Jesus as the Father? Why does it emphasize his fatherhood? The irony is that Latter-day Saints seldom discuss the matter for fear that we will be espousing apostate doctrine, though the Book of Mormon teaches the fatherhood of Christ much more clearly than does the New Testament. (We much prefer to speak of him as our "Elder Brother," though the scriptures *never* use that phrase.) Might this be one of the things the Book of Mormon was meant to restore?

How is Christ the light of the world? How is he its life? (Does answering that question help us understand how he is the Father?) How is he its truth? (Does the answer to the latter question help us understand how the truth is that which persuades men to do good? How might thinking of Christ as the truth force us to rethink what we mean by the word *truth*?)

Verse 13: What are "the greater things" that those who come to Jesus will be shown?

Verse 15: In most places the veil is spoken of as something that is removed. Here it is spoken of as something we must remove. Is this verse talking about the same veil we refer to when we speak of the veil between ourselves and the Father?

Verse 19: How do we remain faithful to the Lord's name? Where in the Book of Mormon did we see a discussion of this? There is a very real sense in which the Book of Mormon's central theme is taking his name on us and remaining faithful to that name. As you read through it next time, you might watch for the places where that theme is mentioned. You'll find, I think, that each of the prophets speaks of it, and you'll find that King Benjamin's sermon is one of the most important documents in the Book of Mormon.

Ether 5

Verses 3–4: What might have caused Moroni to think of three witnesses as he transcribes the book of Ether?

Lesson 46
Ether 7–15

These notes will cover only chapter 12 of Ether.

Ether 12

Verse 3: When Ether says that all things are fulfilled by faith, what does he mean? What kinds of things can be *fulfilled*, and how are they fulfilled through faith?

Verse 4: Ether says that those who believe can hope for a better world. Is he referring only to the "next world"? Is the answer to our present sorrows "Don't worry, it will be better later," or does the gospel change *this* world as well?

How does hope make us sure and steadfast? How does it cause us to be "abounding in good works"?

Verse 6: How does remembering that *trust* is a synonym for *faith* help make what Moroni says more intelligible? For example, why would faith require that we hope for something not seen?

Why would we not receive a witness until after our faith (trust) had been tested?

Verse 7: When Moroni says that Christ showed himself to the fathers by faith, does he mean by their faith or by Christ's?

Verse 8: What heavenly gift is Moroni speaking of?

Verse 9: The wording of this verse indicates that we can partake of the heavenly gift even before our hope is realized. How does trusting in the Lord (having faith) make it possible for us to partake of the gift?

Verses 10–22: What things does Moroni show us with this list?

Verses 26: What is grace? What does it mean to be meek? (A look at a historical dictionary would be helpful here, perhaps the *Oxford English Dictionary* or Webster's 1828 dictionary.)

What does it mean to say that the Lord's grace is sufficient? Sufficient for what?

Verse 27: What kinds of weaknesses is the Lord speaking of? Should we be grateful for our weaknesses?

Why do we need to be humble? How does this contrast with what our culture often teaches us and our children? How might weak things become strong to us?

Verse 28: What's the connection between weaknesses on the one hand and faith, hope, and charity on the other?

What does it mean to say that the Savior is the "fountain of all righteousness"? What does the word *fountain* mean here?

Verse 29: What does it mean to be comforted? (Here, again, a look at a historical dictionary may be helpful.) How would these words have been a comfort to Moroni? *Which* words does he mean by "these words"?

Verses 30–31: Moroni illustrates the idea of faith with examples. How might these examples of faith have served to comfort him? What purpose or purposes do they serve for us?

Verse 32: Here he illustrates hope. How is this example of hope particularly appropriate?

Verses 33–35: Moroni illustrates the meaning of *charity*. He uses humans to illustrate faith, and he uses our relation to the Son to illustrate hope. How is this illustration of charity particularly significant?

Verse 33: What does it mean to say that Jesus laid down his life *so* he could take it up again?

Does the phrase "to prepare a place for the children of men" refer to "laying down of thy life" or to "thou mightest take it again"? In other words, does it mean he laid down his life to prepare a place for us or that he was resurrected to prepare a place for us? What difference in our understanding might each of these make?

Verse 34: This verse, paraphrased, says, "Christ's love is charity, so unless people have charity they cannot inherit a place in the Father's kingdom." What is the connection between the ideas of the two clauses? In the paraphrase, what does *so* (*wherefore* in the verse) tell us?

Verse 36: What does grace have to do with charity?

Verse 37: The Lord tells Moroni he will be made strong because he has seen his weaknesses. Does that mean we must know our weaknesses if we are to be made strong?

What does it mean to know one's weaknesses? How do we discover them?

What is the significance of using the passive voice—"shalt be made strong"—rather than the active—"will become strong"? What does "shalt be made strong even unto the sitting down" mean?

Verse 39: Moroni says that Jesus talked with him "in plain humility." Does this mean that Jesus too is humble, or is the verse describing Moroni? If it is describing Jesus, what would it mean for him to be humble when he has no weaknesses? Does this teach us anything about what our own humility ought to be like?

Lesson 47

Moroni 1–6

Moroni 1

Verse 4: Moroni intended to end the Book of Mormon with his abridgment of Ether. Why do you think he intended that? What would have made Ether an appropriate end to Moroni's record?

Moroni 2

Verses 1–3: Why weren't these words part of the public record of Christ's visit? Why does Moroni include them in the Book of Mormon?

These verses suggest that the authority to give the gift of the Holy Ghost was the most important aspect of the disciples' ordination. Why might that be?

Moroni 3

Verses 1–3: Was the ordination of priests and teachers among the Nephites accomplished by means of the set prayer that we find here? If so, what does it mean to us that we no longer use a set prayer for those ordinations? If not, what makes you think that it wasn't?

Verse 3: What does "the endurance of faith" mean? Does it mean that faith produces endurance? If so, how might that be so? (Ether 12 may be relevant.)

Moroni 4

Verse 3: What does it mean to say that the bread will be blessed and sanctified (made holy) *to the souls* of those who eat it? Why must we remember Christ's body and then his blood? What does the word *may* suggest in the places where it appears in the prayer? To whom does "his Spirit," meaning "Christ's Spirit," refer? If the Holy Ghost, how is that a proper name for him? If it is not the Holy Ghost, what does that phrase mean? Here is one possible diagram of the sacrament prayer over the bread:

According to this diagram, the priest asks the Father to bless and sanctify the bread for three reasons: so that those who eat may eat in remembrance, so that those who eat may become witnesses, and so that those who eat may have "his Spirit" to be with them. Those who partake become witnesses of three things: that they are willing to take the name of the Son on themselves, that they are willing to remember him, and that they are willing to keep his commandments.

Are there other ways to diagram the prayer, ways that yield different understandings of it? For example, is there another way to understand how the last clause fits with the rest of the prayer? In the diagram, it is one of the things that the priest prays for, but it might also be understood as being the result of keeping the commandments. In other words, in the last clause, does "that they may always have his Spirit" mean "we ask thee to bless and sanctify this bread so that they may always have his Spirit" (as this diagram assumes), or does it mean "they keep his commandments so that they may always have his Spirit"? How do you decide between these two possibilities?

Moroni 5

At the end of the prayer over the wine/water, the priest prays that those who drink it "*do* always remember him." In the prayer over the bread, he prays that they *may* remember. Is this difference significant? If so, what does it signify? If not, why is the wording different?

Moroni 6

Verse 1: What fruits show that one is worthy of baptism?

Verse 2: Does this verse answer the question about verse 1, or does it add additional qualifications? Does the word *neither* at the beginning of the verse suggest an answer to that question?

Verse 3: Are taking the name of Christ upon oneself and having a determination to serve him to the end the same thing or two different things? What does it mean, literally, to take Christ's name upon oneself?

Verse 4: Is the wording "received unto baptism" significant? Why does Moroni say that to be numbered among the members of the church, one must have been "wrought upon and cleansed by the power of the Holy Ghost"? Has

345

everyone who has been given the gift of the Holy Ghost been so wrought upon and cleansed?

Why does Moroni think it was important to keep the names of those who joined the people of the church?

How do we nourish members "by the good word of God"? How do we keep each other "in the right way"?

What does it mean to be "continually watchful unto prayer"? How do we keep each other "continually watchful unto prayer"?

The last part of this verse sounds very Protestant: "relying alone upon the merits of Christ, who was the author and the finisher of their faith." What does it mean to rely *only* on the merits of Christ (and, therefore, not on our own merits)? What does it mean to say that Christ is the author—the creator—of our faith? What does it mean to say that he is its finisher?

Verses 5–6, 9: How might the meetings of the Nephite Saints have been different from ours? How similar?

Verses 7–8: Why does Moroni insert the remark about how to deal with transgressors in the middle of his description of Nephite worship?

Lesson 48
Moroni 7–8; 10

Moroni 7

As you read Mormon's sermon, ask yourself what might have been its occasion. Given the content of the first twenty-one verses, why does Moroni say that this is a sermon on faith, hope, and charity (verse 1)?

What question might have prompted Mormon to write this? (Compare Mormon 9:7–21.)

Does the audience that he mentions (verse 3) make a difference to our understanding of his teaching?

What do you make of the order of his sermon? Below is one outline of that order. Use this outline to ask questions about what Mormon says. As you read, construct your own outline. Are there better ways to describe the contents of the verses than I have given—or a better way of showing how the verses relate to each other?

> I. Mormon speaks to the peaceable followers of Christ who have hope for his rest (verses 3–4)
>
> II. The good cannot do evil works, and the evil cannot do good works (verses 5–13)
>
> III. Therefore, we must be careful in our judgments of good and evil (verses 14–18)

IV. We should lay hold on every good thing (verse 19)

V. How to lay hold on every good thing (verses 21–48)

    A. Faith in Christ (verses 21–39)

        1. Christ's saving mission (21–26)

        2. Miracles have not ceased (verses 27–39)

            a. The ministry required of human beings is parallel to the ministry provided them through angels (verses 30–32)

            b. By faith we can do anything, including repent (verses 33–37)

        3. Salvation comes by faith (verses 37–39)

    B. Hope in Christ (verses 40–44)

        1. Faith requires hope for life eternal through Jesus Christ (verses 40–41)

        2. Hope requires faith (verse 42)

        3. Faith and hope require meekness and lowliness of heart (verse 43)

        4. If a person is meek and lowly in heart, then that person will have charity (verse 44)

    C. The charity of Christ (verses 45–48)

        1. The qualities of charity (verse 45)

        2. Without charity, which never fails, we are nothing (verse 46)

        3. Those who have charity, the pure love of Christ, will be well at the last day (verse 47)

4. We should pray with all the energy of our hearts to be filled with charity so that we may be like Christ (verse 48)

Is there a natural flow to Mormon's discussion? Can you use it to explain how we lay hold of every good thing? To explain the relation of faith and hope? To explain how one might learn to be charitable?

A few questions about particular verses:

Verse 5: Compare Moroni 10:25. Why might this theme have been so important to father and son?

Verses 31–32: What do covenants have to do with this sermon? Why are the references to covenants located in the middle of a discussion of our ministry, a discussion that itself is in the middle of an argument that miracles still occur? Can you explain what covenants have to do with miracles?

Verse 39: Does Mormon equate being meek with having faith?

Verses 45, 47: At the end of verse 45, Mormon says that charity endures all things. Then, at the beginning of verse 47, he says that it endures forever. Is there a connection between these? If so, what is it?

Moroni 10

Verse 1: What does it mean to us that the words that follow (up to verse 23) are specifically directed to the Lamanites? What is Moroni's interest in them?

Verse 3: Why is God's mercy to human beings, from Adam to the present, *the* topic on which Moroni wishes his readers to meditate? Why is that an essential preface to the exhortation that follows?

Verses 4–5: Why does knowing the truth of the Book of Mormon require (1) a sincere heart, (2) real intent, and (3) faith in Christ? If these verses are written specifically for the Lamanites, what justifies our use of them for everyone?

Verse 6: Moroni says that anything that is good is also just, as well as true. It isn't difficult to think of things that don't have anything to do with justice but that most of us would say are good. For example, I think it is good to have children, but I wouldn't say it is *just* to have them. I don't know what it would mean to say that it is. What does it mean to say that all good things are just? Similarly, what does it mean to say that all good things are true? Moroni then adds that no good thing denies Christ. How does that follow from the claims that all good things are also both just and true?

Verse 7: When Moroni says, "I would exhort you that ye deny not the power of God," what denial of God's power does he seem to have in mind? How would what he has in mind be a denial of God's power?

Verses 7–18: Why is this exhortation to remember the gifts of God important to Moroni's audience?

Verse 19: Why does Moroni exhort his audience to remember that Christ is the same and that the gifts mentioned are spiritual and will last as long as the world? Why is that exhortation of particular importance to those he is addressing in these verses, namely, the Lamanites?

Verses 20–23: Moroni gives a summary of the things that his father, Mormon, taught in the last part of his sermon (Moroni 7). Moroni has already given us the sermon, so why does he think it needs to be repeated here?

Verse 24–30: In verse 24 Moroni explicitly turns his attention to everyone rather than only to the Lamanites; he makes a general exhortation. What are its main elements? How do those elements compare to what he has said specifically to the Lamanites?

Verse 31: To whom does Moroni now turn? Why does he turn to them last?

Moroni's metaphor moves from clothing ("beautiful garments") to tents ("strengthen thy stakes and enlarge thy borders"). Is that shift in the metaphor significant?

Verse 32: Grammatically the opening of this verse, "Yea, come unto Christ, and be perfected in him," suggests that this verse is parallel to verse 31. Is that right? If so, explain what the parallels are.

Why does Moroni say "be perfected in him" (passive voice) rather than "perfect yourselves in him"? Does the rest of the verse answer that question?

How does Moroni understand what it means to be perfect? How might that be different than our everyday understanding of perfection?

Verse 33: What does this verse promise? Does Moroni use *sanctified* here to mean what we mean when we speak of exaltation, or does it have another meaning? What does this verse add to our understanding of what it means to be perfect?

Verse 34: What kind of mood does Moroni exhibit in this verse? So what?

Appendix 1
Mosiah 4 outline

Verse 1: And now, it came to pass that when king Benjamin had made an end of speaking the words which had been delivered unto him by the angel of the Lord, that he cast his eyes round about on the multitude, and behold they had fallen to the earth, for the fear of the Lord had come upon them.

A. The words of King Benjamin's speech had been given to him by an angel. He said so at the beginning of chapter 3; he says so here. Why is that fact so important?

B. What about King Benjamin's speech in chapter 3 caused the fear of the Lord to come upon the people?

1. The Lord has a message of joy for King Benjamin and his people: Jesus Christ is coming (verses 3–5).

2. He will live and suffer in the flesh (verses 6–7).

3. He will bring salvation (verses 8–9).

4. He will rise from the dead (verse 10).

5. He will do what he does so that a righteous judgment of human beings can be made (verse 10).

6. He will atone for those who have suffered because of Adam's transgression and died in sin because they didn't know the commandments (verse 11).

7. The Lord has sent the prophets to preach to those who rebel because the only way to be saved is through Jesus Christ (verses 12–18). (He repeats the latter fact several times.)

8. The natural man is an enemy to God and will be unless he

   a. yields to the Holy Spirit,

   b. puts off the natural man,

   c. becomes a saint through the Atonement, and

   d. becomes like a child: submissive, meek, humble, patient, and full of love (verse 19).

9. The knowledge of the Savior will spread throughout the world, and when it does only little children will be held blameless (verses 20–21).

10. King Benjamin's people are not blameless (verse 22).

C. What kind of people were King Benjamin's people? (See Mosiah 1:11—"they have been a diligent people in keeping the commandments of the Lord.")

D. The phrase "fear of the Lord" appears in 1 Samuel 11:7; 2 Chronicles 14:14; 17:10; 19:7, 9; Job 28:28; Psalms 19:9; 34:11; 111:10; Proverbs 1:7, 29; 2:5; 8:13; 9:10; 10:27; 14:26, 27; 15:16, 33; 16:6; 19:23; 22:4; 23:17; Isaiah 2:10, 19, 21; 11:2–3; 33:6. (See also: Acts 9:31; 2 Nephi 12:10, 19, 21; 21:2–3; Enos 1:23; Mosiah 29:30; Alma 19:15; 36:7; and Moses 7:17.)

1. Two words are used: *pahad* and *yi'râ*.

   a. *pahad* means, literally, "dread." It is a word used mostly in poetry and may connote awe or reverence.

   b. *yi'râ* means, literally, "fear." It is often associated with an anticipation of something bad happening.

2. Isaiah uses both words in the phrase "the fear of the Lord."

Verse 2: And they had viewed themselves in their own carnal state, even less than the dust of the earth. And they all cried aloud with one voice, saying: O have mercy, and apply the atoning blood of Christ that we may receive forgiveness of our sins, and our hearts may be purified; for we believe in Jesus Christ, the Son of God, who created heaven and earth, and all things; who shall come down among the children of men.

A. To what are King Benjamin's people responding when they cry out?

B. What is meant by "carnal state"? See Mosiah 4:2 and Alma 22:13; 41:11.

   1. In the standard works, this phrase occurs only in the Book of Mormon. So what?

   2. Webster's 1828 dictionary: "pertaining to flesh," "in its natural, unregenerative state," "lustful." Which of these seems most likely in this case?

C. The phrase "dust of the earth" is used in two ways: to indicate multiplicity (as in Genesis 13:16—"I will make thy seed as the dust of the earth: so that if a man can number the dust of the earth, then shall thy seed also be numbered") and simply to refer to dirt and ashes (as in Exodus 8:17—"Aaron stretched out his hand with his rod, and smote the dust of the earth, and it became lice in man, and in beast"). It is not used in the Bible to indicate lowliness, as it is in the Book of Mormon.

D. What has happened to King Benjamin's people? What do they want? What kind of people are they?

Verse 3: And it came to pass that after they had spoken these words the Spirit of the Lord came upon them, and they were filled with joy, having received a remission of their sins, and having peace of conscience, because of the exceeding faith which they had in Jesus Christ who should come, according to the words which king Benjamin had spoken unto them.

A. What have they received *before* King Benjamin speaks to them in chapter 4?

Verse 4: And king Benjamin again opened his mouth and began to speak unto them, saying: My friends and my brethren, my kindred and my people, I would again call your attention, that ye may hear and understand the remainder of my words which I shall speak unto you.

Verse 5: For behold, if the knowledge of the goodness of God at this time has awakened you to a sense of your nothingness, and your worthless and fallen state—

A. What does King Benjamin believe they have learned?

1. The goodness of God.

2. Their own nothingness; their worthless and fallen state.

Verse 6: I say unto you, if ye have come to a knowledge of the goodness of God, and his matchless power, and his wisdom, and his patience, and his long-suffering towards the children of men; and also, the atonement which has been prepared from the foundation of the world, that thereby salvation might come to him that should put his trust in the Lord, and should be diligent in keeping his commandments, and continue in the faith even unto the end of his life, I mean the life of the mortal body—

A. What does King Benjamin say that his people have learned?

1. The goodness of God.

2. His power, his wisdom, his patience, and his long-suffering with people.

3. That an atonement was prepared from the beginning of the world so that those who trust the Lord, keep the commandments, and endure faithfully to the end . . .

B. Why does King Benjamin repeat essentially the same things he says in verse 5?

C. What does he add this time?

Verse 7: I say, that this is the man who receiveth salvation, through the atonement which was prepared from the foundation of the world for all mankind, which ever were since the fall of Adam, or who are, or who ever shall be, even unto the end of the world.

A. To whom does "this is the man" refer?

B. What do verses 6 and 7 together say to us?

C. Why is King Benjamin telling his people these things?

Verse 8: And this is the means whereby salvation cometh. And there is none other salvation save this which hath been spoken of; neither are there any conditions whereby man can be saved except the conditions which I have told you.

Verse 9: Believe in God; believe that he is, and that he created all things, both in heaven and in earth; believe that he has all wisdom, and all power, both in heaven and in earth; believe that man doth not comprehend all the things which the Lord can comprehend.

Verse 10: And again, believe that ye must repent of your sins and forsake them, and humble yourselves before God; and ask in sincerity of heart that he would forgive you; and now, if you believe all these things see that ye do them.

A. How are the requirements that King Benjamin mentions in verses 9 and 10 (believe in God—that he is, that he created everything, that he has all wisdom and power, and that we do not understand all the things that he does) related to the requirements he lists in verses 5–7?

Verse 11: And again I say unto you as I have said before, that as ye have come to the knowledge of the glory of God, or if ye have known of his goodness and have tasted of his love, and have received a remission of your sins, which causeth such exceedingly great joy in your souls, even so I would that ye should remember, and always retain in remembrance, the greatness of God, and your own nothingness, and his goodness and long-suffering towards you, unworthy creatures, and humble yourselves even in the depths of humility, calling on the name of the Lord daily, and standing steadfastly in the faith of that which is to come, which was spoken by the mouth of the angel.

A. What does King Benjamin say here that he has said before?

    1. If you know the glory of God, or

    2. If you have

        a. known his goodness,

        b. tasted his love, and

        c. received a remission of your sins,

    3. then you should remember

        a. his greatness,

        b. your nothingness, and

        c. his goodness and long-suffering,

    4. and you should

        a. humble yourselves while you

            i. pray to the Lord and

            ii. remain faithful.

Verse 12: And behold, I say unto you that if ye do this ye shall always rejoice, and be filled with the love of God, and always retain a remission of your sins; and ye shall grow in the knowledge of the glory of him that created you, or in the knowledge of that which is just and true.

A. What does King Benjamin promise those who do what he has told them (in verse 11) they must do?

1. You will always rejoice.

2. You will be filled with the love of God.

3. You will retain a remission of your sins.

4. You will have great knowledge of the Creator's glory.

a. In other words, you will have greater knowledge of what is just and true.

Verse 13: And ye will not have a mind to injure one another, but to live peaceably, and to render to every man according to that which is his due.

A. To what does the first word of this verse (*and*) connect the verse?

Verse 14: And ye will not suffer your children that they go hungry, or naked; neither will ye suffer that they transgress the laws of God, and fight and quarrel one with another, and serve the devil, who is the master of sin, or who is the evil spirit which hath been spoken of by our fathers, he being an enemy to all righteousness.

A. This continues the promise begun in verse 12. Where does that promise end?

B. What does it mean that this is a promise rather than a commandment?

Verse 15: But ye will teach them to walk in the ways of truth and soberness; ye will teach them to love one another, and to serve one another.

Verse 16: And also, ye yourselves will succor those that stand in need of your succor; ye will administer of your substance unto him that standeth in need; and ye will not suffer that the beggar putteth up his petition to you in vain, and turn him out to perish.

A. Why does King Benjamin's sermon turn to the question of how we deal with beggars?

B. What groups of people does King Benjamin seem concerned with in the last part of this chapter? What might that say to us?

Verse 17: Perhaps thou shalt say: The man has brought upon himself his misery; therefore I will stay my hand, and will not give unto him of my food, nor impart unto him of my substance that he may not suffer, for his punishments are just—

Verse 18: But I say unto you, O man, whosoever doeth this the same hath great cause to repent; and except he repenteth of that which he hath done he perisheth forever, and hath no interest in the kingdom of God.

Verse 19: For behold, are we not all beggars? Do we not all depend upon the same Being, even God, for all the substance which we have, for both food and raiment, and for gold, and for silver, and for all the riches which we have of every kind?

Verse 20: And behold, even at this time, ye have been calling on his name, and begging for a remission of your sins. And has he suffered that ye have begged in vain? Nay; he has poured out his Spirit upon you, and has caused that your hearts should be filled with joy, and has caused that your mouths should be stopped that ye could not find utterance, so exceedingly great was your joy.

Verse 21: And now, if God, who has created you, on whom you are dependent for your lives and for all that ye have and are, doth grant unto you whatsoever ye ask that is right, in faith, believing that ye shall receive, O then, how ye ought to impart of the substance that ye have one to another.

Verse 22: And if ye judge the man who putteth up his petition to you for your substance that he perish not, and condemn him, how much more just will be your condemnation for withholding your substance, which doth not belong to you but to God, to whom also your life belongeth; and yet ye put up no petition, nor repent of the thing which thou hast done.

Verse 23: I say unto you, wo be unto that man, for his substance shall perish with him; and now, I say these things unto those who are rich as pertaining to the things of this world.

Verse 24: And again, I say unto the poor, ye who have not and yet have sufficient, that ye remain from day to day; I mean all you who deny the beggar, because ye have not; I would that ye say in your hearts that: I give not because I have not, but if I had I would give.

Verse 25: And now, if ye say this in your hearts ye remain guiltless, otherwise ye are condemned; and your condemnation is just for ye covet that which ye have not received.

Verse 26: And now, for the sake of these things which I have spoken unto you—that is, for the sake of retaining a remission of your sins from day to day, that ye may walk guiltless before God—I would that ye should impart of your substance to the poor, every man according to that which he hath, such as feeding the hungry, clothing the naked, visiting the sick and administering to their relief, both spiritually and temporally, according to their wants.

Verse 27: And see that all these things are done in wisdom and order; for it is not requisite that a man should run faster than he has strength. And again, it is expedient that he should be diligent, that thereby he might win the prize; therefore, all things must be done in order.

> A. What two things does King Benjamin say we must do in this verse? How are those two things related to each other?

Verse 28: And I would that ye should remember, that whosoever among you borroweth of his neighbor should return the thing that he borroweth, according as he doth agree, or else thou shalt commit sin; and perhaps thou shalt cause thy neighbor to commit sin also.

> A. Why does King Benjamin turn to a trivial thing like borrowing things from one's neighbor at the end of such an elevated sermon?

Verse 29: And finally, I cannot tell you all the things whereby ye may commit sin; for there are divers ways and means, even so many that I cannot number them.

Verse 30: But this much I can tell you, that if ye do not watch yourselves, and your thoughts, and your words, and your deeds, and observe the commandments of God, and continue in the faith of what ye have heard concerning the coming of our Lord, even unto the end of your lives, ye must perish. And now, O man, remember, and perish not.

A. Why does King Benjamin give the two warnings in verses 29–30?

B. How do these warnings reflect the situation we have seen the people in and what King Benjamin has preached to them?

Appendix 2

Alma the Younger's Conversion

Mosiah 27

8 Now the sons of Mosiah were numbered among the unbelievers; and also one of the sons of Alma was numbered among them, he being called Alma, after his father; nevertheless, he became a very wicked and an idolatrous man. And he was a man of many words, and did speak much flattery to the people; therefore he led many of the people to do after the manner of his iniquities.

9 And he became a great hinderment to the prosperity of the church of God; stealing away the

Alma 36

6 For I went about with the sons of Mosiah, seeking to destroy the church of God; but behold, God sent his holy angel to stop us by the way.

Alma 38

7 But behold, the Lord in his great mercy sent his angel to declare unto me that I must stop the work of destruction among his people; yea, and I have seen an angel face to face, and he spake with me, and his voice was as thunder, and it shook the whole earth.

Mosiah 27	*Alma 36*	*Alma 38*
hearts of the people; causing much dissension among the people; giving a chance for the enemy of God to exercise his power over them. 10 And now it came to pass that while he was going about to destroy the church of God, for he did go about secretly with the sons of Mosiah seeking to destroy the church, and to lead astray the people of the Lord, contrary to the commandments of God, or even the king— 11 And as I said unto you, as they were going about rebelling against God, behold, the angel of the Lord appeared unto them; and he descended as it were in a cloud;	7 And behold, he spake unto us, as it were the voice of thunder, and the whole earth did tremble beneath our feet; and we all fell to the earth, for the	

Mosiah 27	Alma 36	Alma 38
and he spake as it were with a voice of thunder, which caused the earth to shake upon which they stood; 12 And so great was their astonishment, that they fell to the earth, and understood not the words which he spake unto them. 13 Nevertheless he cried again, saying: Alma, arise and stand forth, for why persecutest thou the church of God? For the Lord hath said: This is my church, and I will establish it; and nothing shall overthrow it, save it is the transgression of my people. 14 And again, the angel said: Behold, the Lord hath heard the prayers of his people, and also the prayers of	fear of the Lord came upon us. 8 But behold, the voice said unto me: Arise. And I arose and stood up, and beheld the angel.	

Mosiah 27	Alma 36	Alma 38

Mosiah 27

his servant, Alma, who is thy father; for he has prayed with much faith concerning thee that thou mightest be brought to the knowledge of the truth; therefore, for this purpose have I come to convince thee of the power and authority of God, that the prayers of his servants might be answered according to their faith.

15 And now behold, can ye dispute the power of God? For behold, doth not my voice shake the earth? And can ye not also behold me before you? And I am sent from God.

16 Now I say unto thee: Go, and remember the captivity of thy fathers in the land

Mosiah 27	Alma 36	Alma 38
of Helam, and in the land of Nephi; and remember how great things he has done for them; for they were in bondage, and he has delivered them. And now I say unto thee, Alma, go thy way, and seek to destroy the church no more, that their prayers may be answered, and this even if thou wilt of thyself be cast off. 17 And now it came to pass that these were the last words which the angel spake unto Alma, and he departed. 18 And now Alma and those that were with him fell again to the earth, for great was their astonishment; for with their own eyes they had beheld an angel of	9 And he said unto me: If thou wilt of thyself be destroyed, seek no more to destroy the church of God.	

Mosiah 27

the Lord; and his voice was as thunder, which shook the earth; and they knew that there was nothing save the power of God that could shake the earth and cause it to tremble as though it would part asunder.

19 And now the astonishment of Alma was so great that he became dumb, that he could not open his mouth; yea, and he became weak, even that he could not move his hands; therefore he was taken by those that were with him, and carried helpless, even until he was laid before his father.

Alma 36

10 And it came to pass that I fell to the earth; and it was for the space of three days and three nights that I could not open my mouth, neither had I the use of my limbs.

11 And the angel spake more things unto me, which were heard by my brethren, but I did not hear them; for when I heard the words—If thou wilt be destroyed of thyself, seek no

Alma 38

8 And it came to pass that I was three days and three nights in the most bitter pain and anguish of soul; and never, until I did cry out unto the Lord Jesus Christ for mercy, did I receive a remission of my sins. But behold, I did cry unto him and I did find peace to my soul.

more to destroy
the church of
God—I was
struck with such
great fear and
amazement lest
perhaps I should
be destroyed, that
I fell to the earth
and I did hear no
more.

12 But I was
racked with
eternal torment,
for my soul was
harrowed up to
the greatest degree
and racked with
all my sins.

13 Yea, I did
remember all my
sins and iniquities,
for which I was
tormented
with the pains
of hell; yea, I saw
that I had rebelled
against my God,
and that I had not
kept his holy com-
mandments.

14 Yea, and I had
murdered many
of his children, or
rather led

them away unto destruction; yea, and in fine so great had been my iniquities, that the very thought of coming into the presence of my God did rack my soul with inexpressible horror.

15 Oh, thought I, that I could be banished and become extinct both soul and body, that I might not be brought to stand in the presence of my God, to be judged of my deeds.

16 And now, for three days and for three nights was I racked, even with the pains of a damned soul.

17 And it came to pass that as I was thus racked with torment, while I was harrowed up by the memory of my many sins,

behold, I remembered also to have heard my father prophesy unto the people concerning the coming of one Jesus Christ, a Son of God, to atone for the sins of the world.

18 Now, as my mind caught hold upon this thought, I cried within my heart: O Jesus, thou Son of God, have mercy on me, who am in the gall of bitterness, and am encircled about by the everlasting chains of death.

19 And now, behold, when I thought this, I could remember my pains no more; yea, I was harrowed up by the memory of my sins no more.

20 And oh, what joy, and what marvelous light

Mosiah 27	*Alma 36*	*Alma 38*
	I did behold; yea, my soul was filled with joy as exceeding as was my pain!	

Alma 36

I did behold;
yea, my soul was
filled with joy as
exceeding as was
my pain!
21 Yea, I say unto
you, my son, that
there could be
nothing so exqui-
site and so bitter
as were my pains.
Yea, and again I
say unto you, my
son, that on the
other hand, there
can be nothing
so exquisite and
sweet as was my
joy.
22 Yea, methought
I saw, even as
our father Lehi
saw, God sitting
upon his throne,
surrounded with
numberless con-
courses of angels,
in the attitude of
singing and prais-
ing their God; yea,
and my soul did
long to be there.

Mosiah 27

20 And they
rehearsed unto his
father all that had
happened unto
them; and

Alma 38

his father rejoiced, for he knew that it was the power of God.

21 And he caused that a multitude should be gathered together that they might witness what the Lord had done for his son, and also for those that were with him.

22 And he caused that the priests should assemble themselves together; and they began to fast, and to pray to the Lord their God that he would open the mouth of Alma, that he might speak, and also that his limbs might receive their strength—that the eyes of the people might be opened to see and know of the goodness and glory of God.

Mosiah 27

23 And it came to pass after they had fasted and prayed for the space of two days and two nights, the limbs of Alma received their strength, and he stood up and began to speak unto them, bidding them to be of good comfort:

24 For, said he, I have repented of my sins, and have been redeemed of the Lord; behold I am born of the Spirit.

25 And the Lord said unto me: Marvel not that all mankind, yea, men and women, all nations, kindreds, tongues and people, must be born again; yea, born of God, changed from their carnal and fallen state, to a state of righteousness, being

Alma 36

23 But behold, my limbs did receive their strength again, and I stood upon my feet, and did manifest unto the people that I had been born of God.

Alma 38

Mosiah 27	Alma 36	Alma 38

redeemed of God, becoming his sons and daughters;
26 And thus they become new creatures; and unless they do this, they can in nowise inherit the kingdom of God.
27 I say unto you, unless this be the case, they must be cast off; and this I know, because I was like to be cast off.
28 Nevertheless, after wading through much tribulations, repenting nigh unto death, the Lord in mercy hath seen fit to snatch me out of an everlasting burning, and I am born of God.
29 My soul hath been redeemed from the gall of bitterness and bonds of iniquity. I was in the darkest abyss; but

Mosiah 27

now I behold the
marvelous light of
God. My soul was
racked with eter-
nal torment; but I
am snatched, and
my soul is pained
no more.
30 I rejected my
Redeemer, and
denied that which
had been spoken
of by our fathers;
but now
that they may
foresee that he will
come, and that
he remembereth
every creature of
his creating, he
will make himself
manifest unto all.
31 Yea, every knee
shall bow, and ev-
ery tongue confess
before him. Yea,
even at the last
day, when all men
shall stand to be
judged of him,
then shall they
confess that he is
God; then shall
they confess, who
live without

Alma 36

Alma 38

Mosiah 27

God in the world, that the judgment of an everlasting punishment is just upon them; and they shall quake, and tremble, and shrink beneath the glance of his all-searching eye.

32 And now it came to pass that Alma began from this time forward to teach the people, and those who were with Alma at the time the angel appeared unto them, traveling round about through all the land, publishing to all the people the things which they had heard and seen, and preaching the word of God in much tribulation, being greatly persecuted by those who were unbelievers, being smitten by many

Alma 36

24 Yea, and from that time even until now, I have labored without ceasing, that I might bring souls unto repentance; that I might bring them to taste of the exceeding joy of which I did taste; that they might also be born of God, and be filled with the Holy Ghost.

25 Yea, and now behold, O my son, the Lord doth give me exceedingly great joy in the fruit of my labors;

26 For because of the word which he has imparted unto

Alma 38

Mosiah 27

of them.

33 But notwithstanding all this, they did impart much consolation to the church, confirming their faith, and exhorting them with long-suffering and much travail to keep the commandments of God.

Alma 36

me, behold, many have been born of God, and have tasted as I have tasted, and have seen eye to eye as I have seen; therefore they do know of these things of which I

have spoken, as I do know; and the knowledge which I have is of God.

27 And I have been supported under trials and troubles of every kind, yea, and in all manner of afflictions; yea, God has delivered me from prison, and from bonds, and from death; yea, and I do put my trust in him, and he will still deliver me.

28 And I know that he will raise me up at the last day, to dwell with him in glory; yea, and I will praise

Alma 38

him forever, for
he has brought
our fathers out of
Egypt, and he has
swallowed up the
Egyptians in the
Red Sea; and he
led them by his
power into the
promised land;
yea, and he has
delivered them
out of bondage
and captivity from
time to time.
29 Yea, and he has
also brought our
fathers out of the
land of Jerusalem;
and he has also,
by his everlasting
power, delivered
them out of
bondage and cap-
tivity, from time
to time even down
to the present day;
and I have always
retained in re-
membrance their
captivity; yea, and
ye also ought to
retain in remem-
brance, as

I have done, their
captivity.
30 But behold,
my son, this is
not all; for ye
ought to know as
I do know, that
inasmuch as ye
shall keep the
commandments
of God ye shall
prosper in the
land; and ye ought
to know also, that
inasmuch as ye
will not keep the
commandments
of God ye shall be
cut off from his
presence. Now
this is according
to his word.

Scripture Index